NEW FRONTIERS IN EMPIRICAL LABOUR LAW RESEARCH

This edited collection draws together papers delivered at a symposium on New Frontiers in Empirical Labour Law Research held at the University of Cambridge in April 2014. It contains contributions from established and emerging experts across a range of disciplines (including employment relations, industrial psychology, sociology, economics and political science) to consider four broad themes: the case for empiricism in labour law; the potential for mixed methods; methodological possibilities and insights from other disciplines; and practical challenges and words of caution for those conducting empirical research.

This collection seeks to cultivate confidence and competence in empirical methods among both established and young labour law scholars, through an intergenerational and interdisciplinary 'lessons learned' dialogue. It contributes to the broader debate regarding empirical research methods in labour law, and casts light on how empirical research can be conducted in highly contested fields to enhance labour law policy-making. This collection aims to inspire labour lawyers to embark upon new forms of empirical research, both to enrich their existing research projects, and to ask new research questions. It offers the first stage of a collaborative and interdisciplinary dialogue on empirical labour law research, to emphasise the importance of collaboration and intergenerational mentoring in building empirical capacity.

New Frontiers in Empirical Labour Law Research

Edited by
Amy Ludlow
and
Alysia Blackham

• HART •
PUBLISHING
OXFORD AND PORTLAND, OREGON
2017

Hart Publishing
An imprint of Bloomsbury Publishing Plc

Hart Publishing Ltd
Kemp House
Chawley Park
Cumnor Hill
Oxford OX2 9PH
UK

Bloomsbury Publishing Plc
50 Bedford Square
London
WC1B 3DP
UK

www.hartpub.co.uk
www.bloomsbury.com

Published in North America (US and Canada) by
Hart Publishing
c/o International Specialized Book Services
920 NE 58th Avenue, Suite 300
Portland, OR 97213-3786
USA

www.isbs.com

First published in hardback, 2015
Paperback edition, 2017

British Library Cataloguing-in-Publication Data
A catalogue record for this book is available from the British Library.

ISBN: PB: 978-1-50991-706-8
HB: 978-1-84946-678-3

Typeset by Compuscript Ltd, Shannon
Printed and bound in Great Britain by
Lightning Source UK Ltd

ACKNOWLEDGEMENTS

The editors would like to acknowledge the support of the Cambridge Socio-Legal Group, the Centre for European Legal Studies (CELS) and the Centre for Business Research (CBR) at the University of Cambridge in providing funding to hold the symposium that formed the basis for this edited collection.

The editors also gratefully acknowledge the ongoing support and assistance of Professors Catherine Barnard and Simon Deakin at the University of Cambridge.

TABLE OF CONTENTS

Part C: What Do We 'Do' With Empirical Work? Making Empirical Work 'Count'

1

Introduction

ALYSIA BLACKHAM AND AMY LUDLOW*

Labour law has a strong tradition of empirical legal scholarship. As noted by Deakin, 'There have been empirical studies of the effects of labour and employment laws since the inception of modern social legislation'.[1] Given this history, labour law scholars generally have a well-developed appreciation of the benefits of empirical research, recognising its potential to help us better understand the practical effects of legal change, inform evidence-based policy-making and provide new and radical insights into labour law problems. Interdisciplinary and empirical methods can challenge existing assumptions about the effectiveness or impact of legal rules, something that seems particularly important in the current context of austerity driven, deregulatory responses to the global financial crisis. Therefore, there is now (as ever) a demonstrable *need* for empirical labour law research, a fact recognised by the 2006 *Nuffield Report* in the UK:

> There are many fields calling out for empirical research and this is important for reasons of policy, for reform and for deeper understanding of the law and legal processes in action. The field is therefore wide open for researchers and the scarcity of empirical legal research virtually guarantees originality.[2]

While empirical labour law scholarship offers significant benefits to individual researchers, the legal community and policy makers, there is a noticeable reticence to embark upon empirical labour law projects. The *Nuffield Report* noted that 'breaking new ground can be a daunting prospect, especially for aspiring young researchers'.[3] Further, there is serious disquiet as to legal scholars' capacity and skills to conduct empirical research.[4] There are therefore significant practical

* Turpin-Lipstein Fellow and College Lecturer in Law, Clare College, University of Cambridge and College Fellow and Lecturer in Law, Gonville and Caius, University of Cambridge respectively.

[1] S Deakin, 'The Evidence-Based Case for Labour Regulation' (Regulating Decent Work Conference, ILO, Geneva, July 2009) 1.

[2] H Genn, M Partington, and S Wheeler, *Law in the Real World—Improving Our Understanding of How Law Works: Final Report and Recommendations* (London, Nuffield Foundation, 2006) 6.

[3] Ibid.

[4] See n 2, 9.

challenges impeding the advancement of empirical labour law scholarship, as detailed in the *Nuffield Report*:

> Despite the achievements and impact of empirical legal research, there has been increasing concern within the academy and the user community that the current generation of empirical legal researchers is not large enough to meet the existing opportunities and demand. More seriously, there is concern that many of the leading empirical legal researchers may retire during the next decade and that there is not a robust successor generation of trained empirical legal researchers to build on existing achievements and meet future demand for research. The problem is particularly acute in the civil law/justice field where historically there has been lower capacity and less empirical research activity than in criminal justice.[5]

Given the demonstrable *need* for empirical labour law research, and the fact it is seen as a 'daunting prospect' by many legal scholars, the time is right for a debate about the future of empirical labour law scholarship: what it means, what it can (or should) entail, and where it should progress in the future.

To take up this challenge, and initiate dialogue around these issues, this edited collection draws together papers delivered at a symposium on 'New Frontiers in Empirical Labour Law Research' held at the University of Cambridge in April 2014. The symposium focused on four broad themes: (1) the case for empiricism in labour law; (2) the potential for mixed methods; (3) methodological possibilities and insights from other disciplines; and (4) practical challenges and words of caution for those conducting empirical research. The symposium brought together experts across a range of disciplines (including employment relations, industrial psychology, sociology, economics and political science) to consider these 'new frontiers' in empirical labour law research. Given the deficiencies in empirical capacity among lawyers in the UK (as was plainly evident in the *Nuffield Report*), the symposium particularly sought to cultivate confidence and competence among both established and young scholars, through an intergenerational and interdisciplinary 'lessons learned' dialogue.

In this introduction to the collection, we clarify what we mean by 'empirical labour law research', and briefly outline the benefits and challenges of empirical labour law scholarship. We also provide a broad overview of the contributions that follow.

A. What is 'Empirical Labour Law Research'?

Empirical labour law research entails the study of labour law through direct methods[6] to provide more developed and nuanced understandings of how labour

[5] Ibid.

[6] J Baldwin and G Davis, 'Empirical Research in Law' in P Cane and M Tushnet (eds), *The Oxford Handbook of Legal Studies* (Oxford, Oxford University Press, 2003) 880.

law operates in practice. Empirical labour law research recognises the importance of investigating beyond 'law on the books' to consider legal *results*.[7]

While there is a strong tradition of empirical labour law scholarship, it is still unclear where the line should be drawn regarding what is 'empirical'. For Heise, empirical scholarship is defined narrowly as that which 'uses statistical techniques and analyses'.[8] In contrast, Epstein and King see empirical research as 'learning about the world using quantitative data or qualitative information'.[9] Similarly, Cane and Kritzner define empirical research as 'the systematic collection of information … and its analysis according to some generally accepted method'.[10] Using such a broad definition, legal doctrinal research could also be seen as a form of empirical analysis, drawing upon legislation and case law as 'data'. However, Epstein and King argue that purely normative or theoretical legal research is not empirical,[11] and many doctrinal scholars would not regard their research as empirical.[12] Instead, legal doctrinal research may be analogous to a social science literature review[13] that typically *precedes* empirical work. Therefore, we explicitly exclude doctrinal research from our definition of empirical labour law scholarship.

Empirical labour law research is, in our view, best viewed as a subset of socio-legal enquiry. Socio-legal research examines law in its social context, often by utilising perspectives and research techniques from the social sciences.[14] Socio-legal research and theory bring social considerations into legal study as objects of rigorous enquiry[15] and emphasise the importance of approaching legal research as an 'empirical, systematic study of a field of social experience'.[16] While the field of socio-legal research is easily able to accommodate empirical research methods, socio-legal enquiry is not necessarily empirical. Indeed, the *Nuffield Report* made a clear distinction between *empirical* legal research and *socio-legal* research:

> We argue that it is important now to reframe the issue as one of capacity to carry out empirical research, not as one of 'socio-legal studies'. What is missing is not text-based

[7] L Teitelbaum, 'An Overview of Law and Social Research' (1985) 35 *Journal of Legal Education* 465, 466.

[8] M Heise, 'The Past, Present, and Future of Empirical Legal Scholarship: Judicial Decision Making and the New Empiricism' [2002] *University of Illinois Law Review* 819, 821.

[9] L Epstein and G King, 'The Rules of Inference' (2002) 69 *University of Chicago Law Review* 1, 1.

[10] P Cane and H Kritzer, 'Introduction' in P Cane and H Kritzer (eds), *The Oxford Handbook of Empirical Legal Research* (Oxford, Oxford University Press, 2010) 1, 4.

[11] Epstein and King, 'The Rules of Inference' n 9, 3; *cf* I Dobinson and F Johns, 'Qualitative Legal Research' in M McConville and W Hong Chui (eds), *Research Methods for Law, Research Methods for the Arts and Humanities* (Edinburgh, Edinburgh University Press, 2007) 19; L Webley, 'Qualitative Approaches to Empirical Legal Research' in Cane and Kritzer (eds), n 10, 926, 927.

[12] Cane and Kritzer, 'Introduction' n 10, 5.

[13] Dobinson and Johns, 'Qualitative Legal Research' n 11, 22.

[14] A Bradshaw, 'Sense and Sensibility: Debates and Developments in Socio-Legal Research Methods' in P Thomas (ed), *Socio-Legal Studies* (Dartmouth, Ashgate, 1997) 99, 107, 109; P Thomas, 'Socio-Legal Studies: The Case of Disappearing Fleas and Bustards' in P Thomas (ed), *Socio-Legal Studies* (Dartmouth, Ashgate, 1997) 2.

[15] R Cotterrell, 'Subverting Orthodoxy, Making Law Central: A View of Sociolegal Studies' (2002) 29 *Journal of Law and Society* 632, 636.

[16] Ibid, 633.

> studies that allude to law's social context, but studies of how legal processes, outcomes or structures actually are in the 'real world'. Only that kind of empirical study will give us a broader and deeper understand [*sic*] of law outside law books. This is not to argue that text-based studies are not essential, just that this is not the kind of work that is in short supply.[17]

This volume therefore presents contributions that use *direct methods*, either qualitative or quantitative, to investigate the impact of labour law.

B. The Value of Empirical Labour Law Research

Empirical research methods are a key means of furthering research into the 'material realities of everyday life'.[18] As noted in the *Nuffield Report*:

> Empirical legal research helps to build our theoretical understanding of law as a social and political phenomenon and contributes to the development of social theory. Put simply, empirical research helps us to understand the law better and an empirical understanding of the law in action helps us to understand society better.[19]

Empirical labour law scholarship adds value in 'revealing and explaining the practices and procedures of legal, regulatory, redress and dispute resolution systems and the impact of legal phenomena on a range of social institutions, on business and on citizens'.[20] Therefore, empirical labour law research and the use of direct methods can significantly enhance, though not supplant, traditional legal doctrinal scholarship.

C. The Challenges of Empirical Labour Law Research

While empirical labour law research offers significant benefits, legal scholars face major challenges in conducting research via direct methods. First, the *Nuffield Report* identified a serious lack of skills and capacity among UK legal academics for conducting empirical scholarship. Many legal scholars are never trained in research methods, so have to acquire research skills in an *ad hoc* fashion as the

[17] Genn, Partington and Wheeler, *Law in the Real World Improving Our Understanding of How Law Works*, n 2, 46.

[18] P Hillyard, 'Invoking Indignation: Reflections on Future Directions of Socio-Legal Studies' (2002) 29 *Journal of Law and Society* 645, 652.

[19] Genn, Partington, and Wheeler, *Law in the Real World Improving Our Understanding of How Law Works*, n 2, 1; see also E Mertz, 'Conclusion: A New Social Constructionism for Sociolegal Studies' (1994) 28 *Law & Society Review* 1243, 1261.

[20] Genn, Partington, and Wheeler, *Law in the Real World Improving Our Understanding of How Law Works*, n 2, 1.

need arises. This lack of training can impair researchers' confidence and willingness to use new research techniques, with some feeling like 'imposters' in the empirical field. Second, empirical labour law scholarship can be costly and time consuming, and often requires research funding to be viable. In contrast, doctrinal legal scholarship is relatively inexpensive and efficient, making it a more attractive option for legal scholars who need to demonstrate research 'output'. Indeed,

> the traditional culture of legal scholarship is characterised as a law-centred enterprise conducted by lone researchers unused to collaborating with others, undertaking close textual analysis of legal material with the objective of relatively rapid publication of journal articles and text-books.[21]

Individualistic and rapid research, focusing on legal texts, is a world away from the often collaborative, time-consuming, expensive and 'messy' domain of empirical scholarship. Taken together, these challenges may substantially impair empirical legal research, as noted in the *Nuffield Report*:

> There was a common feeling that lack of skills, together with the time and cost involved in empirical legal research as compared with doctrinal, or purely theoretical or philosophical work, deters those with an interest in empirical questions from engaging in empirical legal research.[22]

While these practical considerations are significant, empirical labour law scholarship also raises deeper theoretical concerns, which are developed in the three parts of this volume. *First*, what is the place and value of empirical labour scholarship in the legal academy? What is (or should be) the role of empirical research? Is it to contain or limit the ideological aspects of policy-making, as argued by Bob Hepple in chapter two? Can empirical labour law research be used to predict legal outcomes or results? As highlighted by Lizzie Barmes in chapter three, there is a need to account for intervening factors in assessing the impact of labour law: labour law is complex and interconnected, meaning our research methods also need to be complex. At the same time, how can we match legal and empirical methods and ideologies (as explored by Zoe Adams and Simon Deakin in chapter four)? Indeed, as Lydia Hayes and Roseanne Russell ask in chapter five, and Amy Ludlow has reflected upon in chapter seven, does labour law have a particular ontology?

Second, how can (or should) we go about empirical legal research? What research techniques can we use? How can we use interdisciplinary ideas to enrich empirical labour law scholarship? This issue is taken up by the contributions in Part B of this volume. In this part of the collection, authors have explored the potential of behavioural economics (Ewan McGaughey), ethnographic methods (Amy Ludlow), statistical evidence (Sonia McKay and Sian Moore) and mixed methods (Tish Gibbons) to enrich labour law scholarship. Indeed, many of the

[21] Ibid, 31.
[22] Ibid, 32.

contributions in this volume stem from mixed methods studies (Tish Gibbons, Sonia McKay and Sian Moore, Simonetta Manfredi and Lucy Vickers, and Alysia Blackham), perhaps indicating growth in this area of labour law research. These contributions highlight the ways in which different and complimentary research methods can add value to our understanding of labour law. However, they also note the importance of recognising the limitations of different research methods and interdisciplinary ideas, and the need to relate empirical and interdisciplinary insights to the doctrinal labour law picture.

Third, then, we consider how empirical research can (or should) relate to traditional legal doctrinal scholarship. What value does it add, and how can we cultivate legal 'impact' and practical outcomes via our empirical research? The immense challenges faced by empirical researchers in overcoming 'ideology' with 'evidence' are raised by Hepple's contribution in chapter two. So long as 'ideology' dominates legal policy-making, empirical labour law scholarship may have limited impact. Equally, empirical scholarship may be misinterpreted or misused by policymakers, as noted by Lizzie Barmes in chapter three. While recognising these challenges, the contributions from Alysia Blackham, Abi Adams and Jeremias Prassl, and Simonetta Manfredi and Lucy Vickers in Part C pose a range of ideas for increasing the impact of empirical labour law scholarship, and for linking empirical findings back to the development of doctrinal law. In the words of Simonetta Manfredi and Lucy Vickers, we are posing ways of securing a 'virtuous circle' of knowledge exchange between law, empirical scholarship and those subject to labour law in practice.

D. The Purposes of this Collection

With this collection, we hope to contribute to the broader debate regarding empirical research methods in labour law. We seek to cast light on how empirical research can be conducted in highly contested fields, and to examine how empirical research can enhance and enrich labour law policy-making. In so doing we hope to inspire labour lawyers to embark upon new forms of empirical research, both to enrich their existing research projects, and to ask new research questions.

We also hope this collection will contribute to building a community of empirical labour law scholars, and promote a more collaborative approach to empirical labour law scholarship. The *Nuffield Report* has flagged the fundamental importance of a research community in promoting successful empirical scholarship: in mapping the careers of successful empirical legal scholars, the report found

> [o]ne or two [researchers] undertook intensive research training in social science research methods, but most lawyers learned 'on the job' and often by means of symbiotic collaboration with a social scientist or an established empirical legal researcher … Several of the contributors talk of critical—sometimes chance—relationships with established scholars who had a profound influence on outlook and approach to research. Such 'mentoring'

> relationships laid the foundation for both intellectual and skills development, by offering a different perspective on the study of law and legal processes and demonstrating, by example, how empirical questions about the operation of law might be studied.[23]

In this collection, then, we also offer the first stage of a collaborative and interdisciplinary dialogue about empirical labour law research, to emphasise the importance of collaboration and intergenerational mentoring in building empirical capacity.

[23] Ibid, 16.

2

Foreword: Evidence and Ideology

BOB HEPPLE*

In recent years labour law and policy in the UK has rarely been informed by rigorously established objective evidence. It is not, in the term popularised by the Blair Government, 'evidence-based'. Instead, legislative and policy measures have been led by ideology, that is by systems of ideas which are used to justify the actions of government or employers and to persuade people of the necessity of specific policies and laws.

This has become evident in two main situations. The first is where the objective evidence does not exist but ideology is more or less exclusively relied upon as the basis for supporting or opposing legislation. The second is where empirical evidence clashes directly with the ideology behind the policy or legislation. There are many examples of these conflicts between evidence and ideology in the historical context of British labour law.

A. Ideology Rules

An example of a purely ideological approach can be found in the opposition by some industrialists and economists to nineteenth-century factory legislation. Sidney Webb characterised nineteenth-century factory legislation as 'a century of experiment' and a 'typical example of English practical empiricism'. This followed Jevons' view (1882) that there were no principles of industrial legislation—'legislation must proceed on the grounds of experience, legislation must be Baconian'. The implication that there was some sort of process of 'trial and error'—the hallmark of scientific empiricism—is now generally regarded as mistaken.

> Instead it is in the ebb and flow of struggle by unions and reform groups inside and outside Parliament, and the resistance by powerful groups of employers and the intellectual supporters of laissez-faire that the key must be found to the patchy character

* Emeritus Fellow, Clare College and Professor of Law, University of Cambridge.

of protective legislation, which began with the Regulation of Chimney Sweepers Act 1788 and the Health and Morals of Apprentices Act 1802.[1]

The evidence in support of such legislation was overwhelming from a humanitarian point of view. It came from the anecdotal accounts by writers such as Charles Kingsley, from the hands-on experience of factory owners like Robert Owen, and the evidence given by workers and manufacturers to inspectors, commissions and parliamentary committees. While Kingsley put the humanitarian case for the chimney boys, Owen focused on the business case—his New Lanark mills showed that better working conditions and shorter hours resulted in greater productivity. Their contributions were evidence-based. The opposition was ideological. Sir Leslie Stephens explained that many of the opponents came from the new class of manufacturers who subscribed to the laissez-faire order of ideas. Some of them said the evidence of abuses was exaggerated (a difficult claim to sustain). But in the main their objections were based on the assumption (rather than evidence) that regulation of working hours would harm trade and drive it out of the country, eventually reducing not only the capitalists, but also the workers, to beggary.

Another example is the Ten Hours' Movement, which from 1831 onwards sought to limit the working hours of all employees, not only children and women, to 10 hours per day. From 1840 onwards the Movement focused on the hours of women in factories. The evidence gathered by the short time committees of the detrimental effects of long hours on both men and women was clear and convincing, but the political reality was that change could be achieved only by relying on the emerging ideology of the Victorian middle class that the man was the breadwinner and the wife was the dependent and child-rearer whose condition was a 'social problem' that needed to be regulated. The opposition to reform came from some industrialists and economists, who argued not simply that the evidence of 'evils' was exaggerated, but also from their ideological position that this would be an unwarranted interference with the freedom to trade. In the 1850s the Womens' Rights Opposition also opposed the legislation as a threat to women's employment. Against this the early socialists argued that legislation was needed because women were too weak economically and socially to achieve change through male-dominated unions alone. A similar debate about women was heard right until the 1980s when the special protection for women was repealed. Marx and Engels hailed the Ten Hours Act of 1847 as 'a legislative recognition of the particular interests of the workers, by taking advantage of the divisions among the bourgeoisie itself'.[2] At the same time many of the larger employers were anxious to show their humanitarian concern in order to eradicate competition from a minority of employers gained a competitive advantage from cheap child and female labour. In other words, it was not the evidence of abuses but rather ideological arguments that were dominant.

[1] B Hepple, 'Individual Labour Law' in GS Bain (ed), *Industrial Relations in Britain* (Oxford, Blackwell, 1983) 405.

[2] K Marx and F Engels, *Manifesto of the Communist Party* (1848).

Fortunately, the advocates of restrictions on working hours won, but not without compromises that shaped our law on working time until 1998 when the Working Time Regulations implemented the EU Directive of 1993.[3] Yet even today those Regulations are hotly contested, not on the basis of objective evidence, but because of anecdotal evidence that they are 'burdens on business'.

Let me skip forward a century to the legislation that followed the Report of the Donovan Commission (1968). The Commission itself, guided by leading academics such as Hugh Clegg, Allan Flanders, and Otto Kahn-Freund, set new standards for empirical labour law research, under their research director Bill McCarthy. The 11 research papers, which brought together much of the existing empirical research on unions and union-management relations, framed the conclusions of the Report. These were that the formal system of collective bargaining embodied in official institutions and the informal system created by the actual behaviour of managers and shop stewards were in conflict. This helped to explain why resort to unofficial and unconstitutional strikes was increasing and there was wage inflation damaging to the economy. On the basis of this evidence they proposed a series of reforms to establish 'orderly and effective collective bargaining'. Their solutions were, of course, consistent with the philosophy of 'industrial relations pluralism' which the Warwick school embraced, but their strength lay in the objective evidence on which they relied.

The framers of the short-lived Conservative Industrial Relations Act of 1971 shared the view that collective bargaining was the best way to determine terms and conditions of employment. In addition, they believed that 'legislation has an essential and positive part to play in the improvement of industrial relations'. The Act opened the Pandora's box of individual rights and state control of trade unions which, despite the repeal of the Act in 1974, are now dominant features of British labour law. The attack on trade unions was said to be justified by anecdotal evidence from cases of abuses of the closed shop and restrictive working practices gathered together in publications such as the Inns of Court Conservative Association's *A Giant's Strength*, and in the courts by judges such as Sir John Donaldson, and Lord Denning who saw the individual as the 'David' pitted against the union 'Goliath'.

The seismic shift in ideology came with the Thatcher Government. At first, the Conservatives treaded warily seeking only pragmatic reforms based on evidence as to where collective bargaining was not working effectively, and retaining (with some restrictions) rights against unfair dismissal and discrimination. But then came Hayek and his British disciple, Sir Keith Joseph. The ideology of market fundamentalism became the driving force of labour legislation and policy. It was claimed that the unions had 'privileges' which would before long destroy the whole market order. Unions were 'the biggest obstacle to the raising of living standards of the working class as a whole'. They were the prime source of unemployment.

[3] SI 1998/1833, implementing the Working Time Directive 2003/88/EC OJ L 299, 18.11.2003, 9–19.

As Wedderburn pointed out in his classic article on 'Freedom of Association and Philosophies of Labour Law', these conclusions 'did not depend on surveys or evidence to Royal Commission but upon an avowed discovery of the true nature of industrial society and of "freedom" itself'.[4] Hayek's stance, Wedderburn said, 'is emphatically not based on arguments of empirical inquiry to set against the traditional analysis ... His is a stance of total and at times bitter opposition to that analysis as a whole, couched in terms of truth and error'.[5]

The Blair Government, while maintaining most of the Thatcher regulation of unions and collective bargaining, said they wanted to end 'the ideological led-based decision making for policy making'. The White Paper *Modernising Government* (1999) noted that Government 'must produce policies that really deal with problems, that are forward-looking and shaped by evidence rather than a response to short-term pressures, that tackle causes not symptoms'.[6] This was dubbed 'evidence-based' policy, but in practice it was also heavily biased by a philosophy of labour law that concentrates upon the competitiveness of the employer not upon the welfare of the human being at work. This was the philosophy behind the ill-fated Parts 2 on tribunal reform and Part 3 on dispute resolution of the Employment Act 2002, which had to be repealed when, as predicted by many critics, these provisions proved to be a failure in reducing costs to the employer.

In his celebrated critique of Thatcher's deregulation of employment law, Wedderburn observed that 'since 1982, the trend has been towards legislation by the assertion of truths. Evidence has increasingly taken a back seat'. This trend is renewed under the Coalition Employment Law Review. The Government's specific deregulatory measures are based not on independent impartial research but instead rely on anecdotal 'evidence' and pressures from business organisations that have a (deregulatory) interest in the results.

Adrian Beecroft (described as 'a multi-millionaire who made a career out of cutting jobs'),[7] the British Chambers of Commerce, and Federation of Small Businesses, claim that employment law is one of the principal 'regulatory burdens' on business, and that the law is weighted too far in favour of the employee. Yet the Government concedes that the Organisation for Economic Cooperation and Development (OECD) has found that, along with Canada, the UK has the second most business-friendly framework of labour law in the developed world, after only the US. How are we to account for the differences between employers' perceptions and reality? Although survey data can indicate what employers think about regulation, they do not reveal how employers adapt their employment practices to regulation in taking on, managing and dismissing workers.

[4] L Wedderburn, 'Freedom of Association and Philosophies of Labour Law' (1989) 18 *Industrial Law Journal* 1, 8.

[5] Ibid, 9.

[6] *Modernising Government* (Cm 4310, 1999) 15.

[7] www.independent.co.uk/news/uk/politics/revealed-how-adrian-beecroft-made-a-career-out-of-cutting-jobs-7789303.html (last accessed 1 November 2014).

The data do not indicate the extent of employer awareness and understanding of their legal obligations, and their perceptions are nearly always based on the costs and restraints of regulation not on the benefits. Impact assessments produced by government with each new set of legislative proposal are notoriously unreliable.[8]

The limitations of surveys and impact assessments have led to a wealth of qualitative research about employer perceptions which presents a more nuanced picture. The most recent of these, commissioned by the Government and published in March 2013, is based on in-depth interviews and case studies with a representative sample of employers.[9] This research indicates that employment regulation has little effect on HR practices and that overall employment regulation is seen as necessary. The research does highlight specific areas of concern notably fears of litigation about dismissal (euphemistically described in the consultation and research papers as 'letting people go'). In reality, only about 6.5 per cent of dismissals result in an unfair dismissal claim. Where a claim is lodged employers face an average of £3,700 worth of time and legal representation costs. Only five out of every 100 of those who claim succeed, and the median compensation award has been around £4,000 to £5,000 for the last six years. No evidence had been produced that increasing the qualifying period does lead to more jobs; indeed between 1999 and 2011, when the qualifying period was one year, 1.75 million new jobs were added. In light of these facts, are the Coalition's deregulatory measures an appropriate and proportionate response to the anxieties of employers who are badly informed on this topic? The most significant step was to remove an estimated 2.7 million workers (many of them young workers, migrants and part-time women) from unfair dismissal protection from April 2012 by raising the qualifying period from one to two years.

Why has the Coalition pressed ahead with deregulatory reforms when the evidence for them is largely confined to the subjective perceptions of employers rather than reality? The OECD has said that 'there is no single golden road to better labour market performance'.[10] The Government's own response to the Beecroft proposals acknowledge that the overall effect of reducing employment protection legislation (EPL) on hiring and firing can be ambiguous, and admits that 'there is extensive empirical literature on EPL which finds evidence to suggest EPL can lead to increased investment in skills and increased incremental innovation (positive for productivity and economic growth)'.[11] The Government is locked into a model

[8] See, eg the impact assessment for the Employment Tribunals and the Employment Appeal Tribunal Fees Order 2013 SI 2013/1893, which significantly underestimated the impacts that introducing tribunal fees would have upon claimants taking cases: www.legislation.gov.uk/ukia/2013/1039/pdfs/ukia_20131039_en.pdf.

[9] E Jordan, A Thomas, J Kitching and R Blackburn, 'Employer Perceptions and the Impact of Employment Regulation' (Employment Relations Research Series 123, BIS, March 2013): www.gov.uk/government/uploads/system/uploads/attachment_data/file/128792/13-638-employer-perceptions-and-the-impact-of-employment-regulation.pdf.

[10] OECD, 'Employment Outlook Editorial: Boosting Jobs and Incomes' (Paris, OECD Publications, 2006) 13.

[11] Department for Business Innovation and Skills, 'Dealing with Dismissal and Compensated No Fault Dismissal for Micro Businesses: Government Response' (London, BIS, 2012) 22.

where there is a presumption that regulation interferes with the efficient working of free markets by limiting the employer's freedom to manage and to hire and fire without restraint.

B. Political Obstacles to Empirical Research on Labour Law

The second situation in which the conflict between empirical research and ideology manifests itself is where government is directly or indirectly the paymaster of research. The results of the research may be perceived as subverting the government's intentions or closing some policy options.

One consequence, where government is paymaster, may be to deny funding. Other consequences of political sensitivity may be excessive access and confidentiality requirements. Civil servants may be reticent to reveal the government's intentions and employers and unions may be reluctant to disclose possible breaches of the law. Written records may be inaccessible and time-consuming to go through—documents are of limited value without an explanation of context. Another result of political sensitivity may simply be to ignore the findings of the research, as illustrated earlier. A more drastic possibility is the suppression of the research or not allowing its publication. This happened at the time when the Conservative's Employment Bill 1982, which imposed further drastic restrictions on the closed shop, was being debated. Research, commissioned by the Department of Employment, threw doubt on the premises on which the legislation was based. The Department withheld the research findings from publication until after the Act had been passed.

Another example is the suspension of the Social Science Research Council's (SSRC) Monitoring of Labour Legislation in 1982 following an allegation by the Conservative Peer, Lord Beloff that the SSRC's Industrial Relations Research Unit at Warwick University was 'unfairly biased in favour of unions', a view apparently shared by at least one senior Department of Employment official. Lord Rothschild, who was conducting an inquiry into the SSRC, proposed the investigation of this accusation of bias. He was under the misapprehension that the Monitoring of Legislation Panel (of which I was Chair) was a part of the Unit, and so it was included in the terms of reference. The subsequent inquiry conducted by Sir Kenneth Berrill, found that there was no ground for including the Panel in its terms of reference. But the damage had been done and the Panel was unable to commission the research that it had intended on the operation of the 1982 Act. I was later informed by a senior civil servant that he had requested Lord Rothschild to include the Panel in the terms of reference after this same civil servant had failed to persuade the Panel not to commission research on a particular topic. The intervention with Lord Rothschild paid off because it prevented the research from going ahead.

The Panel was also subject to other political pressures. The SSRC in the late 1970s was anxious to produce 'policy relevant' research findings. The Research Initiatives Board of the SSRC therefore prioritised two politically contentious topics for research. These were picketing and union ballots. They were regarded as important even if the legislation had no impact on actual behaviour. They were ideological and political footballs, on which there was virtually no empirical research. The Panel believed that 'demystifying' them in order to improve political and legal thinking was as important an objective as studying the impact of the legislation itself. A grant was made in respect of the picketing project to a team based in Oxford. One Sunday morning I had an agitated phone call from a civil servant to tell me that the Prime Minister had read a report in the Sunday *Observer* that one of the members of the research team had co-authored a Fabian report critical of the Government. After much to-ing and fro-ing the SSRC provided funding for a second parallel report to be conducted by a team based on Sheffield on the same subject! We should no doubt be pleased that two first-class studies resulted, but the incident shows just how politically sensitive empirical studies can be when they appear to clash with current ideologies.

C. Some Advice to Empirical Researchers

In the light of these experiences, I have some words of advice:

1. Be aware that research into labour law can be very politically sensitive even if it aims simply to reveal the 'facts'. There will not only be attempts at political interference, but civil servants and other respondents may be very reluctant to disclose information they regard as sensitive or confidential.
2. At all times preserve the distinction between valid polemic and valid research—it is necessary to maintain objectivity, otherwise the findings will be dismissed as partisan. Tread warily! It may be difficult to disprove bias if you have expressed views before the research is completed.
3. Labour legislation can be understood only in the wider context of social control and the ideologies of the parties involved in its construction and implementation. The environment in which legislation is implemented can never be static.
4. The time-scale of monitoring legislation has to be long enough to take account of the 'before' and 'after' and of changes in the social and economic environment in which the legislation is implemented.
5. It is fruitless to measure the impact of legislation in terms of 'success' or 'failure'. First, there is the difficulty in establishing the objectives of legislation—stakeholders may have different and conflicting objectives; second, legislation often has unintended consequences which may be more significant than those that were intended.

Part A

Taking Method Seriously: Theoretical Implications

3

Individual Rights at Work, Methodological Experimentation and the Nature of Law

LIZZIE BARMES*

A. Introduction: The Paradox of Individual Rights at Work

A great deal of UK labour and equality law consists in individual rights that 'on the tin' are about ensuring fairness and equality at work. As a practitioner, teacher and researcher I have looked at these from different vantages. The 'big picture' each viewpoint has gestured towards is that, while such laws have emancipatory effects, they also, to a greater or lesser degree, legitimate the basic power structures on which society is built, its dominant ideologies and ways of being. As enacted by political institutions and implemented by courts, this body of law is revealed in its concepts, philosophies and symbols to further worthwhile, transformative goals at the same time as it supports, even extends, existing hierarchies and governing ideologies.

This arguably reflects a deep truth about the nature of law in its capacity concurrently to challenge and to sustain the status quo. That law has this Janus-faced quality has been contended by scholars as disparate as Kimberlé Crenshaw writing about anti-discrimination law in the modern US,[1] and EP Thompson in his famous work on the eighteenth-century Black Acts in England.[2] Yet there are

* Professor of Labour Law, Queen Mary, University of London.

[1] K Crenshaw, 'Race, Retrenchment and Reform: Transformation and Legitimation in Anti-Discrimination Law' (1988) 101 *Harvard Law Review* 1331.

[2] EP Thompson, *Whigs and Hunters: The Origin of the Black Acts* (New York, Pantheon, 1975). See further for an illuminating discussion of varied accounts of the duality in law within liberal and Marxist thought, A Hunt, 'Dichotomy and Contradiction in the Sociology of Law' (1981) 8 *British Journal of Law and Society* 47.

many areas in which that theoretical insight has not been tested through empirical enquiry. Equally, there is much to be done to uncover and map the precise mechanisms by which law operates and produces its contradictory outcomes.[3]

There is undoubtedly a dearth of empirical work in the labour and equality law field, within and beyond the UK, for which various potential reasons may be discerned.[4] Work of this kind is also particularly needed, again not only for the UK, to make sense of the paradox that individual labour and equality rights have proliferated while the capacity to enforce or insist on fair and equal treatment at work has in multiple ways been hollowed out. While the chimerical quality of many individual workplace entitlements is no doubt related to the decline of plural collectivist systems for the regulation of employment relations,[5] there remain important questions about how exactly these two sets of developments interact and whether the design of the law and enforcement systems can make a difference.

Inspired by this theoretical viewpoint and its particular salience for contemporary labour and equality law, I have recently completed a research project that experimented with new means of documenting the operation of individual workplace rights in the UK.[6] In what follows I outline the methodology and briefly touch on the patterns that were revealed. The objective for the purposes of this collection is to extrapolate from this experience about the potential and challenges of empirical work in the labour and equality law field and, to some extent, for investigation of law more generally.

[3] In relation to the need for focused research on 'legal mobilisation' see H Kritzer, 'Claiming Behaviour as Legal Mobilization' in P Cane and H Kritzer (eds), *Oxford Handbook of Empirical Legal Research* (Oxford, Oxford University Press, 2010) 260, 281: 'given the importance of context revealed in extant research, studies focusing on a broad range of justiciable problems are not likely to advance our understanding of legal mobilization behaviours. Rather, it will be necessary to design research projects focused on specific problem contexts and problem types … What this means is that our understanding of legal mobilization is likely to advance fairly slowly, and to be specific to particular problems rather than general to a wide range of issues'. On a similar analysis regarding labour and equality law, see S Deakin, 'Labor and Employment Laws' in P Cane and H Kritzer (eds), ibid, 308–30, 326–27: 'The new literature stresses that the effects of labour laws cannot be predicted in an a priori way, through the use of models with universal application, but depend on the interaction of legal rules with a number of national, regional and industry-specific conditions and with complementary institutions in capital markets and product markets. This implies a need for better and more reliable data on the content of the law, on modes of operation, and on the context in which legal rules are applied. It also suggests a continuing role for case study work in examining the operation of laws at workplace level and assessing claims for causal inference draw from the quantitative literature'.

[4] See further on this phenomenon, potential explanations for it and the case for a change of approach in L Barmes, 'Common Law Confusion and Empirical Research in Labour Law' in A Bogg and A Davies, *The Autonomy of Labour Law* (Portland Oregon and Oxford, Hart, 2015).

[5] See W Brown, S Deakin, D Nash and S Oxenbridge, 'The Employment Contract: From Collective Procedures to Individual Rights' (2000) 38 *British Journal of Industrial Relations* 611, about the positive relationship between collective bargaining and adherence to statutory rights.

[6] See further, L Barmes, *Bullying and Behavioural Conflict at Work: The Duality of Individual Rights* (Oxford, Oxford University Press, forthcoming 2015).

B. Methodological Experimentation with Individual Labour and Equality Rights

I chose behavioural conflicts at work as the medium through which to investigate the functioning of labour and equality rights. By this I mean disputes about how colleagues behave towards one another, whether or not there is also conflict about a particular workplace practice or decision. I chose this as the focus because, first, it covers a sufficiently broad set of situations, factually and legally, to provide general learning about how individual labour and equality rights are working in the UK. Secondly, there has been significant primary research by non-legal scholars of direct relevance that enriches what may be discovered about law and legal process. Thirdly, it was necessary to avoid conceiving of relevant situations wholly on the basis of either legal terms of art (like harassment) or of words that have variable subjective meanings (like bullying). Much as the rise in the use of the word 'bullying' in relation to work assisted to identify relevant judgments, it was important conceptually that like situations were not excluded because they somehow did not match either legal categories or subjective perceptions of what behaviour signifies. The framing I developed enabled me instead to isolate and investigate a stable category of workplace interactions, which are regulated by all sorts of individual labour and equality rights, and in relation to which several associated literatures enhance what can be learned about the operation of law and legal process.

The first strand of the work involved gathering and qualitatively analysing as many as possible of the population of authoritative, precedential decisions about behavioural conflict at work from 1995 to 2010. I did not include Employment Tribunal (ET) judgments because they do not set a precedent, only deciding the legal implications of a particular fact situation, and are subject to being overturned on appeal, either for doctrinal legal error or because the ET factual findings were legally impermissible. That means the higher courts determine the meaning of both statutory and common law concepts for anyone affected by them, not least ET judges in applying the law to the situations that come before them. Study of ET adjudication, therefore, would not have assisted to answer my research question in this aspect of the study, namely 'How does law about behavioural conflict at work operate through authoritative adjudication?' This is not to deny that what I found out about adjudication could usefully be built upon by investigation into, first, how far ETs abide by the rulings of higher courts and, secondly, whether my findings about styles of judging are reflected in purely ET adjudication, as opposed to only such adjudication that has been scrutinised on appeal.

The original sample that emerged from a series of database searches contained several hundred judgments, of which around 150 remained after I had removed decisions in which the reference to behavioural conflict, as defined, was peripheral or incidental. It was this set of judgments that I qualitatively analysed.

The judgments from 1995–99 enabled me to develop my coding systems, which I applied successively to judgments from 2000–04, 2005–09 and 2010, checking in relation to each batch whether the coding needed revision. In terms of facts, this method enabled me to find out if there were recurrent themes, not in the sense of underlying fact patterns, but in the way 'stories' about behavioural conflict at work were presented to courts and retold by judges. This produced data about how this kind of dispute is presented to, and narrated by, judges with the power to make precedential judicial rulings. In terms of law, my approach disclosed clear patterns, irrespective of the particular individual right being litigated, in how authoritative adjudication determines that behaviour between colleagues is unlawful and then either requires or guides organisations to respond to such conduct and to allegations of it.

The second strand in the research project involved interview studies with senior lawyers and senior managers to explore the influence of law and legal process on behavioural conflict at work. My interviewees were gathered mainly through a snowball sampling strategy. This was supplemented by specific invitations to ensure the sample included, first, senior managers from different sectors and varied sizes of organisation, secondly, both barristers and solicitors and, thirdly, a broadly even gender balance. The interviews for both samples were semi-structured. The interview guides were adapted to the different categories of interviewee, but both investigated, first, how people in organisations are affected by law and legal process when either they are involved in, or required to respond to, behavioural conflict at work, and, secondly, what causes such conflict, first, to become litigious at all and, secondly, to become litigious to different degrees. It also became clear after the first couple of interviews that my data on interviewees' ideas about, and experiences of, what causes escalation would be enhanced if I explicitly asked about situations where this does not happen.

This is not the place to provide a detailed account either of my findings or of the theoretical and substantive implications they have.[7] Rather the objective here is to extrapolate from the experience of putting this methodology into practice about the potential and challenges of empirical methodology in the labour and equality field, and perhaps more generally. Briefly then, the research design enabled me to construct an interpretive account of the practical workings of individual labour and equality rights and related legal processes. This provided a basis on which to theorise about law's impact at work, with potential resonance for other spheres of legal activity. Further there were doctrinal, technical implications about the scope for re-configuring individual rights more effectively to enhance fairness and equality at work, crucially implicating systems for their implementation and enforcement. It is clear overall that my findings support the theoretical position I started from, highlighting the immense difficulty, perhaps impossibility, of overcoming law's duality so as to make legal interventions emancipatory in a more thoroughgoing way.

[7] See for this, Barmes, n 6, above.

Features of my data that demonstrated this are the multiplicity of actors and the complexity of mechanisms by which law simultaneously supports and undermines fairness and equality at work. As expected, the significance repeatedly emerged of the convergence between the growth of individualised legal forms, especially enforcement processes, and the marginalisation of pluralist collective regulation of working life, whether via trade unions or otherwise. Yet it was not that collectivism came across as unimportant to working life under individualised workplace rights regimes. Rather, the suggestion was of managerial constructions of workplace collectivism crowding out other versions, with individualised law and legal process feeding into that differentially according to workplace regimes.

This came across as an essential over-arching factor in many working people who encounter problems at work being faced with an invidious choice whether, first, to bring challenges framed in individualistic terms that put them at odds with the 'taken for granted' ways of being at their workplace, with increasing numbers having little support and potential incurring significant costs of various kinds, secondly, to live with the unsatisfactory situation that created their predicament or, thirdly, to exit the workplace. Aside from hypothesising that this dynamic results in many encroachments on individual rights going unchallenged, I perceived corresponding harmful and costly effects beyond the individuals concerned, implicating their employers and society more widely. Not the least of these lies in waste and loss that flow from sub-optimal deployment of law and adjudication to enhance fairness and equality norms that many, including amongst employers and managers, subscribe to.

At a general level this project, therefore, bore out that the contradictory nature of law is fully present in contemporary UK experience of individual labour and equality rights, while my conclusions correspondingly pointed in divergent directions. On the one hand, they suggest a need for individual labour and equality rights to be re-designed in order better to realise the norms they embody, in particular finding innovative ways, whether based on trade unions or other social groupings, to draw on the essentially collective nature of work to breathe life into the day-to-day operation of these legal forms. On the other hand, it appears highly unlikely that there will be change of this kind given the accumulating effects, and sheer contemporary power, of the host of political, economic and social forces undermining expansive, participatory and inclusive notions of collectivism, at work and elsewhere.

C. Potential and Challenges of Empirical Research in law

The potential of empirical work is to some extent implicit in what I have already said about the dearth of empirical work on labour and equality law. Regarding this project specifically I have suggested that, first, primary data is critical to advancing our understanding of how law operates through individual rights. Secondly, the conclusions immanent in my findings illustrate how investigation of this type can advance the theorisation of law and legal process. I will expand on the possibilities more precisely in what follows here.

From a theoretical point of view there is the liberation of moving from philosophical, conceptual analyses to testing the explanatory, interpretive and predictive capacity of the models that kind of reasoning generates. Where a theoretical model successfully translates to 'law in action', in the sense of fitting with what is found, the analytical starting point will make it possible better to understand and account for what is observed. At the same time there may be feedback effects that enable refinement of the starting theoretical model. This arguably has been my experience, in that attention to the propensity of law to face in two directions at once gave me a model that powerfully assisted in making sense of my disparate findings. At the same time, my documentation of the means by which those effects occurred in the particular context investigated has the potential to enrich and extend the underlying theoretical construct.

Where a model does not fit, the logical corollary is that the theory ought to be questioned, at least in relation to that context and perhaps more generally. It is perhaps worth thinking this possibility through in relation to the popularity of systems theory as a means of modelling the influence that legal intervention can have in a variety of situations. For example, work by Fredman and Hepple has shown that pioneering measures in the equality law field have not followed the prescriptions of systems theory for effective regulation, despite having superficial features that resonate with that worldview. The method by which they uncovered this disconnect involved conceptual and qualitative analyses of the underlying legislation, its detailed implementation by politicians and adjudication in judicial review cases. The conclusion drawn was that systems theory, and specifically its manifestation in ideas about 'reflexive regulation', suggests we ought not to expect much of these legislative interventions as currently constituted.[8] Deakin, McLaughlin and Chai have also conducted analyses leading to the view that reflexive regulatory approaches could improve the effectiveness of various gender equality measures.[9]

The premise to such work is that the precepts of systems theory accurately model the impact that law can have on working life and, as a corollary, enable effective diagnosis of what disrupts or inhibits legal influence in different work settings. Yet I would contend that there are major questions for appropriately

[8] B Hepple, 'Enforcing Equality Law: Two Steps Forward and Two Steps Backward for Reflexive Regulation' (2011) 40 *Industrial Law Journal* 315, S Fredman, 'The Public Sector Equality Duty' (2011) 40 *Industrial Law Journal* 405, and S Fredman, 'Breaking the Mould: Equality as a Proactive Duty' (2012) 60 *American Journal of Comparative Law* 265.

[9] S Deakin, C McLaughlin, and D Chai, 'Gender Inequality and Reflexive Regulation: The Potential of Different Regulatory Mechanisms' in L Dickens (ed), *Making Employment Rights Effective: Issues of Enforcement and Compliance* (Oxford and Portland, Oregon, Hart, 2012).

designed empirical work about whether systems theory's predictions or diagnoses are supported in practice.[10] On this view empirical investigation is essential to working out whether this strand of social theorising in its current forms can truly help in the design of more emancipatory workplace rights or if, instead, its starting points need to be revisited, at least so far as working life is concerned. McLaughlin's recent study about the experience in local authorities of trying to address unequal pay is a pertinent example[11] and some of his findings arguably point to the need for the underlying theory to be altered or refined.

In terms of substantive knowledge to be gained from empirical legal research, there are various features of my methodology that are worth picking out to illustrate the potential to extend learning about how law works. One of the things I was most struck by is how far the data illuminated that the cases that get to higher court adjudication are a skewed sample. This is in relation to the vast range both of problems at work and of types of working people who encounter them. That distortion cannot fail to trace through to the adjudication of disputes and the attitudes of everyone affected by this strain of legal process, as well as the authoritative interpretations that emerge from it. Innate bias in the supply of case law, and the implications this has for evolution in law and related practices, are only however visible because of my project's empirical foundations. These features of the case law were also put into relief by the legal enquiry being nested in wider knowledge about who has problems at work, what people do about them and who ends up litigating, as well as through investigation of what happens in the shadow of situations that do not get to the higher courts.

Another striking feature is the knowledge impacts of the fact that empirical work facilitates investigation that neither stops at the written law nor at the decisions that emerge from courts. What is said by people who are the objects of regulation, and those who advise them, about the legal influences they felt and perceived was profoundly challenging to easy assumptions that are frequently made about the direct impact of both written laws and the adjudication of disputes. This data was suggestive of important legal effects, but that were not linear, stable nor necessarily worker protective even where that was apparently the legislative intention. The data also brought into focus the salience of interactions between legal pressures and those of other kinds for how law creates effects.

[10] See in this regard, Fredman, above in 'Breaking the Mold', n 40, 281, concluding from her analysis of judicial application of the 'due regard' standard contained in the Equality Act 2010 Public Sector Equality Duty: 'Courts have escaped the first horn of the trilemma: regulatory resistance cannot be disguised behind formal compliance. Yet courts have fallen onto the second horn. Instead of dynamic decision-making, public bodies must refer to courts to determine whether there has been compliance. It is difficult to tell without more empirical work what effect this has had on internal decision-making and the extent to which the due regard standard has indeed functioned as a form of reflexive law. On the whole, it is unlikely that judicial review on its own is capable of achieving the internal culture change required if equality is truly to be mainstreamed'.

[11] C McLaughlin, 'Equal Pay, Litigation and Reflexive Regulation: the Case of the UK Local Authority Sector' (2014) 43 *Industrial Law Journal* 1.

Finally, it is worth saying something about methodological learning from empirical legal research. Each time empirical experimentation works to produce knowledge, it provides a methodological resource for others, whether from law or other disciplines. This seems to me to have potential to enhance what can be discovered in comparative and transnational analyses of law and legal process especially. I certainly hope that the methodological experimentation in my project will be useful for colleagues elsewhere. Aside from the findings leading to hypotheses for testing, my experience with carrying out the research design might be drawn upon to investigate other contexts that have witnessed the same kinds of shifts as the UK in terms both of law and the conduct of employment relations. The necessary disciplinary cross-fertilisation that comes with empirical investigation of legal phenomena also promises gains. There is a world of experience and learning from other disciplines about how effectively to investigate complex economic, social and political entitles on which legal research can draw and to which it may ultimately contribute.

However demanding empirical legal research may be, therefore, I have been convinced that this is a strand of enquiry that can deliver major theoretical, substantive and methodological advances. This in no way denies, nonetheless, that this is a difficult path for a researcher to take. Again some of the challenges are implicit in what I said above about the specific project I have recently completed. I evidently had to make difficult choices about the shape of the study and of elements within it as I went along, on which the value of what I discovered ultimately rests. Being clear-sighted about such decisions and their implications should enable work to retain its integrity. Still, there is something very scary about the possibility that a methodological misstep could fatally undermine the usefulness of data, especially when these ramifications may not be easily discernible in advance.

This perhaps highlights that a degree of personal courage is necessary for legal researchers to choose this methodological orientation. Arguably, however, that is a feature of all ambitious research whatever the discipline and approach. The most important challenges for empirical legal researchers that I think this points to are those that come, not from the innate difficulty of empirical work, but from the systemic position of individual scholars. The Nuffield Inquiry conducted by Genn, Partington and Wheeler in 2006 provided a highly useful 'tour de horizon' of these issues in the UK.[12] Moreover it was observed that: 'The information we were able to obtain from overseas colleagues makes clear that concern about empirical legal research capacity is not limited to the UK and that some of the factors affecting capacity in the UK are replicated elsewhere'.[13] The Inquiry's findings strongly resonate with my recent (and earlier) experimentation

[12] H Genn, M Partington, and S Wheeler, *Law in the Real World: Improving our Understanding of How Law Works, Final Report and Recommendations of the Nuffield Enquiry on Empirical Legal Research* (London, Nuffield, 2006).

[13] Ibid, 26–27, which also contain brief accounts of the position in Canada, Australia, New Zealand, and the US.

with empirical methodologies in the labour and equality field. In what follows I explain this further, focusing on the research environment in the UK while making some points that have wider purchase.

First there is the fact that legal education and professional training, especially at undergraduate level, tend to be methodologically unsophisticated, as mine most certainly was. The focus is on acquiring legal modes of thinking and reasoning, becoming comfortable with primary legal sources and adept at the techniques that lawyers and judges deploy in handling them. No doubt this is important in that these intellectual tools are constitutive of an insider's perspective on law and legal process and hence necessary to both internal and external examination of these phenomena. A certain amount is moreover typically done in legal education, at both undergraduate and Master's level, to equip students to undertake external analyses. This is achieved, for example, by relating philosophy, social and legal theory to legal rules, practices and institutions. Primary sources are also contextualised to some degree in relation to the use made of law outside legislatures and courts, and by drawing on empirical enquiry into how law functions in different environments.

The considerable problem nonetheless remains that undergraduate legal education, and often that at Master's level, does not systematically equip students themselves to undertake empirical investigations and sociologically to interpret 'law stuff', nor even to evaluate work of this kind by others. At its most basic, law students graduate significantly uneducated about how an entity such as law can be understood and scrutinised other than on its own terms.[14] This is an omission that is to some extent remedied by methods courses on PhD programmes. Further development in this direction may also increasingly create a cleavage between existing and future generations of legal researchers, a development of which this collection, and the conference it originated from, may be a sign. This would be welcome in many ways, not least given serious recent concern that empirical legal research capacity has declined, which indeed prompted the Nuffield Inquiry. Even so, while developments in postgraduate training in law have somewhat changed the equation for more recent entrants to the UK Academy, the broad picture is still that many legal scholars who want to undertake empirical legal research must first educate themselves about how to do so. This presents a massive challenge, while heightening the risks mentioned above and the consequent need for courage to embark on this course.[15] Equally, it sets up an in-built tendency for legal academics

[14] See ibid, generally and in particular at 30–33 on this set of issues and how they interact with other features of the UK Legal Academy to heighten the challenges associated with conducting empirical legal research.

[15] Ibid, 25, the following comment is strikingly resonant with this analysis: 'we also collected a number of biographical pen-portraits from experienced empirical legal researchers. These brief accounts of career paths reveal the often serendipitous entry—and occasionally stumble—into empirical research in civil law and justice. While the social scientists quoted below take for granted their empirical research

to concentrate on non-empirical, secondary research, augmenting the likelihood that empirical legal researchers will be somewhat isolated within their discipline.[16]

The second major challenge that I perceive, not wholly unrelated to the first, is that primary research is extraordinarily time consuming. The time it takes is also probably longer for legal researchers because of the need first to acquire necessary methodological expertise. Forecasting this aspect of a project may also be especially difficult for scholars who are not formally trained in designing empirical studies. The sheer length of my interview study was certainly a shock, adding nearly two years to a four-year project. This factor presents another hurdle for individual legal academics, in that they must invest so much more time than if they used other approaches before seeing any return for their efforts. This is exponentially problematic for early career scholars given the pressure to establish their publications profile and at a very demanding level in terms of quality. This is surely easier to do when research projects are 'bite-sized', for which the design of non-empirical projects will tend to be better adapted. This effect is then likely exacerbated by the Research Excellence Framework, the current UK model for scrutinising university research output, which requires a steady stream of at least one publication ever year or so.

Thirdly, and in a sense bringing together the factors above, would-be empirical legal researchers must contend with a self-reinforcing loop within law schools related to undergraduate teaching needs. As we have seen, many colleagues will naturally chose the more familiar, less time-heavy path of non-empirical research. There are, however, yet more benefits from doing so, this time institutionally in that this kind of research will be better articulated to the teaching that is prioritised in taught law degrees.[17] That will often make traditional legal researchers attractive to law schools needing to cater for the teaching of ever growing numbers of students on taught programmes, while sometimes rendering those scholars' teaching obligations less onerous and freeing up even more time to progress with research.

There is, of course, potential to neutralise these challenges through collaborations, including of an inter-disciplinary kind, since these increase research capacity in terms both of expertise and time. There are also signs of research

skills and tend to focus on the development of their interest in legal issues, the lawyers who have made the transition from legal academic training to empirical legal research, focus more on their cross-disciplinary journey and the acquisition of the skills *and, most importantly, the confidence to undertake empirical projects*. One or two undertook intensive research training in social science research methods, but most lawyers learned "on the job" and often by means of symbiotic collaboration with a social scientist or an established empirical legal researcher'. (Emphasis added.)

[16] See M Siems and D Mac Síthigh, 'Mapping Legal Research' (2012) 71 *Cambridge Law Journal* 651, 666–71 on the distribution of different types of legal research within university law departments. This supports that conduct of traditional legal scholarship is resilient, while at the same time showing that UK legal scholars in appreciable numbers take different, sometimes overlapping, approaches that encompass empirical work.

[17] See Genn, Partington and Wheeler, n 12, 32–33 and 36–37 situating these particular challenges in the context of the UK Legal Academy.

funding supporting group endeavour. Yet this is likely to work better for those at later stages of their careers, who have the experience and intellectual relationships to make collaborations work. This may well not genuinely reduce the challenges at a systemic level therefore, in that people will only get to the point of collaborating if they have anyway overcome the obstacles to conducting empirical research in law.[18] There are also further challenges associated with inter-disciplinary working, in that, first, it is inherently at risk of being undervalued because, by definition, it is unlikely to be in the mainstream anywhere and, secondly, people who have, rationally, eschewed an inter-disciplinary path may well be difficult to communicate with about the value of such work.[19]

D. The Nature of Law and Legal Process

Finally, on top of these systemic issues, it seems to me there is a substantive challenge that empirical work with contemporary labour and equality law highlights, albeit that it is likely reproduced in other areas of law. This is the difficulty of finding a language that effectively, on the one hand, uncovers the weaknesses of existing models of legal intervention to enhance fairness and equality and, on the other hand, enhances law's capacity to promote those norms. In a world that has moved so decisively away from collective, communal understandings of the good, towards individualist, self-regarding conceptions, a particular danger is that critique of the current functioning of fairness- and equality-promoting legal rules becomes, in the hands particularly of politicians, yet more grist to the mill of sustaining and extending unfair and unequal power structures. This resonates with some of Bob Hepple's contribution to this collection (chapter one).

For criticism of law's current functioning to give politicians more bases on which to undermine emancipatory laws would be an ironic, dubious kind of 'impact'. Yet it is perhaps the kind most likely in the contemporary UK for research about labour and equality law and irrespective of what was actually found or argued. One consolation might be that successive UK governmental efforts to render individual labour and equality rights practically unenforceable have finally succeeded to such an extent, especially with the introduction of ET fees, that UK politicians will move on from instrumental deployment of research findings in this

[18] See however ibid, 26 that: 'Finally, the biographies provide some evidence of the challenges facing even well-established legal researchers in making the space and time necessary for empirical work. They reflect both the hard realities of empirical data collection and the tremendous intellectual satisfaction gained from the successful completion of projects'.

[19] See further ibid, 34–36 on this set of issues. Also see generally, R Cotterrell, 'Socio-Legal Studies, Law Schools and Socio-Legal Theory' QMUL School of Law, Research Paper 126/2012 and specifically on funding and inter-disciplinarity at 3–4 and 6.

particular way.[20] Yet this amounts in effect to noticing that it may be safe to expose structural weaknesses in current legal approaches to achieving fairness and equality at work because those flaws have so efficiently been exploited that there is nothing left to lose. As such this is surely better seen as an additional, powerful argument that the spotlight needs to be turned onto how law and legal process really work.

Yet the dilemma adverted to here is even internal to the Academy, in the risk of work being criticised merely for questioning individualised models of legal entitlement and enforcement, given the theoretical promise those forms carry, the gains they have undoubtedly made and that individual rights might well be seen as providing the only countervailing force, whether in legal or other worlds, to the concentration of power and resources in the hands of ever more narrowly drawn elites. A particular issue here is the difficulty of criticising the multiple failures of law to deliver meaningful protections of individual rights without slipping into, or at least seeming to slip into, denying the importance of the underlying entitlements being protected whether or not they are expressed as rights.

The point this leads me to is that this dilemma instantiates another mechanism by which the contradictory nature of law is realised. The more the Janus-faced quality of law and legal process is perceived, the more thinkers and researchers should be cognisant that whatever law says 'on the tin' it will always, somehow or other, reinforce that which it purports to subvert. As soon as you are in the business of uncovering law's deep structure, you are bound on this view to recognise that turning to law and judges for emancipation, whatever the virtuosity of legal design, is in some sense bound simultaneously to achieve the opposite. How much more appealing, then, from so many points of view, instead to emphasise the positive side of law's potential contribution. And it is true that this stance may better navigate the perils of research being misused.

Yet much is also thereby lost. By definition avoiding law's 'dark side' elides arguably the most important critique of legal experience, abandoning thereby a critical aspect of the quest to find ways better to use law's transformative power.[21] Much as law is slippery, mercurial and exasperating as a medium for delivering worthwhile social change, its very duality gives hope that legal mechanisms can strike a better balance between disrupting and upholding the status quo. It is this tantalising possibility that ultimately most convinces me that the challenges of empirical legal scholarship are worth confronting.

[20] See generally on the Coalition changes, B Hepple, 'Back to the Future: Employment Law under the Coalition Government' (2013) 42 *Industrial Law Journal* 203 and Ministry of Justice, *Tribunal Statistics Quarterly, January to March 2014* (June 2014). For recent figures on the dramatic decline in claims see pp 2 and 7–8.

[21] See A Hunt, 'Rights and Social Movements: Counter-Hegemonic Strategies' (1990) 17 *Journal of Law and Society* 309 generally and specifically at 320 for the following argument in favour of rights strategising, although being careful to uncouple this from the use necessarily of litigation: 'A more far-reaching criticism of litigation is that, rather than helping, "law", conceived variously as litigation or legal reform politics, is itself *part of the problem* … Here a hegemonic strategy must insist that it is precisely in the engagement with the actually existing terrain, in particular, with its discursive forms, that the possibility of their transformation and transcendence becomes possible'. This seems to me an attempt to reconcile clear-sightedness about the limitations of rights with finding ways nonetheless to realise their emancipatory possibilities.

4

Quantitative Labour Law

ZOE ADAMS AND SIMON DEAKIN*

A. Introduction

Quantitative approaches to the analysis of labour law have become widespread since the publication of the Organisation for Economic Cooperation and Development's (OECD) index of employment protection laws in the 1990s, followed in the 2000s by the World Bank's *Doing Business Report* indicators. These quantitative measures of labour law rules have been used extensively to study the economic effects of labour market regulations of various kinds and have had a tangible effect on policy. However, they suffer from a number of methodological limitations; in particular, they do not provide a continuous time series of the kind that is needed to test claims of a causal relationship between legal change and economic outcomes. Nonetheless, in this paper we defend the idea that there is an important role for empirical, particularly quantitative, approaches to the analysis of labour law today. We then present findings from the CBR Labour Regulation Index (CBR-LRI), which uses 'leximetric' methods to code labour law rules for over 30 developed and developing countries for the period 1970–2013, extending the more limited, five-county dataset presented in 2007 by Deakin, Lele and Siems.[1] We explain how the CBR-LRI takes a distinct approach to data coding and how this is providing us with new evidence on the long term trends in, and economic effects, of labour laws.

* The authors are respectively Researcher at Centre for Business Research, University of Cambridge and Professor of Law and Director of the Centre for Business Research, University of Cambridge. The authors gratefully acknowledge support from the DFID-ESRC Joint Fund for Poverty Alleviation and the Legal Reform Institute.

[1] S Deakin, P Lele and M Siems, 'The Evolution of Labour Law: Calibrating and Comparing Regulatory Regimes' (2007) 146 *International Labour Review* 133.

B. The Importance of an Empirical and Quantitative Approach to Labour Law

Empirical research has often been criticised for being inappropriate in the context of legal analysis. Such research techniques are criticised for excessive reductionism, for failing to account for the dynamic nature of law, and for ignoring the importance of contextual and historical factors in legal interpretation.[2] In particular, the reduction of values to pure data, as required by quantitative approaches, is seen to run against the very nature of legal analysis. Nonetheless, empirical research techniques offer a considerable resource to enable a better understanding of the discipline. Such an approach makes labour law appear more relevant and accessible to non-lawyers, as well as facilitating a multi-disciplinary approach that enables labour law to draw on concepts and ideas from other fields. It is in this way that labour law can become a key consideration in economic policy.

Furthermore, the distinction between empirical and legal analysis should not be over-emphasised. There are equivalents to 'raw data' and 'coding' to be found in legal research in the form of legislative texts, and the interpretation of findings in light of theory, respectively. While it is true that legal research is primarily concerned with the systematic interpretation of texts, in search of a doctrinal 'meaning' or 'fit', while empirical research involves formulating and testing hypotheses concerning the social world, legal research too has often engaged with social facts in order to test certain claims.

Labour law is traditionally understood as a distinct legal discipline, to be differentiated from social science disciplines touching on the world of work, such as industrial relations or labour economics. However, it was the empirical study of factory labour, collective bargaining, and the 'public organisation' of the labour market through the antecedents of the modern social security system, that provided the material for the legislative reforms which originally gave birth to labour law in the early twentieth century. Labour law developed, therefore, as certain empirical facts began to intrude into the realm of legal thought. Just as the early claims for social legislation were strengthened by reference to surveys and statistics concerning social conditions, modern claims linking aspects of labour law with social and economic outcomes can be supported, and also, where relevant rebutted, through a sustained engagement with empirical research techniques.

Today, labour law may be seen to be in a state of 'crisis'. The assumed facts underpinning traditional labour law discourse have been subject to increasing challenge on the basis of economic and ideological arguments that place labour law and the market in opposition, construing the former as a 'distortion' on the latter. These challenges have called into question many features of national labour

[2] See M Siems, 'Numerical Comparative Law: Do We Need Statistical Evidence in Law in Order to Reduce Complexity?' (2005) 13 *Cardozo Journal of International & Comparative* Law 521.

law regimes, particularly in the context of the EU internal market and the policies of the World Bank and the OECD.

This new orthodoxy claims that labour law has an employment inhibiting effect, and that there is a link between the degree of labour market regulation and economic performance. While at the level of normative theory we can seriously challenge the basis of these claims, such rebuttals are often ignored or misinterpreted at the policy level. In order to be influential in policy-making, the analysis of labour law needs to engage with the empirical claims made by this new orthodoxy. In particular, techniques need to be employed that enable systematic and rigorous analysis of causal influences on economic performance. The evidence then needs to be presented in a way with which policymakers are familiar. Work that is not empirically grounded runs the risk of being written off as 'pure theory'.

Quantitative techniques (explained in more detail below) are particularly useful because they facilitate an investigation into causation, thus enabling labour lawyers to engage with the claimed links between labour laws and specific economic outcomes. In the absence of such evidence, ideological claims may go unchallenged. In addition, the quantification of legal regulation may be useful in facilitating comparative analysis, reducing the complexity inherent in cross-country comparison.[3] This is particularly important today, given that empirical research has proved influential in the policies of the World Bank, and has been used to place pressure on transitional and developing countries to adopt neo-liberal and deregulatory reforms.

The limitations of empirical methodology, particularly quantitative methods, cannot be ignored. However, as we show below, there are methodological steps that can be taken to enable many of these limits to be overcome. Quantitative legal research, precisely because of its capacity to engage with data in other fields (such as finance), and to reduce the complexity of legal argument, is particularly useful in the verification and falsification of hypotheses[4] such as those made by the new economic orthodoxy. Empirical research has proved to be far more influential at the policy level than complex legal argument, making the discipline of labour law more accessible to policymakers. Thus for these various reasons, empirical legal research—and quantitative methods in particular—should be seen as an essential part of the toolkit of labour lawyers.

C. The World Bank (*Doing Business Report*) and OECD Indices

The *Doing Business Report* (DBR) indices purport to assess the quality of a legal system by measuring the extent to which the regulatory climate of a given country

[3] Ibid.
[4] Ibid.

minimises the costs of establishing and running a business.[5] The ranking thus purports to reflect the 'ease of doing business' in each country. Laws and regulations are given a value between 0 and 100, with the higher value representing greater rigidity. The index ranks 180 countries on this basis.

The DBR indices build on the claim that complex and costly legal regulations limiting property rights constitute obstacles to economic development.[6] According to Djankov and Ramalho, the extent of business regulation in a country is not correlated to the presence of market failures, but to a set of socio-economic characteristics including the level of corruption, the degree of democracy, and the stage of economic development.[7] The level at which countries 'entered' a given regulatory environment was also said to be influenced by their common law or civil law legal origin. This particular link was developed by the work of Botero et al in the context of labour law.[8]

The DBR Employing Workers Index (EWI) builds on the initial study of Botero et al. Scores decrease correlatively with the existence of regulations that cause delay or cost to businesses.[9] The sub-indicators covered are: (1) the difficulty of hiring; (2) rigidity of hours; and (3) redundancy costs.

The primary data in the EWI are mostly sourced from survey evidence. Initially, questionnaires were sent to business actors ('local partners') including commercial law firms in the countries concerned. Respondents were asked to rank the rigidity of labour laws applying to a 'hypothetical case' referring to a 40-year-old male worker with 20 years' seniority, employed in permanent factory work in an establishment employing more than 200 workers. The methods used to collect the data have been subjected to a number of criticisms, which include the vagueness of the questionnaires, the irrelevance of the hypothetical case to emerging market settings, and the focus on rigidities at the expense of elements of flexibility in the application of labour laws.[10] Criticism of the EWI culminated in the report of the Manuel Commission, set up by the World Bank itself, which in 2013 confirmed an earlier decision, in 2009, removing the EWI from the main part of the annual

[5] S Benedettini and A Nicita, 'Towards the Economics of Comparative Law: The "Doing Business" Debate' (2010) 1 *Comparative Law Review* 2.

[6] H de Soto, *The Mystery of Capital* (New York, Basic Books, 2000).

[7] S Djankov and R Ramalho, 'Employment Laws in Developing Countries' (Centre for Economic Policy Research (CEPR) Discussion Paper No DP7097, 2008) available at SSRN: ssrn.com/abstract=1344676.

[8] J Botero, S Djankov, R La Porta, F Lopez-de-Silanes and A Shleifer, 'The Regulation of Labor' (2004) 119 *Quarterly Journal of Economics* 1340.

[9] Ibid.

[10] J Berg and S Cazes, 'The Doing Business Indicators: Measurement Issues and Political Implications' (Geneva, ILO Working Paper, 2007), J Berg and S Cazes, 'Policymaking Gone Awry: The Labor Market Regulations of the Doing Business Indicators' (2008) 29 *Comparative Labor Law & Policy Journal* 349, B du Marais, 'Methodological Limits of "Doing Business" Reports' (2009), available at papers.ssrn.com/sol3/papers.cfm?abstract_id=1408605, S Lee, D McCann and N Torm, 'The World Bank's "Employing Workers" Index: Findings and Critiques—a Review of Recent Evidence' (2008) 147 *International Labour Review* 416.

Doing Business Reports, along with a number of changes to its methodology, which included modification of the hypothetical case used to collect country-level data. These steps notwithstanding, the EWI continues to be updated and published, and unmodified data from the early 2000s onwards are still being used in empirical studies of the effects of labour laws.

The OECD index is an index of the 'strictness' of employment protection legislation in the OECD Member States and a number of developing and transition countries. Thus like the EWI, it purports to measure the costs of regulation. It is based on a series of data gathering exercises undertaken in the late 1980s, 1990s and 2003, followed by more regular, annual data collection up to the present day. Since 1999 the scores have been expressed on a 0 to 6 scale, with 6 representing maximum 'strictness'. Three areas of employment protection legislation (EPL) are covered: rules regulating dismissals with regards regular contracts, rules governing fixed-term contracts (FTCs) and temporary work agreements (TWAs), and rules governing collective dismissals. A composite score is arrived at to give an indication of overall strictness for a given country.

The OECD's coding methodology has changed over time.[11] From 1999, the values and scores used were based on a 'variety of national sources', principally 'multi-country surveys' supplemented by additional information from OECD governments. In practice, it appears that the data were derived mostly from government returns, with some verification and updating by OECD staff. This mostly took the form of references to secondary literature; legislation and case law were consulted only in cases of residual uncertainty. Where data were not available, values were often attributed retroactively, and over time many of the scores in the index were corrected and revised.

From 2013, less reliance was placed on governmental surveys, and more emphasis given to primary sources, including, for the first time, collective agreements, which were 'systematically reviewed' in an attempt to improve and correct previous data. The 2013 report claims that the revisions have had little effect on aggregate indicators. However, it is not straightforward to determine what the impact of particular changes in the coding methodology has been on data for earlier years.

A number of new indicators have been incorporated into the OECD index over time. Only from 2008 does a set of weighted scores exist that incorporates indicators covering the time allowed to make an unfair dismissal claim, equal treatment for TWAs, and authorisation and reporting requirements for TWAs. The 'cost' reflected by the score is calculated with reference to the user firm, and not the agency as it is the user which will be assessing the costs of alternative forms of employment.

[11] See OECD, *Employment Outlook* (Paris, OECD, multiple years); OECD, *OECD Jobs Study, Evidence and Explanations, Part I: Labour Market Trends and Underlying Forces of Change* (Paris, OECD, 1994) and D Venn, *Legislation, Collective Bargaining and Enforcement: Updating the OECD Employment Protection Indicators* (Paris, OECD, 2009).

An additional change in the 2013 update is to exclude fault-based dismissals, as opposed to economic dismissals (redundancies or restructurings) from the definition of 'rigidities' affecting employers. This approach had not previously been applied in a consistent way, resulting in misleading data comparisons between countries. A problem remains, however, in that severing this aspect of the definition of 'unfair' dismissal presupposes that such a distinction is made within a country's own legal system. Such distinctions are not always so clearly made. Further, when it comes to analysing the procedural restrictions on dismissal, it is not clear that those procedures that relate most particularly to fault-based dismissals (as do many procedural constraints) have been consistently discounted from the unfair dismissal indicators. In some countries, a distinction is made between a dismissal that is null and void, and one that is merely 'unfair'; whether reinstatement is available or not often turns on this distinction. The OECD coding gives a significant weighting to this 'remedial' aspect of dismissal regulation: it is one-twelfth of the assessment of the 'regular contracts' score, which itself is five-twelfths of the overall EPL score. However, it is not clear that in assessing how likely a court is to order reinstatement account is taken of differences between dismissals that are void and those that are merely unfair.

Consideration of collective dismissals has not been undertaken throughout the entire period. Collective dismissals were not included in the index prior to 1999 and they were not incorporated into the overall EPL indicator until 2013. Collective dismissal scores are calculated by reference to the extent that regulation goes beyond regulation of individual dismissals, and a weighting devised to assess this extra impact. A curious aspect of this, however, is that the indicator for the definition of unfair dismissal in the assessment of individual dismissals absorbs redundancy selection criteria as part of the calculation—which arguably belongs more properly to the realm of collective dismissal and ought to be a distinct indicator.

The 2013 update also made a number of changes in relation to scoring and weighting. A score of '0' has been adopted where an employer can object to reinstatement. This has resulted in revisions to the scores for certain countries (in Luxembourg and Sweden, for example). The OECD tries to take account of enforcement issues in relation to this indicator. Court practice on the issue of the remedy 'usually awarded' appears to be influencing the score given for this indicator. However, it is not clear that this approach is being consistently applied on a cross-country basis.

A further change has been made in relation to the scorings for temporary employment. Previous exercises gave a score of '0' (representing the least 'restrictive' value) in relation to the indicators for equal treatment and maximum number of renewals for temporary agency workers' contracts and fixed term contracts, where such work contracts were illegal in the country concerned. The 2013 update instead adopts the maximum score of '1' if these contracts are not permitted. This has had a tangible effect on the values given for the rules affecting temporary agency work.

D. Empirical Analysis of the DBR and OECD Indices

Recent empirical studies using the DBR and OECD indices do not present a consistent picture. Although some analyses, mostly those using the DBR data, point to a correlation between low regulation and greater flexibility, resulting in lower unemployment, others suggest that the effects of employment protection laws differ according to the characteristics of firms and industries. There is evidence to suggest that stricter employment protection is associated with a stronger employment performance during the recent crisis, and with beneficial impacts on innovation and productivity.

Pierre and Scarpetta have investigated firm responses to high levels of EPL using both the DBR and OECD indices.[12] They have found that levels of EPL do not significantly affect the decisions of larger firms which, having lower levels of employee turnover, tend not to adjust their human resource strategies as the stringency of EPL varies. High EPL impacts mostly upon smaller firms, whose responses usually consist of a combination of training and alternative employment strategies.

Heyes has shown that countries with higher levels of EPL have tended to experience fewer labour market disruptions than those with weaker protections.[13] In relation to the EU15, Heyes concludes that countries with robust employment protection have been effective in cushioning the shock of the economic crisis and have thus experienced fewer job losses.[14] The cushioning effect, however, lasted only in the short to medium term, and did not prevent job losses in later phases. As the crisis continued, countries responded by deregulating their employment protection so as to encourage hiring. Heyes' analysis suggests, however, that these reforms did not lead to improvements in aggregate employment.

Cazes at al have found a small, but positive, link between EPL stringency and employment.[15] They have also found that the gap between the stringency of EPL for regular and temporary contracts is linked to labour market dualism, although they found that this link occurs only at the extremes. For most countries, the gap between EPL for regular and temporary work has almost no effect upon the temporary employment rate. Cazes et al have argued that other factors such as the efficiency of judicial procedures may be driving dualism. The suggestion that EPL is not a conclusive determinant of employment levels is supported by Can who

[12] G Pierre and S Scarpetta, 'Do Firms Make Greater Use of Training and Temporary Employment when Labor Adjustment Costs are High?' (2013) 2 *IZA Journal of Labor Policy* 15.

[13] J Heyes, 'Flexicurity, Employment Protection and the Jobs Crisis' (2011) 25 *Work, Employment & Society* 642.

[14] J Heyes, 'Employment Protection Under Fire: Why Labour Market Deregulation Will Not Deliver Quality Jobs' (Working Paper for the SPERI Inaugural Conference, 16–18 July 2012).

[15] S Cazes, S Khatiwada and M Malo, *Employment Protection and Collective Bargaining: Beyond the Deregulation Agenda* (Geneva, International Labour Organisation, 2012).

has shown that government size and output gap are more important factors.[16] Similarly, Alemán has shown that EPL may complement spending on active labour market policies but that the degree of fit depends upon factors such as the extent of corporatism and union involvement in active labour market policy.[17] Bertane found that EPL is negatively and significantly associated with youth unemployment and lowers the youth unemployment rate, while Sarkar has found no causal connection between EPL and either youth unemployment or unemployment more generally.[18] Cappellari et al have highlighted the unwanted negative effects on productivity in Italian firms following Italy's two recent 'flexibility' based reforms to temporary employment.[19]

Recent research also indicates that different EPL rules may impact to a greater/lesser degree on unemployment than others. Bassanini et al show that the most influential regulatory determinant of labour market flows is practice on reinstatement.[20] They also argue that judicial willingness to grant, and worker incentives to request, reinstatement are influenced by social and cultural practices beyond the law itself. Nuanced distinctions are also necessary when considering the incidence of EPL on labour market mobility. While a high level of EPL is correlated with low levels of *within* industry job-to-job transitions, it has no significant effect on industry composition, or on persistent joblessness.

The selective impact of legal rules also needs to be considered, given that how far a new legal rule impacts on behaviour will depend upon how far the new rule differs from existing practice at firm level.[21] Thus Bassanini et al found that dismissal regulation affects EPL-binding firms (that is firms with a high propensity to dismiss in economic downturn) more than others.[22]

Particular combinations of laws and policies may have distinct effects. Lee has shown that, in the context of long-term unemployment and non-standard employment, a low level of the statutory minimum wage can lead to high levels of non-standard employment in combination with either strict EPL for permanent

[16] R Can, 'The Impact of Employment Protection Legislation on the Unemployment Rate in Selected OECD Countries' (doctoral dissertation, Georgetown University, 2013).

[17] J Alemán, 'Active or Passive? Reforming Employment Benefits in the OECD' (2012) 4 *Review of European Studies* 94.

[18] C Bertane, 'Does Employment Protection Legislation Hinder Youth Employment in OECD Countries?' (Georgetown University, 2011), P Sarkar, 'Impact of Labour Regulation on Unemployment: A Case Study of France, Germany, UK and USA' (University Library of Munich, 2011), P Sarkar, 'Does an Employment Protection Law Lead to Unemployment? A Panel Data Analysis of OECD Countries, 1990–2000' (2013) 37 *Cambridge Journal of Economics* 1335.

[19] L Cappellari, C Dell'Aringa and M Leonardi, 'Temporary Employment, Job Flows and Productivity: A Tale of Two Reforms' (2012) 122 *Economic Journal* F188.

[20] A Bassanini and A Garnero, 'Dismissal Protection and Worker Flows in OECD Countries: Evidence from Cross-Country/Cross-Industry Data' (2013) 21 *Labour Economics* 25.

[21] S Deakin and P Sarkar, 'Assessing the Long-Run Economic Impact of Labour Law Systems: A Theoretical Reappraisal and Analysis of New Time Series Data' (2008) 39 *Industrial Relations Journal* 453.

[22] A Bassanini, L Nunziata and D Venn, 'Job Protection Legislation and Productivity Growth in OECD Countries' (2009) 24 *Economic Policy* 349.

workers or weak EPL for temporary workers.[23] On the other hand, long-term unemployment rates also tend to be higher when high EPL for temporary workers is combined with high levels of statutory minimum wages.

In comparing the unemployment rates of France and Spain during the crisis, Bentolila et al attribute 64 per cent of the increase in unemployment in Spain to its EPL composition.[24] Overall, the OECD scorings for both countries were virtually identical. The 2004 index gives a score of 2.5 to France and 2.6 to Spain for protection for regular employment, and 3.6 to France and 3.5 to Spain for regulation of temporary employment, and 2.1 to France and 3.1 to Spain for collective dismissals. The overall EPL score is 3.0 for France and 3.1 for Spain. There are differences, however, in the strictness of dismissal regulation for permanent contracts and regulation of temporary employment. This then implies that grouping countries with similar EPL scores when making policy recommendations may lead to unwanted and inconsistent results.

Three recent IMF papers report empirical evidence, using data from the Fraser Institute, which are themselves derived from the EWI, to show that more flexible labour markets are negatively associated with employment elasticities.[25] They conclude that large-scale reforms of labour market institutions, aimed towards increasing flexibility, may help to reduce unemployment. However, the results are almost certainly a function of the dataset being used here, which contains several unexplained discontinuities.[26] The Fraser Institute dataset contains breaks in its time series which are caused by methodological changes in data collection and questionable data aggregation.[27] It also double counts many individual components. This leads to overestimates in the 'rigidities' attributed to particular countries. The positive 'reforms' to which the studies point as indicators of the benefits of increasing flexibility cannot be replicated when the breaks in the date series are accounted for.

[23] S Lee, 'Examining Policy Configurations as Conditions for Long-Term Unemployment and Non-Standard Employment in OECD Countries Using Fuzzy-Set Analysis' (2013) 47 *Quality & Quantity* 3521.

[24] S Bentolila, P Cahuc, J Dolado and T Le Barbanchon, 'Unemployment and Temporary Jobs in the Crisis: Comparing France and Spain' (Working Paper 2010-07, 2010).

[25] D Furceri, 'Unemployment and Labour Market Issues in Algeria' (IMF Working Paper 12/99, 2012), E Crivelli, D Furceri and J Toujas-Bernaté, 'Can Policies Affect Employment Intensity of Growth? A Cross-Country Analysis' (IMF Working Paper 12/218, 2012), L Bernal-Verdugo, D Furceri and D Guillaume, 'Crises, Labour Market Policy, and Unemployment' (IMF Working Paper 12/65, 2012), published as: 'Banking Crises, Labour Reforms, and Unemployment' (2012) 41 *Journal of Comparative Economics* 1202.

[26] M Aleksynska, 'Deregulating Labour Markets: How Robust is the Analysis of Recent IMF Working Papers?' (ILO Working Paper, 2014).

[27] In 2010 the Fraser Institute introduced some methodological changes in its data by introducing new components. Thus, the database is revised back to 2002—but prior to this, data on old components are still reported in the 2010 edition of the database. The minimum wages subcomponent is a replication of the World Bank's Difficulty of Hiring Index, but only for the years 2002–08. Thus the subcomponent for hiring regulations and minimum wages represents a mixed data series. Similar issues exist in relation to the mandated cost of hiring subcomponent. These changes, taken together, mean that 2002 is an important break in series in the Fraser Institute data. In addition, the composite scores are formed on the basis of averages drawn from different types of data. See Aleksynska, n 26.

Some of the so-called 'reforms' are instead false indicators caused by changes in the data collection methods used by the World Bank. Aleksynska has shown that if observations with missing data for the subcomponents from the Fraser sample are excluded, only 17 out of 53 of the reforms identified in the dataset should be included. If the 'conscription' subcomponent is excluded (as it should be if the focus is on EPL), only 8 of the recorded 53 reforms can be relied on. When a more complete time series is used, the negative results of the IMF studies cannot be replicated.[28]

The problems associated with using an incomplete time series in the context of the IMF papers apply equally to a number of studies using the OECD data. Bassanini et al attempt to compensate for gaps in the OECD data by using country-level labour market surveys in relation to a number of OECD countries, but acknowledge that for many countries, data are still not available for the entire period.[29] In an attempt to compensate for missing data in relation to collective dismissals, for example, they have substituted the EPL score for individual dismissals of regular workers. To compensate for the lack of collective bargaining coverage in the times series, they have substituted union density for that variable. Baumann et al appear to rely solely on the data from OECD's 2004 codings.[30]

E. The Extended CBR-LRI: Theoretical Foundations, Coding Methods, and First Results

The DBR and OECD indices both assume that costs to firms can be imputed from the existence of regulations of particular types. Formally, at least, they purpose to measure these costs—the 'rigidity' and 'strictness' of rules—rather than the intrinsic character of legal rules. There are inherent problems with this approach. It assumes that in the absence of worker-protective labour laws, the market is in a unique equilibrium, which legal intervention 'disturbs'. Relatedly, it takes no account of the extent to which labour law rules codify or crystallise practices of firms. How far a particular rule constitutes a 'constraint' or a 'cost' will vary across firms. An alternative approach is to attempt to code for the degree of protection which, in principle, is conferred on a worker by a given rule, using an ordinal scale that compares the content of different norms. A purely text-based approach will not be able to capture actors' perceptions of the strength or weakness of particular rules, but it may offer greater consistency and clarity of coding than methods that combine de iure and de facto aspects of rules.

The CBR-LRI is one of a number of databases developed at the Centre for Business Research in Cambridge since the mid-2000s that provide longitudinal

[28] Aleksynska, n 26.

[29] A Bassanini and A Garnero, 'Dismissal Protection and Worker Flows in OECD Countries: Evidence from Cross-Country/Cross-Industry Data' (2013) 21 *Labour Economics* 25.

[30] F Baumann, M Mechtel and N Stähler, 'Employment Protection and Temporary Work Agencies' (2011) 25 *Labour* 308.

data on changes in labour and company law using 'leximetric' coding methods.[31] The methods used to construct the CBR-LRI reflect a certain theoretical conception of the relationship between legal rules and social structure. This is based on their endogeneity, mutability, and formality.

By referring to law's partial endogeneity, we mean the sense in which legal rules reflect economic conditions as well as shaping behaviour. Legal systems co-evolve alongside developments in the economy and the political system.[32] Thus quantitative economic analysis must be able to take on board the possibility of reverse causation or of multi-directional causal flows between legal and economic variables. It further follows that econometric analysis of law should be longitudinal. Cross-sectional analyses can indicate correlation but not, normally, causation.

A second relevant feature of legal rules is their mutability. Legal rules rarely have a completely fixed meaning or unique interpretation. Thus the application of a legal rule is rarely a matter of 'either/or'. Binary variables, which purport to measure the presence or absence of a legal rule using a simple (0, 1) coding scheme, may well not be an appropriate way of conceptualising the operation of regulatory norms.[33]

A third feature to consider is the formality of law, that is, the gap between 'law on the books' and 'law in action'. The formal enactment of a legal rule may tell us something about its practical effects, but legal rules are not self-enforcing. If a given legal rule reflects an existing social consensus, it may well take effect without the need for regular enforcement. In other contexts, general respect of the law, the efficiency of the court system and the amount of resources devoted to enforcement may be critical variables to add into the analysis.[34]

From these theoretical starting points, leximetric method involves breaking down the process of index construction into a series of stages, beginning with the identification of a *phenomenon* of interest ('labour law') which can be expressed as a conceptual *construct* ('regulation', from the viewpoint of the employer, or 'protection', from that of the worker). Then one or more *indicators* or *variables* are identified which, singly or together, express the construct in numerical terms. A *coding algorithm* is then devised, setting out a series of steps to be taken in assigning numerical values to the primary source material. The algorithm incorporates a *measurement scale* of some kind. Finally, a decision must be taken on whether and/or how to apply *weights* to the individual variables or indicators.

[31] M Siems and S Deakin, 'Comparative Law and Finance: Past, Present, and Future Research' (2010) 166 *Journal of Institutional and Theoretical Economics* 120, J Buchanan, D Chai and S Deakin, 'Empirical Analysis of Legal Institutions and Institutional Change: Multiple-Methods Approaches and their Application to Corporate Governance Research' (2014) 10 *Journal of Institutional Economics* 1.

[32] J Armour, S Deakin, P Lele and M Siems, 'How Legal Norms Evolve: Evidence from a Cross-Country Comparison of Shareholder, Creditor and Worker Protection' (2009) 57 *American Journal of Comparative Law* 579.

[33] J Armour, S Deakin, P Sarkar, M Siems and A Singh, 'Shareholder Protection and Stock Market Development: An Empirical Test of the Legal Origins Hypothesis' (2009) 6 *Journal of Empirical Legal Studies* 343.

[34] S Fagernäs, 'Labor Law, Judicial Efficiency and Informal Employment in India' (2010) 7 *Journal of Empirical Legal Studies* 282.

The result is an *index* that provides a measure of the phenomenon of interest, which can be used in statistical analysis.

The Cambridge indices use coding algorithms that indicate not just the presence or absence of a worker-protective law in a given country, but estimate magnitudes concerning the degree of protection conferred by a given legal rule. These are represented using graduated scores between zero (indicating little or no protection) and one (indicating high protection). The coding algorithms, along with the primary sources for the codings and the values given to particular indicators on country/year basis, are reported on an open-access website that is regularly updated.[35]

The LRI contains 40 indicators in all, grouped into five sub-indices.[36] These cover, respectively, the regulation of alternative employment contracts (self-employment, part-time work, fixed-term employment and temporary agency work); working time (daily and weekly working time limits and rules governing overtime); dismissal (procedural and substantive rules on termination of employment); employee representation (rules on collective bargaining, the closed shop and codetermination); and industrial action (the extent of legal support for the right to strike, including rules on secondary and political strikes).

The indicators in the LRI can be combined in various ways. For the purposes of the present analysis we will take the nine indicators in the LRI dismissal law sub-index and add two further indicators from the employment representation sub-index, relating to aspects of codetermination (employee information and consultation, and employee participation at board level). This enables us to construct a sub-index of the LRI that approximately corresponds to the OECD-EPI for laws governing individual and collective dismissals. It also makes it possible to compare the LRI scores for employment protection and codetermination combined with data from the CBR-SPI, another of the CBR datasets, which codes for minority shareholder rights. These comparisons are useful for suggesting certain properties of the LRI and the uses to which it might be put in statistical analysis.

Figures 1 and 2 show that shareholder protection scores have risen steadily over the period since 1990, and that the increase has been particularly marked in civil law countries, which have now more or less converged with common law countries. When the sample of countries is broken down by level of development, developed countries are shown to have higher levels of shareholder protection over most of this period than either transition or developing countries, but here again there has been convergence, with transition systems in particular catching up with developed systems.

Figures 2–4 show trends in employment protection and codetermination from 1970. Now, civil law countries have consistently higher scores than common law countries. Otherwise the story is similar: developed countries have higher levels of protection than developing countries, and transition systems have largely

[35] See: www.cbr.cam.ac.uk.

[36] S Deakin, P Lele and M Siems, 'The Evolution of Labour Law: Calibrating and Comparing Regulatory Regimes' (2007) 146 *International Labour Review* 133.

converged with (and in some cases overtaken) developed systems. There is no evidence of a general trend towards deregulation of employment protection laws.

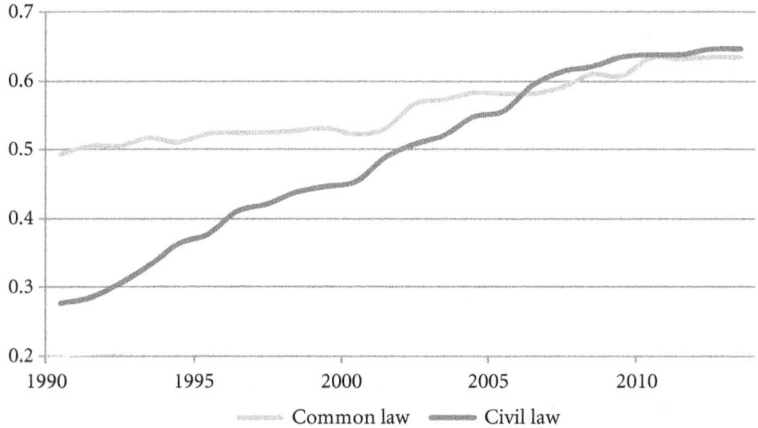

Figure 1: Shareholder protection in 30 countries, 1990–2014, comparing common law and civil law origin countries
Source: CBR-SPI, CBR Leximetric Database: (www.cbr.cam.ac.uk)
Note: the countries in the dataset are Argentina, Austria, Belgium, Brazil, Canada, Chile, China, Czech Republic, Cyprus, Estonia, France, Germany, India, Italy, Japan, Latvia, Lithuania, Malaysia, Mexico, the Netherlands, Pakistan, Poland, Russia, Slovenia, Sweden, South Africa, Spain, Switzerland, Turkey, UK and the US. The scale used is 0–1.

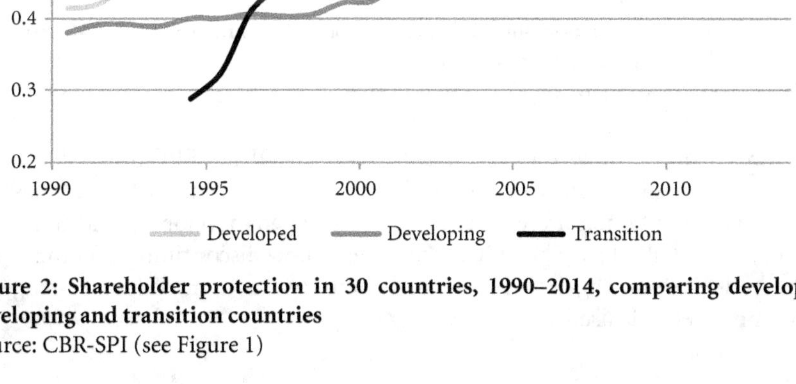

Figure 2: Shareholder protection in 30 countries, 1990–2014, comparing developed, developing and transition countries
Source: CBR-SPI (see Figure 1)

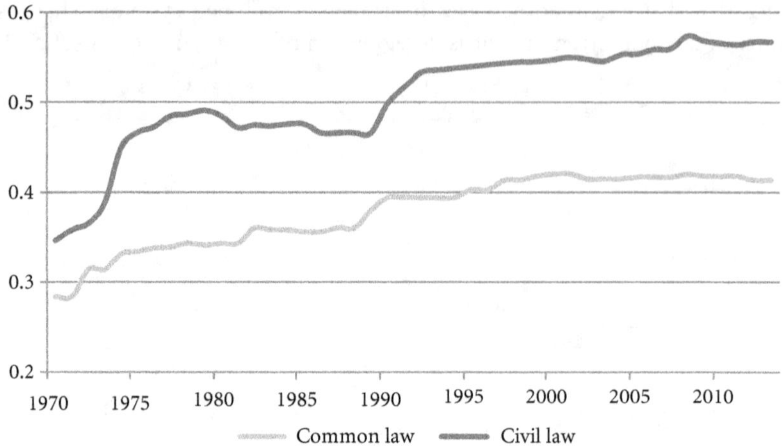

Figure 3: Dismissal protection and co-determination in 30 countries, 1970–2014, comparing common law and civil law origin countries
Source: CBR-LRI (see Figure 1)

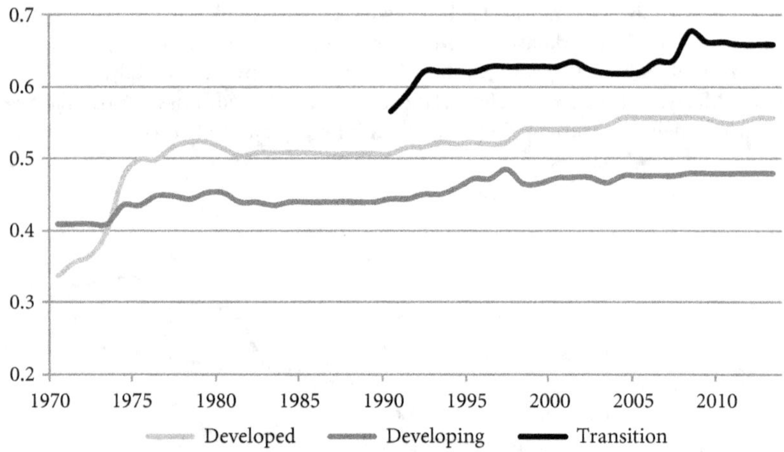

Figure 4: Dismissal protection and co-determination in 30 countries, 1970–2014, comparing developed, developing and transition countries
Source: CBR-LRI (see Figure 1)

Figures 5 and 6 show comparable data from the OECD EPI from 1990. These data record a higher score for civil law countries than common law countries, but do not show the same differences between developed, developing and transition systems as the CBR-LRI. The OECD scores also show discontinuities in the scores in the mid-2000s and again in 2013, which seem to be accounted for by changes in the coding methods used.

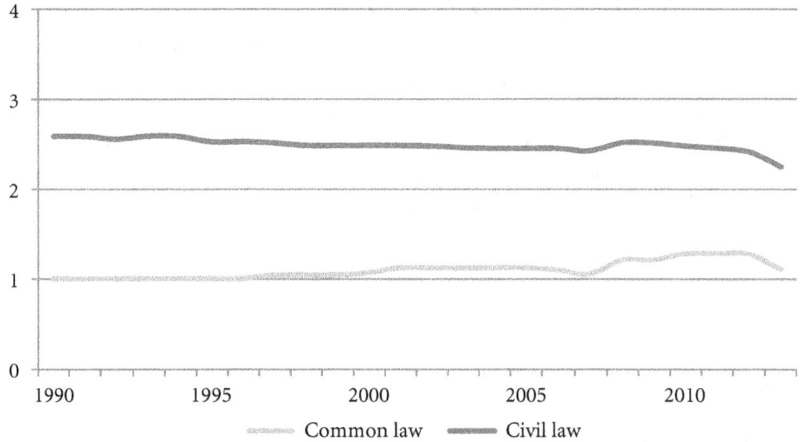

Figure 5: Individual and collective dismissal protection in 42 countries 1990–2013, comparing common law and civil law countries
Source: OECD-EPI, OECD iLibrary
Note: the countries in the dataset are Argentina, Austria, Belgium, Brazil, Canada, Chile, China, Czech Republic, Cyprus, Denmark, Estonia, France, Germany, Greece, Hungary, Iceland, India, Ireland, Italy, Japan, Latvia, Luxembourg, Malaysia, Mexico, the Netherlands, Pakistan, Poland, Russia, Saudi Arabia, Slovakia, Slovenia, Sweden, South Africa, Spain, Switzerland, Turkey, UK and the US. The scale used is 0–6.

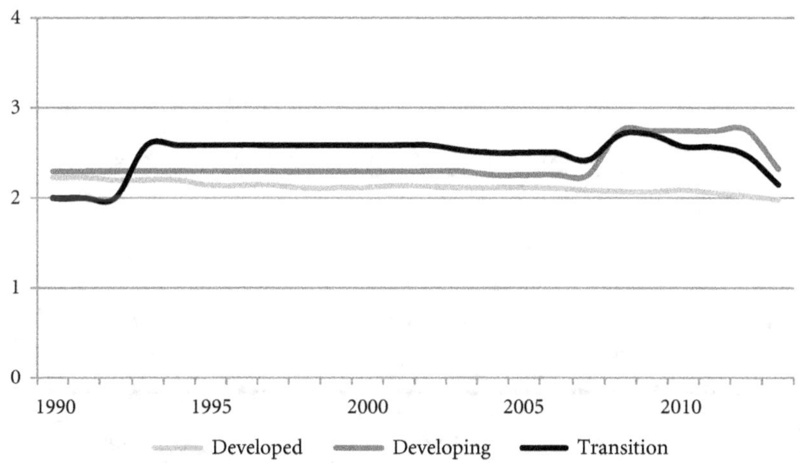

Figure 6: Individual and collective dismissal protection in 42 countries 1990–2013, comparing developed, developing and transition countries
Source: OECD-EPI (see Figure 5)

Figures 7 and 8 compare the scores for Germany, the UK and the US for the OECD EPI and the CBR-LRI. The OECD data show the UK and US to have similarly low scores. The CBR-LRI, by contrast, shows the UK in between Germany and the US in terms of the degree of protection conferred on workers. It is possible that the OECD index has been consistently underscoring the UK on the basis of the survey and questionnaire returns received from local sources, in contrast to the content-based leximetric coding of the CBR-LRI.

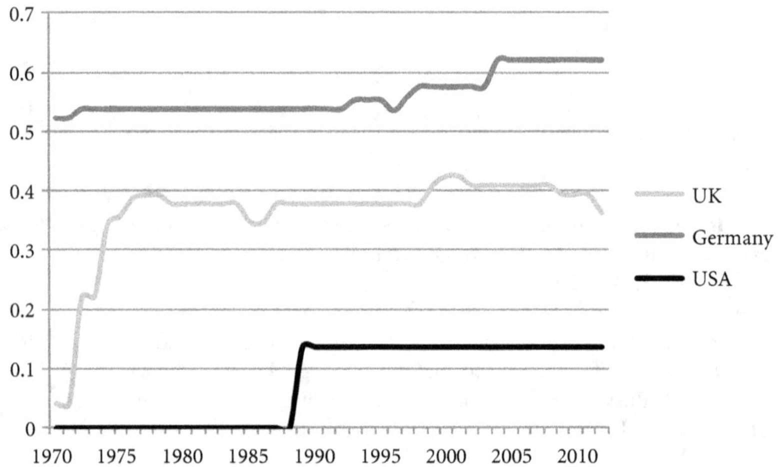

Figure 7: Dismissal protection and co-determination in the UK, Germany and the US, 1970–2014
Source: CBR-LRI (see Figure 1)

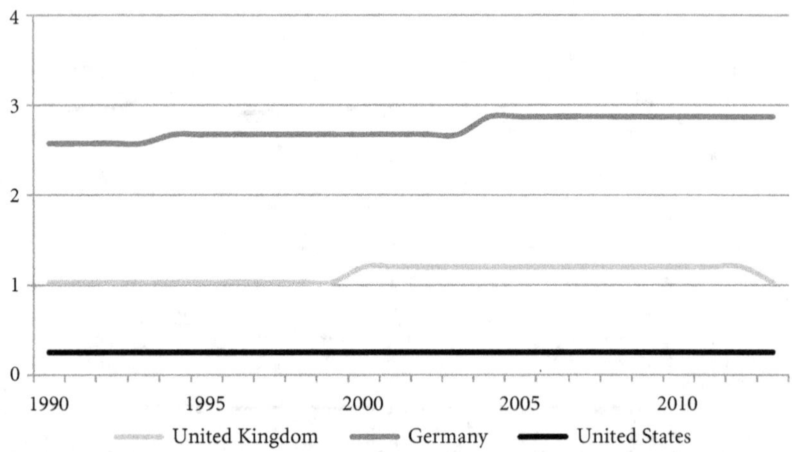

Figure 8: Individual and collective dismissal protection in the UK, Germany and the US 1990–2013
Source: OECD-EPI (see Figure 5)

F. Empirical Analysis of the CBR Index and Related Research on Productivity, Innovation and Inequality

Five countries were initially coded in the CBR index (France, Germany, India, the UK and US) and more have been added over time.[37] The resulting dataset can be put to use in panel-data and time series econometric analysis, to study the effects of legal change, and to identify the direction of causality in the law–economy relation. Control variables can include the World Bank Rule of Law Index, which measures the general, de facto implementation of laws in a given country, and GDP growth, which will take cyclical economic effects into account. Allowing for these controls, if the law–economy relation is essentially one of co-evolution, statistical methods should be capable of identifying two-way causal flows, and of indicating when a change in the law induces a long-run shift in the evolutionary path of the economy or just a temporary adjustment after which the economy resumes its previous path. Vector autoregression (VAR) and vector error correction (VEC) models, which can distinguish between the short-run and long-run effects of a change in legal rules and identify the direction of causal flows, are particularly appropriate here and well suited to the statistical properties of the CBR datasets.[38] Difference-in-differences approaches to panel data analysis can also be used in conjunction with CBR data.

A particular focus of statistical analysis using the CBR datasets has been on the relationship between employment protection laws and innovation. Acharya, Baghai-Wadji and Subramanian have used the dismissal protection variables in the CBR-LRI to examine the effects of changes in EPL over time on patenting activity and citations to patents in four industrialised countries (France, Germany, the UK and the US).[39] Using a difference-in-differences approach, they found a positive correlation, which can be interpreted as a causal relationship, with greater employment protection laws stimulating higher innovation based on employee input into new products and processes.

In a separate study, using state-level US data on employment laws, Acharya, Baghai-Wadji and Subramanian found that the states with the greatest concentration of high-tech firms, namely California and Massachusetts, are among those with the most significant exceptions to the employment at will rule (the 'implied good faith exception'), and that following the tightening of wrongful discharge laws in these states there was an increase not only in patenting activity but in the number of entrepreneurial start-ups and in the numbers employed in innovative

[37] Ibid.

[38] K Juselius, *The Cointegrated VAR Model: Methodology and Applications* (Oxford, Oxford University Press, 2006).

[39] V Acharya, R Baghai-Wadji and K Subramanian, 'Labor Laws and Innovation' (2014) 56 *Journal of Law and Economics* 997.

firms.[40] The study also reported positive effects on patenting activity in California following the adoption of the federal WARN law of 1988 on notice and severance pay. This finding replicates Deakin and Sarkar's analysis of positive productivity effects of the WARN law, using the CBR-LRI.[41] They also found positive productivity effects of a tightening of dismissal and working time laws in Germany and France.[42]

These findings on the positive link between employment protection, productivity and innovation are being replicated in other studies. A cross-national study by Belloc reports evidence that a combination of low EPL and high shareholder protection is correlated with reduced innovation, measured in terms of patenting and patent citation rates.[43] Belloc used OECD data for EPL and the CBR-SPI, as well as World Bank data, as a measure of shareholder rights. In studies using the OECD-EPI, Koeniger found that a high level of EPL at country-level is associated with more innovation-related firm-level training.[44] Griffith and McCartney report a correlation between high EPL and investments by multinational firms engaging in incremental innovation (involving the adaptation of existing technologies), although they also find that low EPL attracts cross-border investments by firms pursuing radical innovation (developing new technologies).[45] Zhou, Decker and Kleinknecht find, in an econometric study of Dutch firms in a range of sectors including manufacturing, that firms adopting 'Rhineland' style job security practices had stronger innovation performance (measured in terms of sales of new or improved products) than those with 'Anglo-Saxon' hire-and-fire type practices.[46] Temporary contracts were positively correlated with 'imitative' (follower) strategies on the part of innovating firms, but negatively correlated with strategies of market-leading firms. They interpret their findings as support for a theoretical model within which innovating firms offer 'functional flexibility', combining job security with a high degree of firm-specific training and intra-organisational mobility on the part of workers, rather than 'numerical flexibility', which relies on temporary contracts and redundancies to meet fluctuations in labour demand. On this basis they caution against policies of labour market deregulation, arguing that they will reduce pressures on weaker firms to upgrade their performance.

[40] V Acharya, R Baghai-Wadji and K Subramanian, 'Wrongful Discharge Laws and Innovation' (Working Paper, NYU-Stern Business School, 2012) available at: pages.stern.nyu.edu/~sternfin/vacharya/public_html/WDL_Innovation_paper_withnames_30Apr2012.pdf.

[41] S Deakin and P Sarkar, 'Assessing the Long-Run Economic Impact of Labour Law Systems: A Theoretical Reappraisal and Analysis of New Time Series Data' (2008) 39 *Industrial Relations Journal* 453.

[42] Ibid.

[43] F Belloc, 'Law, Finance and Innovation: The Dark Side of Shareholder Protection' (2013) 37 *Cambridge Journal of Economics* 863.

[44] W Koeniger, 'Dismissal Costs and Innovation' (2005) 88 *Economics Letters* 79.

[45] R Griffith and G Macartney, 'Employment Protection Legislation, Multinational Firms, and Innovation' (2014) 96 *Review of Economics and Statistics* 135.

[46] H Zhou, R Decker and A Kleinknecht, 'Flexible Labour and Innovation Performance: Evidence from Longitudinal Firm-Level Data' (2011) 20 *Industrial and Corporate Change* 941.

A second strand of research is looking at the impact of labour law on inequality and on possible trade-offs between equality and unemployment. Deakin, Malmberg and Sarkar carried out a dynamic panel data analysis on the CBR-LRI for six OECD countries (France, Germany, Japan, Sweden, the UK and the US), using a range of different approaches for dealing with unobserved cross-country heterogeneity.[47] They found that higher scores on the sub-indices for alternative employment contracts, working time protection and employee representation are correlated with a higher share of national income for labour (the 'labour share', which is conventionally associated with equality). The dismissal law sub-index is not correlated with higher equality using the labour share as a measure, but nor is it correlated with higher unemployment. There is a positive impact on employment of stronger laws for employee representation.

Deakin, Fenwick and Sarkar used the CBR-LRI to study the impact of collective labour laws on inclusive development in the BRICS countries (Brazil, Russia, India, China and South Africa), using a panel data approach with fixed-effects and random-effects models to deal with cross-country heterogeneity and changes over time.[48] They found that higher scores on the employee representation sub-index are correlated with greater equality, as indicated by a lower Gini coefficient, with no disemployment effects. Deakin and Sarkar, in a time-series study of India, found no long-term disemployment effect from the adoption of pro-worker dismissal laws, and some evidence of short-term positive impacts on unemployment.[49]

These findings, pointing to the effects of labour regulation in terms of reducing inequality, are consistent with other research that has demonstrated the role of collective bargaining and union presence in narrowing the earnings dispersion.[50] It also tallies with studies suggesting that policies of emphasising shareholder rights at the expense of worker protection lead to greater inequality.[51]

G. Conclusion

In this chapter we have sought to illustrate the importance of a quantitative approach to labour law research. We explained the theoretical and methodological

[47] S Deakin, J Malmberg and P Sarkar, 'Do Labour Laws Increase Equality at the Expense of Higher Unemployment? The Experience of Six OECD Countries, 1970–2010' (2014) 153 *International Labour Review* 1, forthcoming.

[48] S Deakin, C Fenwick, and P Sarkar, 'Labour Law and Inclusive Development: The Economic Effects of Industrial Relations Laws in Middle-Income Countries' in M Schmiegelow (ed), *Institutional Competition between Common Law and Civil Law: Theory and Policy* (Frankfurt, Springer, 2014).

[49] S Deakin and P Sarkar, 'Indian Labour Law and its Impact on Unemployment, 1973–2006: A Leximetric Study' (2011) 53 *Indian Journal of Labour Economics* 607.

[50] R Freeman, 'Labor Market Institutions without Blinders: The Debate over Flexibility and Labour Market Performance' (NBER Working Paper No 11286, 2005).

[51] O Sjöberg, 'Corporate Governance and Earnings Inequality in the OECD Countries 1979–2000' (2009) 25 *European Sociological Review* 519.

limitations but also the advantages of such an approach, and have used the CBR-LRI index to illustrate its potential. We reported first results from the extension of the CBR-LRI from the original five-country study to cover 30 developed, developing and transition countries. The extension of the dataset shows that civil law countries are more worker-protective than common law countries, and that developed countries are more worker-protective than developing countries. Transition countries have also seen a high rate of adoption of pro-worker labour laws since the mid-1990s.

Because it provides a continuous time series using consistent coding, the CBR-LRI can be used to identify both short-run and long-run effects of labour laws, and to distinguish between causation and correlations, thereby remedying limitations in the main alternative indices, the Doing Business Report Employing Workers Index, and the OECD Employment Protection Index. Early results suggest that worker-protective labour laws tend to increase equality, and have positive effects on innovation. Their overall effect on employment appears to be neutral or slightly positive. There is more work to be done in mapping labour law systems around the world through leximetric techniques and in refining our understanding of causation and correlation in statistical analysis, but these early results suggest that this is a research field with considerable potential, not least for reshaping policy debates.

5

Women in Labour Law: The Use and Implications of Empirical Methods

LYDIA HAYES AND ROSEANNE RUSSELL*

In this chapter we discuss how women have been variously included and represented in academic work published in the UK's *Industrial Law Journal* from 1972–2013. On a historic view, the frequency with which women have been included as the subjects of research arguably coincides with contemporaneous social and political concerns. Their inclusion is also heavily dependent upon legal context and varies according to the application of empirical and/or doctrinal methods. Women are principally the subjects of research in stereotypical contexts relating to motherhood, marriage and a gendered perception of their participation in the labour market as problematic. Their representation in relation to such a constrained range of topics may impede the potential for labour law scholarship to conceive of women as workers more broadly. However, when this labour law scholarship engages strongly with issues of gender we find it is frequently enriched by empirical data and applies insights drawn from disciplines outside of law. Further, there is evidence to suggest that labour law scholars are increasingly using empirical methods to gather their own original data and develop specific, evidence-based critique. This latter approach appears particularly likely to explore gender from the perspective of the work women are employed to perform, and the contractual terms under which they are engaged. The implication is of a labour law empiricism moving beyond its 'magpie' traditions of using data from elsewhere, which seeks instead to explore gender as a social relation constructed *through work*. We argue that the trajectory of women in labour law scholarship examined here points towards the possibility of a more rounded account of women as subjects of labour law.

A. Introduction

Labour law has been accused of demonstrating an 'unquestioned acceptance' that its subjects are 'male workers'.[1] While the subjects of labour law are not necessarily

* Journal of Law and Society Research Associate, Cardiff Law School and Lecturer, Cardiff Law School respectively.

[1] R Hunter, 'Representing Gender in Legal Analysis: A Case/Book Study' (1991) 18 *Melbourne University Law Review* 305, 305.

explicitly characterised as male, gender-neutral representations of workers act to exclude and marginalise women. Equality law in the UK tackles sex difference between men and women on the basis of individual characteristics. However, 'gender' is an organising principle of the labour market; it is the expression of sex as social status.[2] If workplaces are legally regarded as gender-neutral spaces, and if labour law is established as a realm where gender is not part of the picture, then the law denies the existence of social hierarchy based on sex.[3] Under these circumstances, scholars of labour law might probe beneath the surface and expose the disconnections between legal rationality and real-life in order to critique legal assumptions of gender-neutrality.[4] The most obvious examples emerge when the law assumes workers are free from the demands of domesticity. Legal reasoning thus proceeds from the conceptual starting point of an 'ideal worker' to whom women are much less likely to correspond than men.[5] It is the false assumption in law, of workers as gender-neutral legal subjects, that has given rise to an extensive critique of labour law as 'gender blind'.[6] However, it need not follow that labour law *scholarship* is similarly afflicted by a disregard for gender. In scholarship, the inclusion of women as *research subjects* may differ from their construction as *legal subjects* through the texts, doctrine and practice of law.

Our research design explicitly sought to understand the position of women in labour law scholarship. Asking 'the woman question' is a method that aims to explore sites of exclusion or marginalisation in legal, social or institutional systems.[7] We deliberately avoided comparing the representation of women with the representation of men. Rather we were guided by this question: *When* women are included in published work, *how* are they represented? We hoped to be able to elaborate on the assertion that labour law is gender blind by observing how women are constructed as subjects in published research, both in relation to legal issues and through the research methods used.

In the first part of this discussion we provide a retrospective overview of the shape and extent of the inclusion of women in labour law research. Our historic assessment suggests that the frequency of their inclusion is influenced by legal and political development as well as social change.

[2] EN Glenn, 'Gender, Race, and Class: Bridging the Language-Structure Divide' (1998) 22 *Social Science History* 29.

[3] For a conceptual overview, see J Conaghan, *Law and Gender* (Oxford, Oxford University Press, 2013); on the construction of gender, see DM Figart et al, *Living Wages, Equal Wages: Gender and Labour Market Policies in the United States* (London, Routledge, 2002) 55–60.

[4] KT Bartlett, 'Feminist Legal Methods' (1990) 103 *Harvard Law Review* 829; J Scott, *Gender and the Politics of History* (New York, Columbia University Press, 1999).

[5] C Pateman, *The Sexual Contract* (Cambridge, Polity, 1988) 131, J Williams, *Unbending Gender: Why Family and Work Conflict and What to Do About It* (New York, Oxford University Press, 2000) 20.

[6] J Conaghan, 'Gender and the Idea of Labour Law' (2014) 4 *feminists@law* 1, J Fudge, 'Labour Law as a "Fictive Commodity": Radically Reconceptualizing Labour Law' in G Davidov and B Langille (eds), *The Idea of Labour Law* (Oxford, Oxford University Press, 2011) 120, 131. See more generally, J Conaghan, 'Reassessing the Feminist Theoretical Project in Law' (2000) 27 *Journal of Law and Society* 351.

[7] See Bartlett, n 4. Asking the 'woman question' is a method that spans three centuries and dates back to Mary Wollstonecraft's *Vindication of the Rights of Women* (1792).

In the second part, we look at the issue of legal context. In a large majority of instances women have been represented in relation to marriage, maternity and variations thereof (including non-standard working patterns and highly feminised occupations such as caring and cleaning). Since the inclusion of women appears aligned to and constrained by these themes, there is a risk of gender being regarded as an aspect of social life which is merely imported into employment relations. On this view, women are 'gendered' through family structures and are put to work in the labour market in ways that naturally reflect a pre-existing sex-based hierarchy. However, family, home and kinship are not the only places where gender is shaped and the confinement of gender analysis to the family is itself a form of male bias.[8] This raises questions about how scholarship might rightly pay attention to central statutory reference points relating to gender, without reinforcing the marginalisation of women as workers.

In the third part, we discuss how research methods are used. The labour law scholarship we examined appears highly likely to be informed by empirical data when it engages most strongly with issues of gender. However, the ways in which scholars have aligned empirical data with doctrinal assessment has shifted over time. In our sample, from the 2000s onwards, scholarship that engages strongly with issues of gender appears unlikely to rely solely upon doctrinal methods. There has been a corresponding movement towards combining doctrinal discussion with empirical data generated in the fields of economics, social policy and sociology. This opens up opportunities for evidence based critique of the gender blind assumptions set out in labour law. In more recent years, we find that primary empirical methods, in which the author generates original empirical data, are increasingly likely to be used. We identify an emerging trend for primary empirical methods to position women research subjects in the context of atypical work and traditionally gendered occupations. It therefore seems that this turn to empiricism coincides with increased concern for women as subjects of labour law who are gendered *through work*.

B. Women as Research Subjects in Labour Law Scholarship

Our enquiry focused on scholarship published in the UK's *Industrial Law Journal* (*ILJ*) because it is 'the leading periodical in its field'.[9] It has published work since labour law was in its infancy as a distinct discipline, has traditionally taken a broad view of the discipline's scope, and from its outset aimed to promote theoretical

[8] N Kabeer, *Reversed Realities: Gender Hierarchies in Development Thought* (London, Verso, 1994).

[9] Taken from the *ILJ*'s introductory web page: www.oxfordjournals.org/our_journals/indlaw/about.html (last accessed 1 November 2014).

scholarship that was informed by practice, 'the one helping to fashion the other and in turn being refashioned itself'.[10] We searched the *ILJ* for published material that made explicit use of the terms 'woman or women' or a female pronoun 'she or her', to identify where women were included in research, whether as primary or secondary subjects or in central or peripheral ways.[11] We identified 844 relevant papers.[12] Methodological limitations mean we cannot make general claims for 'the state' of empiricism in labour law scholarship or the position of women within the discipline on the basis of our findings. Searching for a limited range of words and phrases in a single publication is a blunt instrument, yet we are satisfied that the size of our sample is sufficiently large as to provide useful insights. Figure 1 shows the annual spread of these papers.

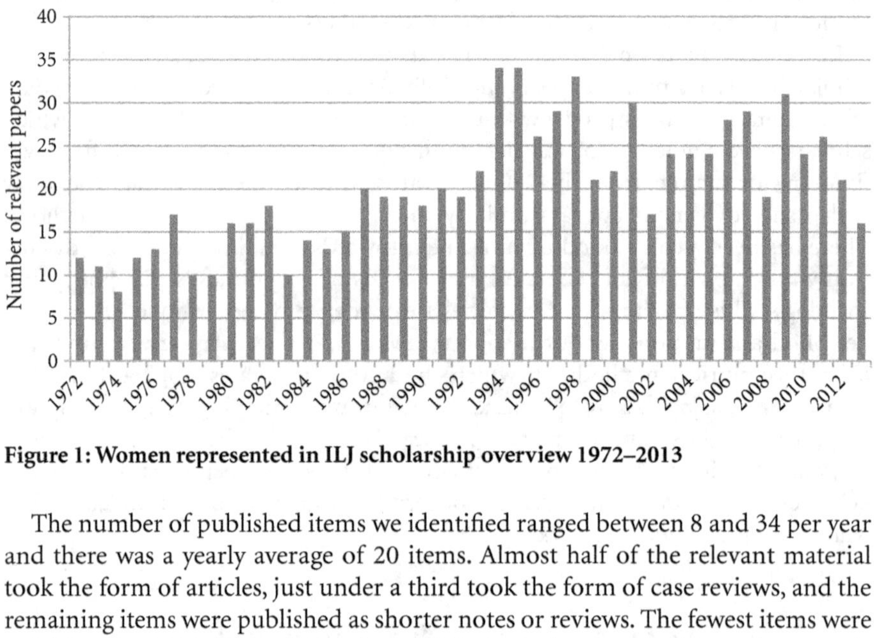

Figure 1: Women represented in ILJ scholarship overview 1972–2013

The number of published items we identified ranged between 8 and 34 per year and there was a yearly average of 20 items. Almost half of the relevant material took the form of articles, just under a third took the form of case reviews, and the remaining items were published as shorter notes or reviews. The fewest items were published in 1974. The mid-section of Figure 1 shows a significant increase in frequency in the mid to late 1990s, with a high point of 34 items reached in 1994 and 1995. It is notable that in the period following the financial crisis in 2008, the presence of women as research subjects in labour law scholarship appears to be in decline. Figure 2 offers an alternative representation of the annual total data as a series of peaks and troughs, showing smaller totals towards the centre of the grid.

[10] B Hepple, 'Our Aims' (1972) 1 *Industrial Law Journal* 1, 1.

[11] For similar enquiry in the fields of psychology and industrial relations, see P Hegarty and C Buechel, 'Androcentric Reporting of Gender Differences in APA Journals: 1965–2004' (2006) 10 *Review of General Psychology* 377, and J Wajcman, 'Feminism Facing Industrial Relations in Britain' (2000) 38 *British Journal of Industrial Relations* 183.

[12] We are grateful to Cardiff Law School for financial assistance and to Abi Walbridge for her excellent research assistance.

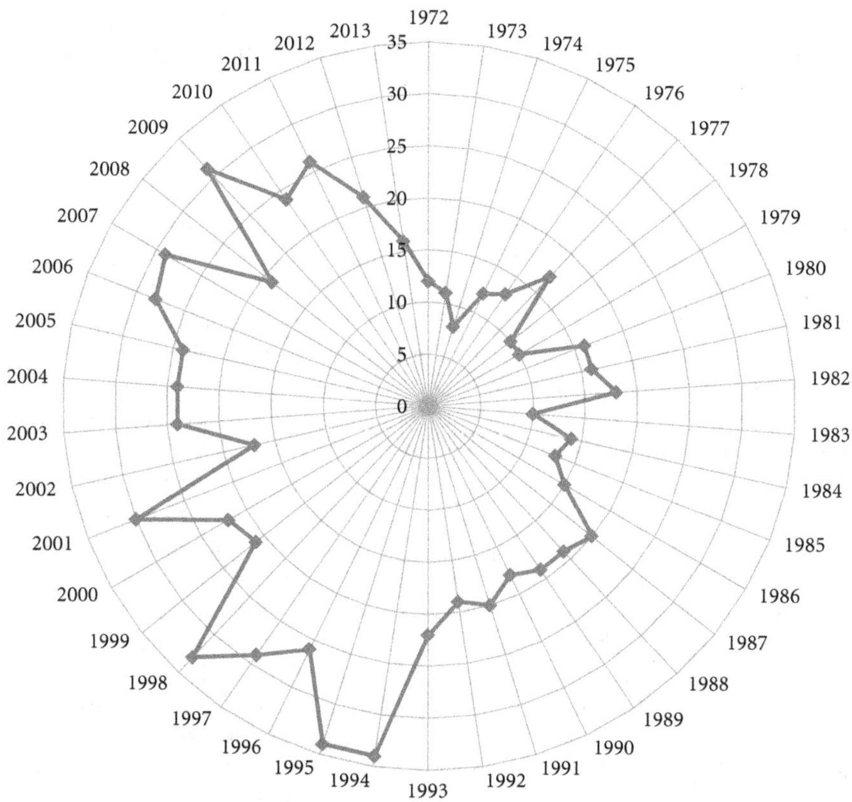

Figure 2: Frequency of representation of women in published scholarship 1972–2013

The number of published items referring to women is considerably higher in the 1993–2013 period shown on the left-hand side than in the earlier period from 1972–1993 shown on the right. Structural factors such as evolving social mores and changes in the surrounding political landscape may account for periods of greater or lesser engagement with women as research subjects. We are cautious not to ascribe a causative link between the representation of women and political and legal influences; not only because of an appreciation that publication is influenced by editorial preference but also in light of the 'time lag' between political interest, policy development and legislative action.[13] However, in order to explore the credibility of our findings we make a number of observations. Based on the patterns in our data, we have organised our assessment over four specific time periods. These are: the period between 1972–87 in which the frequency with which women

[13] R Inglehart and P Norris, 'The Developmental Theory of the Gender Gap: Women's and Men's Voting Behaviour in Global Perspective' (2000) 21 *International Political Science Review* 441, 446.

are represented is comparatively low; the period between 1987–2000 when representation grows strongly; the consolidation period of 2001–08; and the 2008–13 period of financial crisis in which the frequency of representation is in decline.

1. Low Representation: 1972–87

This time period takes account of material published during the Labour governments of Wilson and Callaghan and in the context of Margaret Thatcher's election victories in 1979, 1983 and 1987. From the perspective of industrial relations these were difficult and turbulent years in which 'The oil crisis, the new radicalism of the trade union leaders and Britain's entry into the EEC all shook British politics'.[14] Thatcher's policies pursued the restriction of trade union power through law, the de-regulation of the individual employment relationship, and turned towards individualism in the structuring of employment rights.[15] *ILJ* published scholarship reflected this shifting labour relations landscape and centred on the shift towards individual contractual rights, procedural changes and heightened scrutiny of trade union activity. Our findings suggest women were not frequently included in the context of these considerations. This is not to say that women and their engagement with law and the workplace were absent from academic scrutiny at this time,[16] but rather they were missing from discussions in the *ILJ* of concerns that might be characterised as 'mainstream' or central to the discipline.

This period was also a time of intense and sustained change for women in the workplace and society more generally. The Equal Pay Act 1970 was developed, partly in anticipation of the UK joining the then EEC,[17] but also motivated by increasing political agitation and social justice demands for the assimilation of women into the workplace on the same terms as men. The political ambitions of feminist lawyers and activists aspired to achieve much more than 'a piece of the pie for women', but they made significant headway in promoting equal opportunities and protection from less favourable treatment on grounds of sex.[18] The Equal Pay Act 1970 and the Sex Discrimination Act 1975 came into force on 29 December 1975 and the increased reference to women in *ILJ* material in the late 1970s and

[14] R Vinen, *Thatcher's Britain: The Politics and Social Upheaval of the 1980s* (London, Simon & Schuster, 2009) 75.

[15] J Clark and Lord Wedderburn, 'Modern Labour Law: Problems, Functions and Policies' in Lord Wedderburn, R Lewis and J Clark (eds), *Labour Law and Industrial Relations: Building on Kahn-Freund* (Oxford, Clarendon Press, 1983) 127, 130–44, P Davies and M Freedland, *Labour Legislation and Public Policy* (Oxford, Clarendon Press, 1993) 529.

[16] See, eg WB Creighton, *Working Women and the Law* (London, Mansell, 1979) and A Sachs and JH Wilson, *Sexism and the Law: A Study of Male Beliefs and Legal Bias in Britain and the United States* (Oxford, Martin Robertson, 1978).

[17] C McCrudden, 'Equal Pay for Work of Equal Value: the Equal Pay (Amendment) Regulations 1983' (1983) 12 *Industrial Law Journal* 197.

[18] H Eisenstein, 'A Dangerous Liaison? Feminism and Corporate Globalization' (2005) 69 *Science & Society* 487, 495.

across the 1980s would therefore seem commensurate with a legislative period of specific relevance to women.[19]

However, if legislative attempts to combat the impact of sex discrimination in the workplace are to explain the steady rise in scholarship through the 1980s credibly, we must also account for the sharp fall in published material representing women in 1974, 1979, and 1983. It is interesting that each of these occasions was an election year. This may suggest that women were afforded lesser prominence in the context of political priorities lying outside of the formal boundaries of law during this period.

2. Period of Rapid Growth: 1987–2000

Post-1987 the inclusion of women in labour law scholarship increased markedly and retained its prominence. This development appears to reflect two key issues. First, an intense *political* focus on the restructuring of the labour market and the privatisation of public services; secondly, an intense *legal* focus on gender equality—evident in ground-breaking case law developments relating to equal pay and sex discrimination.[20] The 'significant structural change' that took place in the labour market is reflected in sustained scholarly engagement with issues of gender and inequality during this period.[21] The post-war paradigm of the full-time, permanent worker became increasingly strained by women's engagement with the paid labour market on part-time and fixed term bases. Apparently neutral practices and labour market policies were contested.[22] As a result, the importance of indirect discrimination provisions came to the fore in *ILJ* scholarship and case law developments at this time.[23] There were major concerns about the particular disadvantage faced by women in a political climate that sought increased labour market competition, the fragmentation of established patterns of collective bargaining and the exposure of public sector services to tendering and cost-comparison regimes in order to facilitate wage reductions.[24]

19 See, eg M Richards, 'The Sex Discrimination Act—Equality for Women?' (1976) 5 *Industrial Law Journal* 35.

20 Notable examples include *Bilka-Kaufhaus GmbH v Weber von Hartz* [1986] IRLR 317; *Rainey v Greater Glasgow Health Board* [1987] IRLR 26; and *Hayward v Cammell Laird Shipbuilders Ltd* [1988] ICR 464.

21 S Deakin, 'Labor and Employment Laws' in P Cane and H Kritzer, *The Oxford Handbook of Empirical Legal Research* (Oxford, Oxford University Press, 2012) 308, 310. An example of such engagement is S Deakin, 'Equality under a Market Order: The Employment Act 1989' (1990) 19 *Industrial Law Journal* 1.

22 *R v Secretary of State for Employment ex parte Seymour-Smith and Perez* [1999] 2 AC 554; *R v Secretary of State for Employment ex parte Seymour-Smith and Perez* [2000] ICR 244.

23 Eg see *Pearse v City of Bradford Metropolitan Council* [1988] IRLR 379; *Greater Manchester Police Authority v Lea* [1990] IRLR 372; and *Jones v Adjudication Officer* [1990] IRLR 533.

24 M Jaffe et al, *Equal Pay, Privatisation and Procurement* (Liverpool, IER, 2008); L Hayes, 'Women's Voice and Equal Pay: Judicial Regard for the Gendering of Collective Bargaining' in A Bogg and T Novitz (eds), *Voices at Work: Continuity and Change in the Common Law World* (Oxford, Oxford University Press, 2014).

There is a significant quantitative leap forward in the frequency of women's representation in the *ILJ* from 1994, the year in which the success of Pamela Enderby in her equal pay claim is reported.[25] Indeed, 1994–95 is the period during which women are most frequently represented. It is marked by strong discussions of women in relation to equality law and pensions, part-time employment, equal pay and equal treatment.[26] This high prominence precedes the 1997 election of the first Labour Government in Britain since the 1970s. Later peaks in frequency in 1998 and 2001 appear to correspond to the introduction of protections for part-time and fixed-term workers and the establishment of the UK's first ever statutory minimum wage.[27]

A significant proportion of material in this period draws on EU law. As shown in Figure 3, between 1987–92 the quantity of published material concerned with women in the context of UK jurisdictional issues remained fairly constant. However, it is in this period that the profile of women as subjects of EU law became markedly prominent. A significant explanatory factor for the increased reference to women as research subjects from 1987 to 2000 is the turn to EU law.

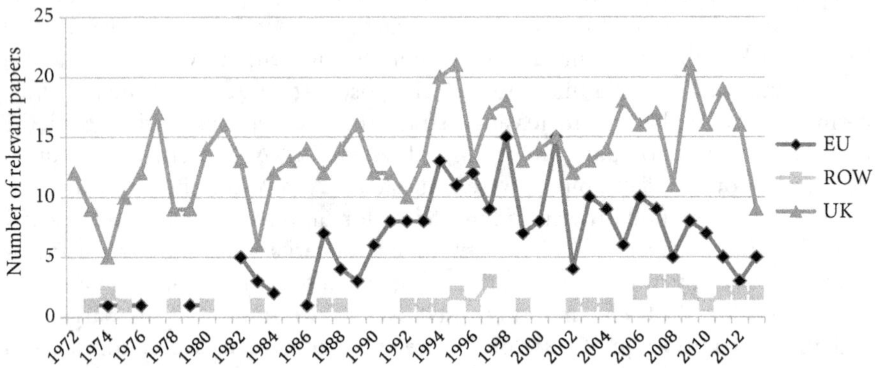

Figure 3: Jurisdictional basis of scholarship in which women are represented: UK, EU or rest of world (ROW)

3. Consolidation: 2001–08

In this period the inclusion of women in labour law research remained consistently high. It is likely to be a reflection of the policy initiatives and statutory zeal

[25] *Enderby v Frenchay Health Authority and Secretary of State for Health* [1993] IRLR 591.

[26] Such as discussion of Council Directive 92/85/EEC concerning the implementation of measures to encourage improvements in the safety and health of pregnant workers, workers who have recently given birth and women who are breastfeeding (OJ L 348, 28.11.1992, 1–8).

[27] Council Directive 97/81/EC of 15 December 1997 on part-time work (OJ L 14, 20.1.1998, 9–14); National Minimum Wage Act 1998; The Part-time Workers (Prevention of Less Favourable Treatment) Regulations 2000 (SI 2000/1551); and The Fixed-term Employees (Prevention of Less Favourable Treatment) Regulations 2002 (SI 2002/2034).

of the Labour Governments of 1997–2001 and 2001–05. Increasingly, the rate of women's labour market participation was a key plank of economic and social policy which subsequently has been characterised as carrying a 'preoccupation with flexibility and employability'.[28] It was with a wider economic and political objective of reducing child poverty, through parental engagement in paid work, that a new right to request flexible working was introduced with the purported intention that it would ease the challenges of combining paid work with caring responsibilities.[29] Moreover, for the first time fathers were permitted statutory entitlement to paternity leave.[30] The introduction of such 'family friendly' legislation is a central feature of scholarship in this period. Throughout the 2000s the balance of *ILJ* content shifts towards an increased proportion of full articles to case notes. The impact is that individual items of published research are longer and discussion of women is consequently less frequent but more sustained (where it occurs).

4. The 'Austerity' Period: 2008–13

Our final observation is of a marked reduction in the frequency of material following the 2008 financial crisis. In the context of recession and austerity women are less frequently included as research subjects. Of note in the political backdrop to this period has been the Fawcett Society's (unsuccessful) challenge to the budget reforms adopted by the Conservative/Liberal Democrat Coalition Government.[31] Scholars of gender and labour law have noted that a sacrificing of equality has taken place in the name of austerity.[32] Indeed, the development or regression of gender equality policy in the UK has been demonstrably linked to national economic performance.[33] It may be the case that less frequent placing of women within labour law scholarship is a consequence of recession.

However, from the perspective of legal discourse, the potential to frame labour rights as human rights following the Human Rights Act 1998 may have promoted a partial supplanting of explicit reference to women by the gender-neutral inclinations of human rights law.[34] A further explanation may lie in the turn towards a more pluralistic approach to matters of equality and anti-discrimination reflected

[28] T Novitz and P Skidmore, *Fairness at Work: A Critical Analysis of the Employment Relations Act 1999 and its Treatment of Collective Rights* (Oxford, Hart, 2001) 11, Lord Wedderburn, 'Labour Law 2008: 40 Years On' (2007) 36 *Industrial Law Journal* 397, 411–12.

[29] D Piachaud and H Sutherland, 'Child Poverty in Britain and the New Labour Government' (2001) 30 *Journal of Social Policy* 95. Flexible Working (Eligibility, Complaints and Remedies) Regulations 2002 (SI 2002/3236).

[30] Paternity and Adoption Leave Regulations 2002 (SI 2002/2788).

[31] H Conley, 'Using Equality to Challenge Austerity: New Actors, Old Problems' (2012) 26 *Work Employment and Society* 349.

[32] J Fudge, 'Women Workers: Is Equality Enough?' (2013) 2 *feminists@law* 1, 16.

[33] C Annesley and F Gains, 'Investigating the Economic Determinants of the UK Gender Equality Policy Agenda' (2012) 15 *British Journal of Politics and International Relations* 125.

[34] V Mantouvalou, 'Are Labour Rights Human Rights?' (2012) 3 *European Labour Law Journal* 151.

in the establishment of the Equality and Human Rights Commission and subsequent Equality Act 2010. These developments reflect a prevailing view about the ineffectiveness of treating equality on a single-strand or 'silo' basis.[35] A more conscious embrace of intersectionality has coincided with political scepticism at the idea that women can be identified with sufficient homogeneity as to genuinely constitute a social group.[36] Fewer explicit mentions of women in the *ILJ* suggest that the employment experiences of men and women are no longer necessarily accepted as self-evidently different on the basis of sex; but may have polarised more sharply on the basis of age, race, ethnicity and migrant status.[37] However, on an empirical basis it is evident that women's distinctive contribution as providers of *unpaid* labour within the family continues to situate them differently to men within the labour market, however marginalised men or women may also be on grounds of race, ethnicity, migrant status or disability.[38] In the context of the post-2008 financial crisis, it appears reasonable to echo concerns that specific issues of gender will become subsumed in a broader, over-arching approach to equality in labour law scholarship.[39]

C. Motherhood, Marriage, Cooking and Casuals? The Contextual Limits of Women's Inclusion

Frequency alone is a crude measure of women's representation in labour law scholarship. It tells us nothing about how fully women are represented and does not establish the manner of their inclusion. Therefore we devised search terms from words and phrases relating to issues that are frequently associated with gender stereotyping. These were:

— Relational: women's social roles in relation to men and children as wives, mothers, widows, etc. The search terms were wife OR mother OR spouse OR widow* OR marri* OR family* OR child*.
— Biological: women's distinctive biological characteristics relating to pregnancy, maternity and breastfeeding. The search terms were matern* OR pregnan* OR breast*.

[35] I Solanke, 'Infusing the Silos in the Equality Act 2010 with Synergy' (2011) 40 *Industrial Law Journal* 336.
[36] S Archer Mann and DJ Huffman, 'The Decentering of Second Wave Feminism and the Rise of the Third Wave' (2005) 69 *Science & Society* 56.
[37] Fudge, n 32, 10.
[38] Fudge, n 6, 131.
[39] C O'Cinneide, 'The Commission for Equality and Human Rights: A New Institution for New and Uncertain Times' (2007) 36 *Industrial Law Journal* 141, 143.

- Traditional occupation: women's propensity for paid employment within a narrow range of occupations traditionally associated with unpaid work in the home such as cleaning, clerical, care and catering work.[40] The search terms were domestic OR cook* OR clean* OR care* OR caring OR clerical OR secretar* OR cater* OR cashier.
- Atypical workers: women's employment on the basis of atypical contractual terms, deviating from assumed norms of full time, permanent work through part-time working hours and 'flexible' forms of engagement.[41] The search terms were 'part time'* OR part-time* OR casual OR temp* OR flex* OR vulnerab*.

We investigated how frequently these terms applied in the 844 published items that included women as research subjects. As shown in Figure 4, although our range of search terms was limited, we could account for 74 per cent of all scholarship about women with these four lines of enquiry. Roughly a quarter of the material in which women were included also engaged in discussions about their relational identities in respect of marriage and motherhood (22 per cent). Mentions of pregnancy, maternity or breastfeeding placed women in the context of biological issues in 12 per cent of the research material. Women were constructed in the context of traditional occupations such as cleaning, caring and catering in almost a fifth of instances (18 per cent). In respect of our fourth gender category, atypical work, women were represented as research subjects in the context of discussions

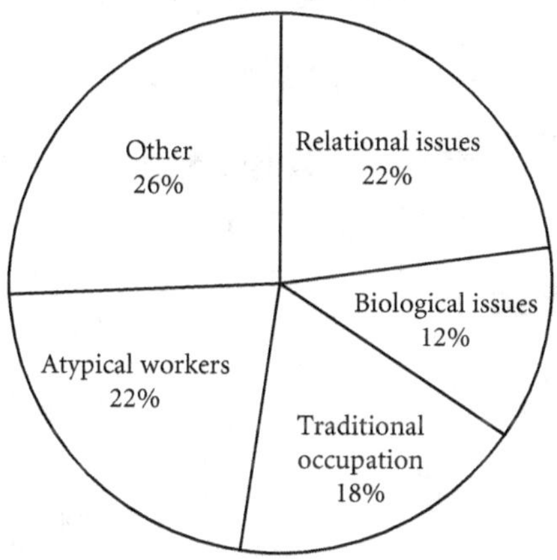

Figure 4: Context of women's inclusion 1972–2013

[40] On occupational segregation generally, see WT Bielby and JN Baron, 'Men and Women at Work: Sex Segregation and Statistical Discrimination' (1986) 91 *American Journal of Sociology* 759, 760.

[41] J Williams, 'The Family-Hostile Corporation' (2002) 70 *The George Washington Law Review* 921, 929, S Fredman, 'Women at Work: The Broken Promise of Flexicurity' (2004) 33 *Industrial Law Journal* 299, and D Bovill, 'Patterns of Pay: Estimates from the Annual Survey of Hours and Earnings, UK, 1997 to 2013' (London, ONS, February 2014) 5.

about part-time hours, temporary or casual contracts, flexible working and vulnerability in 22 per cent of the material. A quarter of the material (26 per cent) fell outside our gendered search terms and is categorised as 'other'. A small element of this 'other' material discusses women as sexual subjects in the context of harassment claims but it is mainly concerned with issues that are likely to be assumed as gender-neutral, such as unfair dismissal.

In Figure 5, the results are shown by decade to illustrate how contextual emphasis has changed over time. Since our research covers the period 1972–2013, and the number of available years in the 1970s and 2010s are less than 10, we have presented the material on the basis of percentages in order to make comparisons

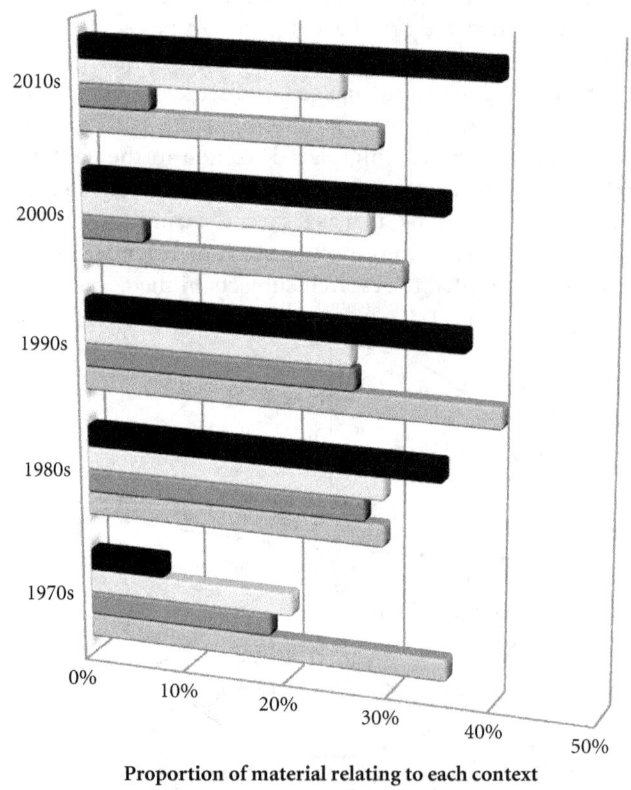

	1970s	1980s	1990s	2000s	2010s
■ Atypical workers	8%	35%	37%	35%	40%
□ Traditional occupation	20%	29%	26%	28%	25%
▪ Biological issues	18%	28%	27%	6%	7%
□ Relational issues	35%	29%	41%	31%	29%

Figure 5: Gendered contexts in which women are represented as research subjects. Comparison by decade

meaningful (note that material can fall into more than one category and therefore percentages will not add up to 100 per cent).

There are marked differences across the time periods. Viewed by decade, we can assert that, whilst our gendered categories are salient throughout, they have the greatest explanatory power regarding *ILJ* research published during the 1990s. However, viewed on the basis of each individual line of gender enquiry, it is apparent that there was a sharp variation of interest in atypical work between the 1970s and 1980s; a relatively stable regard for women in respect of traditional occupations across all time periods; a sharp decline in interest in biological issues between the 1990s and 2000s; and a sustained yet variable pattern of research about women in the context of relational issues, notwithstanding a particular increase in interest between the 1980s and 1990s. These results illustrate that at different times (and no doubt in response to different legal conundrums or statutory initiatives), the focus of labour law research on women and issues of gender is uneven.

Variations in the frequency with which labour law scholars have taken up issues reflects legal and political concern for the economic and cultural dynamics of gender expressed in relation to work and employment. As noted above, women barely feature in the context of discussions about atypical work in the 1970s; yet by the 2010s, 40 per cent of material in which women are research subjects places them in relation to issues of atypical working. Whereas women in the 1970s were frequently engaged in (what we would now label as) atypical labour market situations,[42] labour scholarship concerns about atypical work focused on casualisation in traditionally male occupations such as dock work and the disruption of employment relations through temporary layoffs in manufacturing and engineering.

A significant increase in the representation of women in the context of both atypical employment and traditional occupations occurred in the 1980s. Much of this related to the dismantling of women's jobs in the public sector and associated legal claims which arose in respect of outsourcing, redundancy and TUPE transfers. Part-time work was perceived as a dominant paradigm through which women were disadvantaged as atypical workers.[43] Discussion of women in relation to flexible hours was limited, although the notion of 'flexible work patterns' is raised by Ewing in relation to poor pay, unpleasant conditions and a lack of employment security for women in homeworking occupations.[44] However, in relation to temporary work, it is evident that even in the late 1980s discussion centres on women's periodic entry and exit from the labour market in association with childbearing. There is little indication that women's temporary working was regarded as a mainstream labour market issue.

[42] S Connolly and M Gregory, 'Women and Work since 1970' in N Crafts et al (eds), *Work and Pay in Twentieth Century Britain* (Oxford, Oxford University Press, 2007).

[43] Eg G Pitt, 'Individual Rights Under the New Legislation' (1980) 9 *Industrial Law Journal* 233, C Hakim, 'Employment Rights: A Comparison of Part-Time and Full-Time Employees' (1989) 18 *Industrial Law Journal* 69.

[44] KD Ewing, 'Homeworking: A Framework for Reform' (1982) 11 *Industrial Law Journal* 94.

Through the 1970s, 1980s and 1990s there was a sustained interest in including women as research subjects in the context of biological issues. It reflects growing awareness of the incompatibility of working norms with the circumstances of pregnancy and maternity which were thrown into sharp relief by Upex and Morris in 1981.[45] In their critique of the maternity rights regime, they demonstrated that few women were capable of benefitting from these rights due to length of service and national insurance contributions requirements. In conclusion, they caution against 'arguments about the burden on the hard-pressed small business', which points to the burgeoning trajectory of economic influence that we see in labour market considerations of the 1980s.[46]

An engagement with women as research subjects in the context of biological characteristics falls sharply between the 1990s and 2000s to 6 per cent from its prior position at 27 per cent of research which includes women. From the 2000s onwards we see a general decline in the representation of women in the context of both biological and relational issues. However, whilst the scholarship may have moved on this has not corresponded with an improvement in the real-life treatment of pregnant workers. In 2005, the Equal Opportunities Commission found that almost half of all pregnant workers in Great Britain would experience 'some form of disadvantage at work'.[47] In November 2013, the Equality and Human Rights Commission announced that it will conduct a fresh comprehensive inquiry into the scale of pregnancy and maternity discrimination in light of concerns that the problem has not improved.[48]

We found that 35 per cent of the material published in the 1970s considered women in the context of their social roles and relations to men in the domestic sphere as wives, widows or mothers. Applying the lens of gender, scholarship often took an interest in women's status in the context of these relational identities and subjected social security regimes to examination, critique and doctrinal investigation.[49] It is in the 1990s that discussion of women in the context of their relation to men and families is at a height. There is a concentration of scholarship in relation to pension reform and motherhood. Issues relating to biological issues crystallise in discussions about the Pregnant Workers Directive[50] and a raft of claims for protection from dismissal due to pregnancy or pregnancy-related illness.[51] In the 2000s, discussions of so-called family friendly legal provisions such as the right to request flexible working are reflected in the positioning of women in the context

[45] R Upex and A Morris, 'Maternity Rights: Illusion or Reality?' (1981) 10 *Industrial Law Journal* 218.

[46] Ibid, 238.

[47] EOC, 'Greater Expectations: EOC's Investigation into Pregnancy Discrimination' (Manchester, EOC, June 2005).

[48] R Dunstan, 'Overdue: A Plan of Action to Address Pregnancy Discrimination Now' (London, Maternity Action, December 2013).

[49] Eg D Gilling-Smith, 'Occupational Pensions and the Social Security Act 1973' (1973) 2 *Industrial Law Journal* 197.

[50] Council Directive 92/85/EEC concerning the implementation of measures to encourage improvements in the safety and health of pregnant workers, workers who have recently given birth and women who are breastfeeding (OJ L 348, 28.11.1992, 1–8).

[51] *Webb v EMO Air Cargo (UK) Ltd* [1994] QB 718; *Brown v Rentokil Ltd* [1998] IRLR 445.

of domestic relations. Scholarship published in the current decade of the 2010s retains a similar level of concern for women as research subjects in the context of their familial relations as wives, widows and mothers as scholarship did back in the 1970s. However, conceptions of women as financial dependents appear to have shifted away from a focus on their reliance on male partners to a focus on their dependence upon state support and wage subsidy.[52]

Our findings, in respect of relational and biological aspects of gender, suggest that women have been defined sharply in labour law scholarship by social roles and relations that are ostensibly *external* to the workplace and located in familial structures. In recent years, however, there has been a decline in the representation of women in the context of biology and relational status. By contrast, a concern for women in the context of traditional occupations and atypical work has increased. It is particularly in the 2010s that labour law scholarship positions women as research subjects in relation to gendered issues arising on account of the type of work that women do and the way in which they participate in the labour market. These two aspects of gender are conceptually anchored within the workplace. It is arguable, therefore, that women are increasingly represented in labour law scholarship on the basis of the construction of gender *through* work.

D. The Use of Empirical Methods

To examine the methodological approaches in use we selected a sub-set of 60 papers from our original sample on the basis of being the items that most strongly engaged with gender. We assessed all 60 papers on an individual basis to identify a dominant methodological approach in order to classify each paper within one of three deliberately broad categories:

— Doctrinal: centred on textual analysis of cases and legislation, concerned with 'what the law is' and, classically, appearing to stand apart from the social realities of lived existence.[53]

— Law in context: legal analysis drawing upon empirical insights emanating from outside the law. This method sets law in its broader societal, historical, political or industrial relations context and is often used to critique the law's adequacy in reflecting or responding to the lived experiences of its subjects.

— Primary empirical: where the author engages in the construction of original empirical data. This could take a number of forms, such as qualitative enquiries on the basis of participant interviews or focus groups or fresh analysis of pre-existing quantitative datasets to produce entirely new insights.

[52] W Chan, 'Mothers, Equality and Labour Market Opportunities' (2013) 42 *Industrial Law Journal* 224.

[53] P Chynoweth, 'Legal Research' in A Knight and L Ruddock, *Advanced Research Methods in the Built Environment* (Oxford, Wiley-Blackwell, 2008) 28, 30.

The 60 papers were chosen on the basis of being those in which our search terms for gender issues were found most frequently. It is perhaps unsurprising that the two years in which the very highest scoring papers were found were published during the 1990s. However, the annual spread of the 60 papers shows a clear trend towards research with a *strong* gender focus being published in more recent years (see Figure 6). We can infer from this that, despite the post-financial crisis reduction in the *frequency* with which women are explicitly recognised as subjects of research, more recent scholarship which has engaged with women has done so in a manner which affords gender a central or sustained focus.

Our assessment of method found that a majority of work did not take a solely doctrinal approach (see Figure 7). Either through the use of 'law in context'

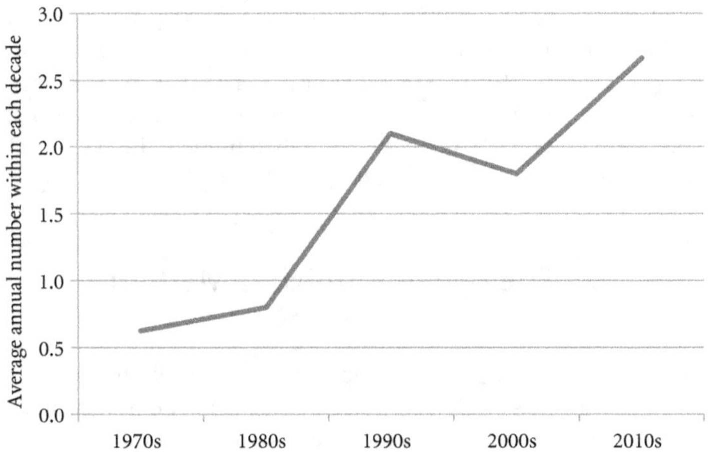

Figure 6: Frequency of published work that strongly engages with gender issues

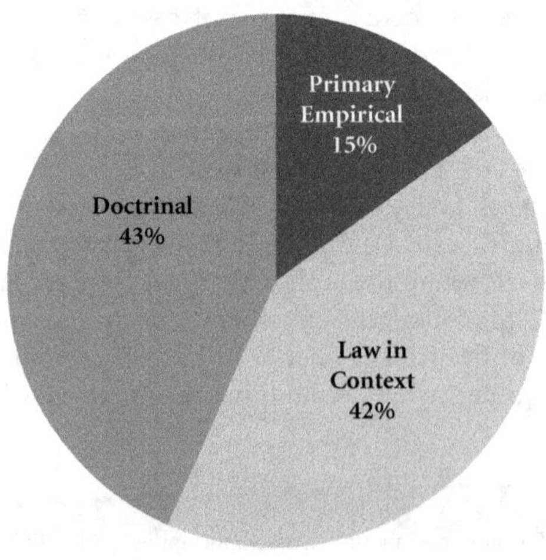

Figure 7: Methods used in work that was highly engaged with gender issues

methods (42 per cent) or through the application of 'primary empirical' methods (15 per cent) scholarship was largely empirically informed (combined total 57 per cent). 'Law in context' methods were particularly prominent and occurred most frequently in discussions about equality law. 'Law in context' methods were based on gathering empirical insights developed outside of the formal boundaries of law to foreground or contextualise a discussion of gender and issues of women's labour market participation. Public policy reports, peer-reviewed social science journal articles and government commissioned research all featured centrally.

A critical site of convergence amongst feminist lawyers is the commitment to interrogate flawed assumptions of institutional or structural gender neutrality.[54] Conaghan has argued that it is virtually impossible to make a gendered critique of law without 'some engagement with the lives and experiences of "actual women"'.[55] It is through the application of empirical data that the realities of the labour market and experiences of employment can inform a gendered assessment of labour law. Our findings in respect of 'law in context' methods mark out a 'magpie' tendency within the discipline. It appears that labour law scholars are keen to draw on empirical knowledge generated elsewhere, in recognition that work/employment is not only a legal issue but also 'a broader social activity' that is about more than economics alone.[56]

The number of examples where 'primary empirical' methods were used was small and represented just 15 per cent of material. However, this scholarship notably placed women at the centre of the research through techniques that included reassessing pre-existing quantitative data from a distinctly feminist perspective, directly quoting the words that women used to describe their lived experiences or by gathering original interview data.[57] In research that used 'primary empirical' methods, labour law scholars were finding ways to generate their own assessments of the realities of working life for women and combine this with doctrinal knowledge. Simon Deakin has suggested that empirical research undertaken by labour lawyers can provide a more complete account of the impact of labour law than is possible by drawing on assessments made by researchers in other fields. For example, scholars of industrial relations focus on aspects of the labour market where regulation is prominent but do not give prominence to the regulatory role of law, sociologists consider law as a form of social ordering that is largely external to the workplace, while economists tend to view the impact of law as self-reinforcing and

[54] D Reaume, 'What's Distinctive about Feminist Analysis of Law?' (1996) 2 *Legal Theory* 265.

[55] J Conaghan, 'Reassessing the Feminist Theoretical Project in Law' (2000) 27 *Journal of Law and Society* 351, 370.

[56] J Browne, 'Resolving Gender Pay Inequality: Rationales, Enforcement and Policy' (2004) 33 *Journal of Social Policy* 553, 567.

[57] E Albin, 'The Case of Quashie: Between the Legalisation of Sex Work and the Precariousness of Personal Service Work' (2013) 42 *Industrial Law Journal* 180; L Flynn, 'Gender Equality Laws and Employers' Dress Codes' (1995) 24 *Industrial Law Journal* 255; N Busby and M McDermont, 'Workers, Marginalised Voices and the Employment Tribunal System: Some Preliminary Findings' (2012) 41 *Industrial Law Journal* 166.

without sufficient consideration of how rights are actually claimed, behaviours changed or legal rules accommodated in labour market decision-making.[58]

In our sample, 'primary empirical' methods were most likely to be used to examine women as research subjects in the context of atypical work (see Figure 8). This suggests there are connections between how women are regarded as *legal subjects* and how they are constructed as *subjects in research*. Primary empirical methods reveal and support the proposition that atypical work, an apparently gender-neutral concern of hours, pay and contractual variation, is in fact an intensely gendered construct. Through the empirical examination of atypical work, women are framed as subjects of *all* labour laws (or at least as equally their subject as men) including mainstream contractual concerns.

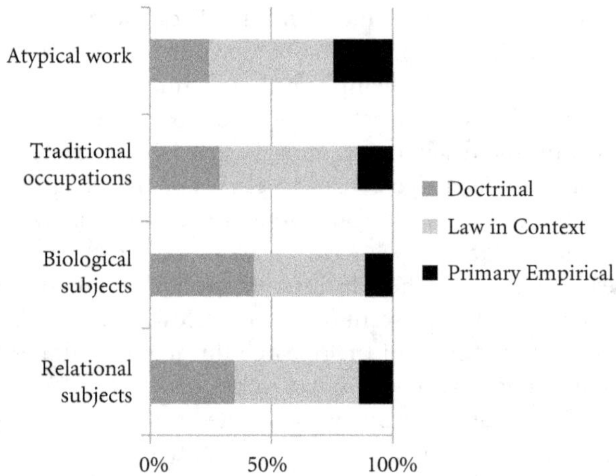

Figure 8: Method in use and gender context

By way of contrast, it was the research that only applied doctrinal methods, which was most likely to consider women in respect of biological issues. Doctrinal scholarship was also the least likely to place a discussion of women in the context of atypical work. This is an interesting finding, not least because it supports our assessment of 'primary empirical' techniques as inclined towards a conception of women that is broader than as subjects of a narrow category of laws relating to maternity rights or equal treatment. Solely doctrinal research that was highly engaged with issues of gender tended to view women as an explicit group of rights-holders in relation to marriage, maternity and familial structures. Notwithstanding its undoubted merits in providing a robust critique of legal provisions, its methodological form followed the law in incorporating women as a social group with distinct needs who rely on distinct legal provision to facilitate their participation in the labour market.

[58] S Deakin, 'Labour and Employment Laws' in P Cane and H Kritzer (eds), *The Oxford Handbook of Empirical Legal Research* (Oxford, Oxford University Press, 2012) 308, 309.

It is widely understood that qualitative empirical study by labour law scholars in the 1960s, 1970s and 1980s was fundamental to understandings of employment and industrial relations in Britain.[59] However, as discussed earlier, women were less frequently represented in the ground-breaking research work of this period. Yet the results of analysis set out in Figure 9 show that when research in this period was highly focused on gender, it was most likely to take an empirical approach through 'law in context' methods. This reflects Deakin's observation that the core of labour law is 'interdisciplinarity'.[60]

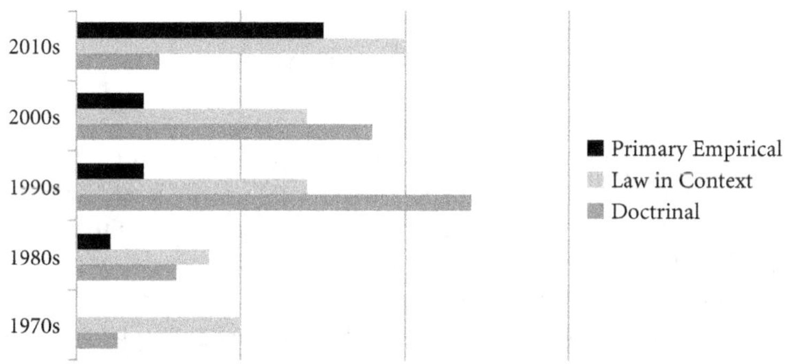

Figure 9: Methods used by decade

Nevertheless, it is particularly striking that the use of doctrinal methods increases so rapidly in our sample between the 1980s and 1990s. This finding illustrates that it was not until the 1990s that the main body of scholarship with a strong gender focus conceived of women solely through the use of doctrinal methods. It suggests a legacy of claims-making through the courts in matters of gender equality during the period, reflected in scholarship recognising women as subjects of labour law without reference to external sources but instead attempting to give doctrinal coherence to the large number of judicial decisions at this time.

Subsequently, it seems that empirically informed methods became a more popular way to include women in research which is highly engaged with gender. Deakin notes that it was in the 1980s that labour law scholarship observed a general shift towards quantitative data that reflected the growing influence of economic approaches,[61] as well as political expectations for evidence that labour law reforms met social policy objectives including flexibility, efficiency, employability, productivity and employment. Certainly by the mid-1990s, the influence of women's participation in paid work on labour market structures, and the turn towards

[59] Ibid, 310.

[60] S Deakin, 'A New Paradigm for Labour Law?' (2007) 31 *Melbourne University Law Review* 1161, 1169.

[61] S Deakin, 'Labour and Employment Laws' in P Cane and H Kritzer, *The Oxford Handbook of Empirical Legal Research* (Oxford, Oxford University Press, 2012) 308, 311.

quantitative, comprehensive workforce studies, were acknowledged in labour law scholarship, often in the same work.[62]

It is, however, most notable that it is against a background of declining frequency of the inclusion of women in the post-financial crisis years that 'primary empirical' methods are most likely to be used. It appears to be increasingly likely that scholars of labour law are exploring gender as an empirical consequence of the forms of employment contract that women enter into, the types of work they typically are engaged in and the dynamic relation of labour law to their working lives.

E. Conclusion

Our analysis of 40 years of labour law scholarship in the *Industrial Law Journal* shows that through their participation and engagement as research subjects, woman are very much part of the labour law scholarship story in the UK.

The gender-blind traditions and reputation of labour law itself has not prevented the representation of women on the basis of historical and legislative developments. However, their inclusion as research subjects has varied by subject matter and method and is firmly associated with gendered discussions that typically focus on motherhood, marriage and variations thereof. Latterly, in the context of atypical work and female-centric occupations such as care work and cleaning, such representation is more likely to address the indirect rather than the direct 'biological' basis of women's perceived difference from men. Furthermore, scholarship about women is largely reflective of statutory provisions which might be characterised as 'gender specific' because they purportedly promote the inclusion of women in the labour market.

We find that from the 2000s there has been a marked decrease in research that seeks to understand gender by solely relying upon doctrinal analysis. It appears that the majority of labour law scholarship engaging with gender is empirically informed, often drawing on data and insights from outside law to foreground or contextualise subsequent analysis. To a lesser extent, we observed scholars engaging in the construction of primary empirical data. While our analysis demonstrates the visibility of women within the discipline, the contexts of their representation tends to be anchored in discussions of aspects of gender that have served to stereotype women, exclude them and subject them to less favourable treatment. The discipline has, rightly, paid attention to the position of women in respect of gender-specific concerns. It would seem that without attention to method, such a narrow focus paradoxically impedes the potential for labour law scholarship to conceive of women as workers more broadly. Our findings attest

[62] S Fredman, 'Labour Law in Flux: The Changing Composition of the Workforce' (1997) 26 *Industrial Law Journal* 337; and S Fredman, 'The Poverty of Equality: Pensions and the ECJ' (1996) 25 *Industrial Law Journal* 91.

to the importance of empirical work in revealing sites of women's exclusion and speaking to the lived realities of women workers.

Our own method consciously avoided a comparison between the representation of women and the representation of men as the subjects of labour law research. We have found it more satisfactory to anchor an assessment of women as research subjects to a consideration of women as subjects of labour law. The benchmark then is not that the representation of women is quantitatively 'equal' to men but that it is sufficiently 'full' to enable labour law scholarship to effectively critique the repertoire of law as it relates to all work and all workers.

Labour law scholarship appears highly likely to be informed by empirical methods when it engages most strongly with issues of gender. To an increasing extent, labour law scholars are combining doctrinal insight with primary empirical study and original empirical data. This suggests that empirical methods have the potential to include working women as research subjects in ways that more roundly perceive them as the subjects of labour law. The implication is that labour law scholarship can move beyond its empirical 'magpie' approach of using data from elsewhere. The trajectory of women in labour law scholarship points to the possibility of a fuller account of women as subjects of labour law.

Part B

Taking Methodological Inspiration from Other Disciplines

6

Can Behavioural Psychology Inform Labour Law?

EWAN McGAUGHEY*

A. Introduction

Empirical research is unlikely to interest someone who views labour law's justifications as being based solely on the protection of fundamental human rights. For a strict rights theorist, basic labour standards like those in the Universal Declaration of Human Rights,[1] ought to be guaranteed by law because they represent moral absolutes, and the consequences are irrelevant. The very character of being 'universal', 'basic', or 'fundamental' embodies a foundational and authoritative normative assertion. It must put an end to further enquiry.[2] This ideal has its roots both in natural law and justice[3] and in modern times (ironically) in the experience of humanitarian tragedy.[4] It takes the priority of certain rights as self-evident, or at least as evident upon careful reflection.[5]

The mere assertion that 'labour rights are fundamental' rarely persuades people whose preferred list contains conflicting norms, such as the right to a business,[6] to freedom of contract,[7] or freedom of establishment.[8] Consequentialist reasoning,

* Lecturer in Private Law, King's College London.

[1] Universal Declaration of Human Rights 1948. See, eg Art 23 (right to work, in just and favourable conditions, to unemployment protection, no discrimination, just pay, to form trade unions and take collective action), Art 24 (right to rest and leisure), and Art 25 (right to social security).

[2] *Cf* Sophocles, *Antigone* (441 BC).

[3] F Kessler, 'Natural Law, Justice and Democracy—Some Reflections on Three Types of Thinking about Law and Justice' (1944) 19 *Tulane Law Review* 32–61.

[4] Charter of the United Nations 1945, Preamble: 'We the Peoples of the United Nations determined to save succeeding generations from the scourge of war, which twice in our lifetime has brought untold sorrow to mankind, and to reaffirm faith in fundamental human rights'.

[5] J Finnis, *Natural Law and Natural Rights* (Oxford, Oxford University Press, Clarendon Law Series, 1980) ch 2.

[6] *Quinn v Leathem* [1901] AC 495, 534, per Lord Lindley, criticised by WN Hohfeld, 'Some Fundamental Legal Conceptions as Applied in Judicial Reasoning' (1913) 23 *Yale Law Journal* 16, 42. Note its re-surfacing in C-426/11 *Alemo-Herron v Parkwood Leisure Ltd* ECLI:EU:C:2013:521 under the Charter of Fundamental Rights of the European Union, Art 16.

[7] *Lochner v New York*, 198 US 45 (1905).

[8] C-438/05 *The Rosella* or *International Transport Workers Federation v Viking Line ABP* ECLI:EU:C:2007:772.

as opposed to deontological reasoning, then becomes useful in the art of persuasion. For example, it can be contended that the 'real concern' underpinning business, contract or establishment rights is a concern for economic growth. To achieve economic growth, it can be said that rights like those in the Universal Declaration are indispensable to preclude value-decreasing competition,[9] or to stimulate effective aggregate demand.[10] But mooting consequences entails predictions, and predictions must be substantiated by empirical evidence about the effects of different policies. This 'positive methodology' has been regarded as essentially the same as in any physical science.[11] But when two phenomena (for instance, the minimum wage and changes in employment) correlate in empirical data, how can causation be deduced? Explicit or not, there is necessarily a theory of human behaviour. Our theories of behaviour will explain *why* a policy drives people to react in a way that leads to the consequences we predict (for instance, higher wages encourage skilled workers to enter the labour market at the margin). We are still very far away from perfecting a 'science of man',[12] but behavioural psychologists have significantly advanced our understanding of the workplace, and also what labour law should be doing. Above all, we now have compelling evidence about the connection between human motivation and productivity, and the importance of fairness for efficiency.

The behavioural psychology method has been around for some time,[13] and can be regarded as a *tertium quid* in empirical research, on top of quantitative data correlation and qualitative surveying or interviewing. It seeks to test how real people *generally* react in response to incentives in isolated experiments. It generates new data (rather than observing existing phenomena), and identifies why people *generally* react to incentives (regardless of what people subjectively think or say). In this chapter, three groups of experiments and the implications for labour law will be discussed: (1) the effect of fair terms and conditions on productivity, (2) the effect of security in pay, and jobs, on productivity, and (3) workplace participation and productivity. This chapter's central argument is that the evidence proves beyond reasonable doubt that the classic goals of labour law—to counteract inequality of bargaining power, improve security, and embed worker participation in economic institutions—do promote economic productivity and growth.

[9] See, eg S Webb, 'The Economic Theory of a Legal Minimum Wage' (1912) 20 *Journal of Political Economy* 973, and S Webb and B Webb, *Industrial Democracy* (London, Longmans, Green and Co, 1920) Pt III, ch 2.

[10] See, eg JM Keynes, *The General Theory of Employment, Interest and Money* (Cambridge, Macmillan Cambridge University Press, for Royal Economic Society, 1935) ch 24, and MS Eccles, *Beckoning Frontiers: Public and Personal Recollections* (New York, Knopf, 1951) 76–77.

[11] M Friedman, 'The Methodology of Positive Economics' in M Friedman, *Essays in Positive Economics* (Chicago, University of Chicago Press, 1953) chs 1,4.

[12] F Kessler, 'Natural Law, Justice and Democracy—Some Reflections on Three Types of Thinking about Law and Justice' (1944) 19 *Tulane Law Review* 32, 60.

[13] See, eg S Milgram, 'Behavioral Study of Obedience' (1963) 67 *Journal of Abnormal and Social Psychology* 371, on obeying orders to electrocute people.

The evidence from behavioural psychology conflicts with rational economic choice theories. For example, in 1984 Richard Posner memorably wrote in 'Some Economics of Labor Law' that:

> [B]ecause labor law is (as we shall see) founded on a policy that is the opposite of the policies of competition and economic efficiency that most economists support, the field is unlikely to attract as a subject for teaching and scholarship, the lawyer who is deeply committed to economic analysis; it is likely to repel him.[14]

Thus, a standard view in law and economics came to be that inequality of bargaining power had 'no economic basis',[15] that anything other 'at-will' employment was economically inefficient,[16] and collective action to any end by a union was virtually indistinguishable from a price-fixing cartel.[17]

But was this all true? Does labour law undermine a competitive economy? In 1998 Posner wrote that behavioural psychology could not present 'an alternative theory' to rational choice because 'it is profoundly unclear what "behavioral man" will do in any given situation'.[18] However this view, even if it was accurate then, is wrong now because a growing number of specific experiments are creating a superior positive understanding of how people act in economic affairs. Case-by-case experimentation can always be repeated, which means that unlike rational choice theory,[19] the theories it generates are built on falsifiable evidence.[20]

Many labour lawyers will not be surprised to hear that their subject is not economically or socially destructive. But this does not mean that engagement with hard-line law and economics is unimportant, or that it is sufficient to repose on the easy pillow of rights based rhetoric. Nor is it good enough to say that human behaviour is *so intrinsically* 'contextual' or 'constructed' or 'embedded',[21] that the territory of predicting how people generally react to changes in labour policy is abandoned. Context does change behaviour, but general tendencies can

[14] RA Posner, 'Some Economics of Labor Law' (1984) 51 *University of Chicago Law Review* 988, 990.

[15] RA Posner, 'Reflections on Consumerism' (1973) 20 *University of Chicago Law School Records* 19, 24–25. See also, OE Williamson, *The Economic Institutions of Capitalism* (New York, The Free Press, 1985) 237–58.

[16] RA Epstein, 'In Defense of the Contract at Will' (1984) 51 *University of Chicago Law Review* 947

[17] RA Posner, *Economic Analysis of Law* (New York, Little Brown and Co, 1973) ch 11, effectively restating the view of the US Supreme Court in *Loewe v Lawlor*, 208 US 274 (1908).

[18] RA Posner, 'Rational Choice, Behavioral Economics and the Law' (1998) 50 *Stanford Law Review* 1551, 1559–60. Note the examples of elaborate reasoning to deduce what 'rational man' would do hypothetically: RA Coase, 'The Problem of Social Cost' (1961) 3 *Journal of Law and Economics* 1, and OE Williamson, *The Economic Institutions of Capitalism* (New York, The Free Press, 1985).

[19] *Cf* A Smith, *Theory of Moral Sentiments* (London, A Millar, 1758) 1.

[20] The evidence also indicates that some conclusions of behavioural law and economics previously, notably of Cass Sunstein and Christine Jolls, cannot realistically be supported. See further, E McGaughey, 'Behavioural Economics and Labour Law' (LSE Working Paper Series 20/2014, 2014): papers.ssrn.com/sol3/papers.cfm?abstract_id=2460685.

[21] *Cf* M Granovetter, 'Economic Action and Social Structure: The Problem of Embeddedness' (1985) 91 *American Journal of Sociology* 481. It is worth noting that economists themselves are partly contextualised thought processes. See, RH Frank, T Gilovich and DT Regan, 'Does Studying Economics Inhibit Cooperation?' (1993) 7 *Journal of Economic Perspectives* 159.

still be identified within different contexts. Hard-line law and economics is profoundly influential, both politically and ideologically. Its claims must be carefully scrutinised in their own terms. Everything rests on the claim that economic theories make good predictions. And so long as political decisions are made through deliberative, democratic channels, it remains important to improve our method of predicting policy outcomes, to build a better theory of labour law.

B. Behavioural Studies and the Workplace

1. Fairness and Productivity

One of the most important contributions that behavioural economics has made to social science relates to our understanding of human motivation at work. The motivation to work matters because it naturally affects the productive efficiency of people and the organisations they work in. The normative relevance this has is that if a first institutional arrangement tends to demotivate people, and leads to less productive outcomes compared to a second, the first may be classified as a market failure.

Probably the most important experiment in this respect was conducted by Alain Cohn, Ernst Fehr, Benedikt Hermann and Frédéric Schneider. This was an experiment 'in the field' as opposed to a laboratory. The criticism has been made that laboratory conditions can deviate from real life and so be capable of explaining less about the real world.[22] In fact, results in laboratories may both over- and under-illustrate the various contextual pressures that exist in the real world. Either way, experiments in the field can generally be taken to be even more conclusive. The test participants were temporary workers who got jobs for two weekends in two German towns.[23] These workers did not know they were part of an experiment, and worked in pairs, handing out cards to pedestrians on the High Street for entry into nightclubs and bars. They had to either sell the cards for €5 or would give out the cards for free in return for the customer's information. There were a total of 96 workers in 48 pairs, and they were subjected to three different treatments. A first group worked at a wage of €12 an hour. A second group were hired at €12 an hour, but then were told shortly into their first shift that both workers in the pair would be receiving a wage cut to €9 per hour. The third group, most importantly, were also hired at €12 an hour but were then told the following: 'Worker 1 continues to earn €12 per hour while worker 2 receives €9 instead of €12 per hour. This was the manager's decision'. Obviously, worker two could do

[22] See, eg RA Posner, 'Rational Choice, Behavioral Economics and the Law' (1998) 50 *Stanford Law Review* 1551, 1570.

[23] A Cohn, E Fehr, B Herrmann and F Schneider, 'Social Comparison in the Workplace: Evidence from a Field Experiment' (2014) 12 *Journal of the European Economic Association* 877.

very little, except leave at this point. It was that or unemployment, and so they had very little bargaining power against 'the manager's decision'. The terms of the employment contract allowed for variation.[24] The productivity of the workers was measured both in terms of the number of cards distributed, and in the accuracy of the customer information that was recorded.

Among the second group, where wages were cut to €9 an hour, there was a 15 per cent drop in productivity for both workers in the pair, compared to workers in the first group who stayed on €12 an hour. In the third group, where only one participant's wage was cut, there was an overall drop of 34 per cent in productivity between the participants in the team. This was entirely due to the one team member whose wage was cut to €9. The average worker who remained with pay of €12 continued to work as normal. So, the effect of cutting one worker's wage was a greater productivity loss than if both workers' wages were cut. The conclusion of the German nightclub card study authors is that, not only absolute levels of pay matter for performance, but also relative pay matters. In short, people's motivation to work is affected by their perception of fairness of their pay relative to other people in their group.

This study has important implications for one of the central issues in labour law, because it shows the connection between motivation to work and fairness in pay: a direct consequence of the capacity that employees have to bargain with employers. Mainstream economic thought had, from Adam Smith onwards, recognised the relevance of inequality of bargaining power.[25] This means the weaker negotiating position people have when they hold relatively fewer resources, and so have fewer alternatives. Practically speaking, this is true in most cases when a person bargains with a corporation. Wealth inequality infects the terms of market transactions. To the extent that inequality of bargaining power is not recognised as an unjust factor in transactions, inequality will grow at a geometric rate in income, and an exponential rate in wealth.

However, in a radical departure from orthodox understanding, some strands of law and economics argued that inequality of bargaining power was either non-existent or irrelevant,[26] or that its relevance is only to affect distribution of income. It was said to have no impact on efficiency.[27] As Richard Epstein put it in

[24] Although the express terms of the contract allowed for the variation, the change in the experiment probably amounted to a breach of an implied term in employment contracts. In Germany, this is called 'Treu and Glauben' (see Civil Code (BGB) §242) and is referred to as either 'good faith' or 'mutual trust and confidence' in the Commonwealth and the United States. In the UK, see *Transco plc v O'Brien* [2002] EWCA Civ 379.

[25] A Smith, *An Inquiry into the Nature and Causes of the Wealth of Nations* (London, Methuen & Co Ltd, 1776) Book I, ch 8.

[26] RA Posner, 'Reflections on Consumerism' (1973) 20 *University of Chicago Law School Records* 19, 24–25: 'The argument of "exploitation" based on "unequal bargaining power", however, lacks, so far as I can see, any economic basis'. OE Williamson, *The Economic Institutions of Capitalism* (New York, The Free Press, 1985) 237–58.

[27] RA Coase, 'The Problem of Social Cost' (1961) 3 *Journal of Law and Economics* 1, 5, discussed below, probably triggered this line of thought by remarking, in the course of discussing a settlement in a tort dispute that 'an agreement would not affect the allocation of resources but would merely alter the distribution of income and wealth'.

1984, bargaining power influences 'which side will appropriate most of the surplus in any negotiations' between the employer and employee.[28] When sharing the joint surplus, a workforce with more collective voice could take a larger share of the product than an individualised workforce would,[29] and otherwise the larger share is automatically appropriated by the employer.[30] But if 'efficiency is driving organizational outcomes', wrote Oliver Williamson, 'modes that are efficient under one distribution of income will normally remain efficient under another'.[31] Distribution of income and wealth did not, it was said, affect whether contracts were concluded.[32] Rational actors will still pay enough to ensure that economically efficient activity takes place. So inequality of bargaining power was not in the limited categories of market failure.[33] Of course, it is true that every modern society views inequality of bargaining power a problem that labour law must correct. Law and economics theory contended, however, that things like the protection of collective bargaining, the right to a minimum wage, or upper-limits on working time,[34] must really be concerned with redistribution of wealth on non-economic grounds, and are probably driven by special interests whose motives diverge from the social good. There is no market failure to correct.

Is it true that labour law, when it mitigates inequality of bargaining power, is concerned merely with distribution and not with economic efficiency? There are, of course, multiple reasons why specific labour rights can have positive efficiency consequences, and these have been extensively discussed before.[35] These discussions have concerned labour law's reduction of collective action problems, information asymmetries, transaction costs, improving aggregate demand, and mitigating monopsony.[36] Yet it also seems the German nightclub card study

[28] RA Epstein, 'In Defense of the Contract at Will' (1984) 51 *University of Chicago Law Review* 947, 973–76.

[29] SJ Schwab, 'The Law and Economics Approach to Workplace Regulation' in BE Kaufman (ed), *Government Regulation of the Employment Relationship* (Cornell, Cornell University Press, 1997) and WS Jevons, *Theory of Political Economy*, 3rd edn (London, Macmillan and Co, 1888) ch 4, §74.

[30] It is an implied term of employment contracts that the employer appropriates the benefits of labour. See, eg *Stevenson, Jordan & Harrison v MacDonald & Evans* [1952] 1 TLR 101, copyright over lectures belonged to the employee because they were composed outside the course of employment, under the Copyright Act 1911, s 5(1). The same goes for all benefits of work, whether recognised as property or not.

[31] OE Williamson, *The Economic Institutions of Capitalism* (New York, The Free Press, 1985) 258.

[32] RA Epstein, 'In Defense of the Contract at Will' (1984) 51 *University of Chicago Law Review* 947, 976.

[33] See also, FH Easterbrook and DR Fischel, 'The Corporate Contract' (1989) 89 *Columbia Law Review* 1416, 1435.

[34] In the US, UK and EU, see examples in the National Labor Relations Act 1935, §1, *Autoclenz Ltd v Belcher* [2011] UKSC 41 [35], and C-397/01–C-403/01 *Pfeiffer v Deutsches Rotes Kreuz, Kreisverband Waldshut eV* ECLI:EU:C:2004:584.

[35] See, eg S Deakin and F Wilkinson, 'Labour Law and Economic Theory: A Reappraisal' in H Collins, P Davies and RW Rideout (eds), *Legal Regulation of the Employment Relation* (Kluwer Law International, 2000).

[36] On this, see A Manning, *Monopsony in Motion: Imperfect Competition in Labor Markets* (Princeton, Princeton University Press, 2003). Manning's theory models how a monopsonistic labour market produces sub-optimal results, and contends that labour markets are always monopsonistic. Unpacking why labour markets fit into this model of monopsony, however, is a tricky issue that must be left for another time. It would seem that, as Manning suggests in ch 1, it is a specific example of the general phenomenon of inequality of bargaining power.

indicates why counteracting inequality of bargaining power has important and positive consequences for productive efficiency in itself. If workers as a group perceive themselves to be paid unfairly compared to their co-workers then the likely outcome is a drop in their productivity. Unfair wages in this context represent a market failure. Whenever inequality of bargaining power produces unfair distribution of rights in the workplace this represents a market failure, because it undermines the motivation to work. None of this should come as a dramatic surprise for economic thought, because it is experimental confirmation of much of what Alfred Marshall in 1890,[37] or Adam Smith in 1776,[38] had already realised.

It is important to see exactly how this differs from the assumptions made in prominent strands of law and economics. The motivation to work is affected by assignment of legal rights (like pay) whether or not we are in a hypothetical world without transaction costs.[39] Ronald Coase had made the contention in 'The Problem of Social Cost' that if there were no transaction costs, and so long as it was known who owned rights, economically efficient outcomes would always be reached through people trading their rights in a market. This was a radical break with mainstream economics at the time, which had indeed seen distribution and efficiency as interlinked. But as Coase put it, 'the ultimate result (which maximises the value of production) is independent of the legal position [ie distribution of legal rights] if the pricing system is assumed to work without cost'.[40] For illustration, Coase made specific reference to a number of cases, including *Sturges v Bridgman*,[41] where a doctor succeeded in claiming an injunction to prevent his neighbour, a confectioner, from operating his machinery. Coase contended that whatever way the court decided, the use of the property could be traded to the person who wanted it the most without any detriment to economic efficiency if transaction costs did not exist.[42] Coase did not acknowledge bargaining power as any kind of impediment, which is a little curious given that the person who developed the transaction cost concept, John R Commons, knew about it all too well.[43]

Coase sometimes seems to have had 'allocative efficiency' foremost in mind when he wrote about efficient results, though he was also plainly concerned with productive efficiency.[44] In fact, a mugs and money study was conducted in 1990 by Daniel Kahneman, Jack Knetsch and Richard Thaler to show that people would not trade rights to the point where the rights were most valued because (even in a world without transaction costs) we tend to overvalue, and hold onto, the things

[37] A Marshall, *Principles of Economics*, 3rd edn (London, Macmillan and Co Ltd, 1895) Book VI, ch 4, 649.

[38] A Smith, *An Inquiry into the Nature and Causes of the Wealth of Nations* (London, Methuen & Co Ltd, 1776) Book 1, ch 8, §§43 and 47.

[39] RA Coase, 'The Problem of Social Cost' (1961) 3 *Journal of Law and Economics* 1.

[40] Ibid, 8.

[41] *Sturges v Bridgman* (1879) LR 11 Ch D 852.

[42] Coase, n 39, 15.

[43] JR Commons, 'Institutional Economics' (1936) 26 *American Economic Review* 237, on the original concept of transaction costs, and note JR Commons and JB Andrews, *Principles of Labor Legislation* (New York, Harper & Brothers Publishers, 1916) chs 1 and 9.

[44] RA Coase, 'The Problem of Social Cost' (1961) 3 *Journal of Law and Economics* 1, 5.

that we are 'endowed' with (or possess initially).[45] The 'endowment effect' meant that, to take just one example, in a study with 44 students at Cornell, who were randomly given mugs and money tokens, and then asked to trade, many more people chose to hold onto what they had, simply because they already had it. This already suggested that *allocative* efficiency cannot automatically be presumed in a transaction cost free world. Rights are not always traded to their most valued use.

But more than this, the nightclub card case suggests why *productive* efficiency cannot be presumed either, whenever distribution of legal rights could affect the motivation to work. Suppose that the confectioner in *Sturges v Bridgman*, after losing an appeal against the injunction, bargained with the doctor to continue operating his machinery because it generated more profits overall. Suppose the doctor required that to continue operating the machinery, the confectioner would have to pay 99 per cent of all profits beyond a subsistence income, and suppose the confectioner had no better alternative. This would probably affect the confectioner's motivation to work, particularly as he saw his output being appropriated. Being aggrieved and demotivated would probably not even be irrational.[46] Could the doctor calculate what the precise deduction would be to maximise the confectioner's effort? The answer appears to be 'no' in any situation where the confectioner reasonably thought that a penny of the doctor's enrichment would be unjust.[47] It might be true to say that the confectioner *should* ignore the unfairness, cut his losses, and work productively anyway, just as the workers whose pay was reduced to €9 might have done. Perhaps unfair distributions of legal rights *should* not affect productive efficiency. But to say that economic production is maximised *whatever* the initial distribution of legal rights (even in a world without transaction costs) is inaccurate. Fairness in distribution necessarily affects productive efficiency because it affects motivation. Thinking only about transaction costs simply leads to inaccurate predictions.

[45] D Kahneman, J Knetsch and R Thaler, 'Experimental Tests of the Endowment Effect and the Coase Theorem' (1990) 98 *Journal of Political Economy* 1325.

[46] There is an analogy here to the 'ultimatum game' experiments. These are revealingly discussed by RA Posner, 'Rational Choice, Behavioral Economics and the Law' (1998) 50 *Stanford Law Review* 1551, 1564: '"Why won't he take the penny?" For the same reason that I would not kiss Professor Sunstein's feet for $1,000. The offer of the penny would signal to the respondent the proposer's belief that the respondent holds a low supposal of his own worth, that he is grateful for scraps, that he accepts being ill-used, that he has no pride, no sense of honor. This weak-spirited creature is just the type who in a prepolitical, vengeance-based society would have been stamped on by his aggressive neighbors and, thus deprived of resources, have left few offspring'.

[47] To give just one numbered example, suppose the doctor can make up to £1,000 pa in income, the confectioner up to £2,000 pa, there are no alternatives, and each needs a minimum of £100 pa to survive. Suppose (1) the confectioner is not given an injunction, and the doctor cannot continue his practice. There will be £2,000 pa in production. Or, suppose (2) the doctor wins the injunction. The doctor knows he can stop working now and make a large profit, if only he can find the right balance. Effectively the doctor is in a position to make the confectioner his employee. He could offer the confectioner any amount, except that the doctor will take some fraction. But whatever that fraction is (1% or 99%), the confectioner could rationally react by depriving them both of a gain. The total product is therefore likely to be less than £2,000.

It is true, however, that a lack of motivation from unfair treatment, which can result from unequal bargaining power, might be mitigated in a number of ways. An employer could, for example, introduce a close system of productivity monitoring, coupled with sanctions for under-performance. The employer could spend money on organisational brand promotion to ensure that its workforce comes to identify more closely with their work, and to hold up morale. However, such strategies all come with costs, typically known in management science literature as 'agency costs'. Agency costs are often referred to as the costs of monitoring or bonding, and aim to align the interests of the 'agent' with those of the 'principal'.[48] When inequality of bargaining power produces unfair pay, and lower motivation, this inevitably affects productivity. But an employer will often have a private incentive not to correct the fairness in distribution of the company product, even though it produces a social cost. Instead, further social costs will be incurred as the employer over-invests in monitoring or bonding devices which attempt to mimic (but probably never match) the socially efficient solution.

It may be pointed out that the German nightclub card study concerned workers who, given their context, would have regarded themselves as being in similar situations. Would the outcomes differ if workers had grounds to believe they received an unfair share of the gains compared to people in dissimilar situations, such as management, or the shareholders of an organisation? There is not an experiment on this yet, but it would be surprising if there were no effect at all. It would seem that just as people can make comparisons between themselves and people who are in a similar position, they can also compare themselves with people in other positions (eg the company CEO) with some sense of proportionality.

There is one more main question raised by this experiment. Unfair wages diminish the productivity of the person who feels relatively undervalued, but could there be any effect on people who are substantially overvalued? Much of the modern agency cost literature, since Michael Jensen and William Meckling's work in 1976, has become concerned with the fact of agency costs existing, for instance when a director is not sufficiently accountable to shareholders and uses the opportunity to unjustly enrich himself or herself.[49] Yet in law and economics terms this might also be described as an issue 'merely' affecting distribution and not efficiency. Originally, however, the matter was indeed posed as a question of the damaging efficiency consequences, namely by AA Berle and Gardiner Means in *The Modern Corporation and Private Property*. Berle and Means pointed out that if they were unaccountable, company directors could 'serve their own pockets better by profiting at the expense of the company than by making profits for it'.[50]

[48] The best known discussion is M Jensen and W Meckling, 'Theory of the Firm: Managerial Behavior, Agency Costs and Ownership Structure' (1976) 3 *Journal of Financial Economics* 305.

[49] A Smith, *An Inquiry into the Nature and Causes of the Wealth of Nations* (London, Methuen & Co Ltd, 1776) Book V, ch 1, §107.

[50] AA Berle and GC Means, *The Modern Corporation and Private Property* (New York, The Macmillan Company, 1932) 114.

So overvaluation, unjust enrichment at the expense of others, was an economic efficiency issue, not simply a distributive issue, because it would lead to less productive effort by the person who was unjustly enriched.

The same line of reasoning would appear to fit with all cases where individuals or firms are capable of using their unequal bargaining power to extract excessive gains. This does concern work, but goes beyond labour law. This could include any contracting partner, including in consumer contracts,[51] residential tenancy agreements,[52] and contracts to buy shares or other financial products. An empirical study regarding this hypothesis remains an interesting direction for future research. Yet the view of Berle and Means, not to mention the legislation which exists worldwide in those areas, would seem to be a natural extension of the idea that fairness of income positively affects productivity.

2. Security and Productivity

A second issue, for which behavioural psychology has interesting implications, concerns not just the distribution of rights at work, but the security of rights: particularly security of pay, and potentially job security. In the Madurai game studies designed by Dan Ariely, Uri Gneezy, George Loewenstein and Nina Mazar, a group of people were asked to play six different games and depending on their performance, they would get different rewards.[53] The experiment was conducted by a group of Masters students at Narayanan College, in Madurai, which is in Tamil Nadu, India. In total, 87 residents of the town took part. Each person played the six games, and at the start of each a dice was rolled to determine at random whether person would receive a 'low', 'medium' or 'high' reward for their performance. The high reward was set at 400 rupees per game, and so 2,400 rupees was the maximum possible winnings, equivalent to around five months of the average per capita consumer expenditure of the locality.[54] The games required creative thinking, memory and motor skills of one kind or another, for instance, guiding a metal ball through a tiltable labyrinth which has holes in it that the ball should avoid.[55] They found that for all of the games, the participants who were told they could receive the high reward performed the worst.[56]

In a variation of the experiment, the same games were set up where participants were first given the maximum amount of money they could win, and were told it would be taken away again in proportion to how far their score fell below the

[51] See, eg EU Unfair Terms in Consumer Contracts Directive 93/13/EC, Recital 16 (OJ L 95, 21.04.1993, 29–34).

[52] See, eg *Attorney General of Canada v Nav Canada* [2008] FC 71 [19] per Hugessen J.

[53] D Ariely, U Gneezy, G Loewenstein and N Mazar, 'Large Stakes and Big Mistakes' (2009) 76 *Review of Economic Studies* 451.

[54] Ibid, 454.

[55] The six games were called 'Packing Quarters', 'Simon', 'Recall Last Three Digits', 'Labyrinth', 'Dart Ball', and 'Roll-Up'.

[56] Ariely et al, n 53, 458 and the graphs therein.

highest possible. The idea here was to see if people performed differently if they felt they already had something which they could then lose. 'Loss aversion' is a well-established phenomenon which means that changes which appear to make things worse loom larger in people's minds than changes which appear to be gains.[57] On average people prefer avoiding losses to making gains of the same magnitude by a factor of two to one.[58] Unfortunately, as Dan Ariely later reported, the experiment could not be completed. The first test participant was given the money, performed poorly and then left the test room politely. The second participant, however, 'was so nervous that he shook the whole time and couldn't concentrate'. He then ran away with all of the money.[59] It was thus felt to be inappropriate to continue.

Why did the prospect of a large money payment negatively affect people's performance in the tests? 'Increased motivation', wrote the authors,

> tends to narrow individuals' focus of attention on a variety of dimensions … including the breadth of the solution set people consider. This can be detrimental for tasks that involve insight or creativity, since both require a kind of open-minded thinking that enables one to draw unusual connections between elements.

In fact, the authors had expected that on the games which required only memory skills, the higher payment would induce better performance, but even this prediction was proven to be unsound.[60] In a subsequent experiment with 24 MIT students, they found there was a statistically significant difference in performance between participants who did a task where they hit either the 'N' or the 'V' key on a keyboard, and those who did a task having to find numbers in a matrix that added up to 10.[61] This led to the conclusion that if work involves absolutely no thought, no creativity, no 'cognitive resources and effort', but instead 'requires only physical effort', then higher stakes can motivate better performance.

There are several important and immediate implications from this line of work, and several very interesting questions raised by it. First, the test was designed with the problem of bonus pay in mind. It had previously been thought, and prominently advocated in a large amount of law and economics literature, that it would be desirable to give company directors, senior managers, and perhaps all employees, significant variable components in their pay. An old preconception was that if the incentives of people at work were aligned with shareholders, which took the residual profits in a firm, then people would become more productive.[62] From

[57] D Kahneman, JL Knetsch and RH Thaler, 'Anomalies: The Endowment Effect, Loss Aversion, and Status Quo Bias' (1991) 5 *Journal of Economic Perspectives* 193, 199.

[58] A Tversky and D Kahneman, 'Loss Aversion and Riskless Choice: A Reference Dependent Model' (1991) 106 *Quarterly Journal of Economics* 1039.

[59] D Ariely, *The Upside of Irrationality* (New York, Harper Collins, 2011) 33.

[60] D Ariely, U Gneezy, G Loewenstein and N Mazar, 'Large Stakes and Big Mistakes' (2009) 76 *Review of Economic Studies* 451, 458–59.

[61] Ibid, 460–61.

[62] For a general discussion of some of the origins of this view, see E McGaughey, 'British Codetermination and the Churchillian Circle' (UCL Labour Rights Institute On-Line Working Papers—LRI WP 2/2014, 2014): www.ucl.ac.uk/laws/lri/papers/2%20-2014%20British%20Codetermination%20and%20the%20Churchillian%20Circle.pdf.

the late 1970s, the theory was promoted for company directors,[63] and then for employees generally according to their relative position within the firm.[64] This led to an increasing amount of pay coming in the form of share options, and discretionary bonuses that were notionally performance related. In the UK, the theory was followed in government reports,[65] and the practice was written into the UK Corporate Governance Code.[66]

Importantly, people working in systemically important financial services could frequently expect the majority of their income to be 'performance' linked, and thus insecure. But in practice people would develop a psychological expectation that they would receive their bonus. For example, in *Keen v Commerzbank AG* a proprietary trading employee argued that it would be unlawful for his employer to irrationally exercise its discretion to not award a bonus in 2005. Mr Keen had a salary of £120,000, but in the last two years had received €2.8m and €2.95m in bonuses. He argued that it was a reasonable expectation that he should not be deprived of his bonus, although this was precisely what his contract stated could be done.[67] The Court of Appeal rejected his claim, though other claimants in different situations have been successful.[68] The legal issue of whether the implied terms of a contract must follow the reasonable expectations of the parties, as they surely must,[69] is less important for this purpose than the actual psychological expectations of the parties. Structures which encourage very insecure payment potentially encourage more conflicts (as *Keen* shows), worse performance, and greater risk taking. If people perceive something to be theirs already, then it may encourage cheating as people try to hold onto what they have got.

The theory that bonuses and performance related pay could be economically beneficial has not just been restricted to corporate boards and financial services. A tipping culture has become an increasingly important part of food catering work, many service industries have introduced discretionary or performance related elements to their work, and there has been a concerted attempt to promote employee share schemes. This is not to say that things like tipping, or employees buying stocks are *necessarily* bad, but laws which subsidise overindulgence in these practices are. That has happened with tipping, whenever pay from tips can be used

[63] M Jensen and W Meckling, 'Theory of the Firm: Managerial Behavior, Agency Costs and Ownership Structure' (1976) 3 *Journal of Financial Economics* 305, 328. See also, MC Jensen and KJ Murphy, 'Performance Pay and Top-Management Incentives' (1990) 98 *Journal of Political Economy* 225.

[64] E Lazeer and S Rosen, 'Rank-Order Tournaments as Optimum Labor Contracts' (1981) 89 *Journal of Political Economy* 841.

[65] See, eg Higgs Review, *Review of the Role and Effectiveness of Non-Executive Directors* (London, DTI, 2003) 56–58: www.ecgi.org/codes/documents/higgsreport.pdf.

[66] UK Corporate Governance Code 2010, D.1.1 and Sch A.

[67] *Keen v Commerzbank AG* [2006] EWCA Civ 1536.

[68] Contrast *Clark v Nomura International plc* [2000] IRLR 766, and *Dresdner Kleinwort Ltd v Attrill* [2013] EWCA Civ 394.

[69] In the UK, see *Equitable Life Assurance Society v Hyman* [2000] UKHL 39.

to subsidise the employer's payment of the minimum wage,[70] and it has happened through tax advantages for employee share schemes.[71] All these measures make people's income less secure, particularly share schemes which fail the first rule that any prudent investor must follow: diversify. In doing so they lead to consequences opposed to what is desired. Going by the Madurai game studies, unless someone is doing a job which requires no cognitive effort, the impact of such practices (if any) will probably be negative. Even if someone's job does involve purely mechanical actions a human is not a resource, and treating people like they are no better than cogs in need of oil damages the moral character of the employer.

The outcomes of the Madurai game studies when loss aversion was brought into the equation points toward an interesting question about job security. Would there be similar results if future tests looked at not simply high stakes in pay, but high stakes in keeping one's job? There should be little doubt that, when the decision is made by one's peers or an impartial judge, dismissal is a necessary final sanction for poor job performance and is necessary to respond to changes in economic demand. But if people work under a constant threat of dismissal, how does this affect their performance and productivity? One of the beliefs that supports labour market 'flexicurity' in Europe, or at-will employment in the United States, seems to be that if a trumped up authority figure can bark 'you're fired' when they like, staff will be encouraged to work properly. The reality may well be that the irrational threat of losing one's job has the same impact that any high stake has for productive output. In addition to important issues of justice and fairness,[72] it may damage rather than improve productivity.

3. Participation, Satisfaction and Productivity

A third major finding of behavioural studies sheds light on the importance of participation in workplace management and productivity. Shedding light on participation was not, however, the intended consequence of the original Hawthorne experiments, which were probably the first of their kind in the workplace. In 1924, an Australian researcher at Harvard Business School called Elton

[70] In the UK this was true until an amendment in the National Minimum Wage Regulations 1999 (Amendment) Regulations 2009 (SI 2009/1902) reg 5. Before this see *Revenue and Customs Commissioners v Annabel's (Berkeley Square) Ltd* [2009] EWCA Civ 361. A challenge to the European Court of Human Rights, on the basis that employers' taking tips to pay the minimum wage, was found to be within a Member State's margin of appreciation in *Nerva v United Kingdom* (2003) 36 EHRR 4. In the US, tips still form a large part of people's pay in most service industries because the Fair Labor Standards Act 1938 allowed for deviations, particularly since the Small Business Job Protection Act 1996.

[71] See, eg in the US, the Employee Retirement Income Security Act 1974, §407(d)(6) and Internal Revenue Code, §4975(e)(7).

[72] For a discussion of competing values, see H Collins, *Justice in Dismissal* (Oxford, Oxford University Press, 1992) 13–23.

Mayo formulated an experiment with the employees at the Hawthorne Works of the Western Electric Company. Mayo's work competed with the studies (real or apparent)[73] carried out by Frederick W Taylor in 1899, that later developed into the 'scientific management' movement. Taylor had reported that he had been able to improve the productivity of workers who moved piles of pig iron to different places for the Bethlehem Steel Company by studying and then changing working patterns and break times, coupled with various monetary incentives.[74] Taylor's approach was different because he viewed each worker he observed and manipulated as something like an 'intelligent gorilla', and so quite comparable with an animate but barely conscious object.[75] Mayo's studies, by contrast, intently recorded reactions, opinions and thoughts of the people in his experiments, although the goal of securing greater productivity was similar to Taylor's.

In the Hawthorne experiments, Mayo wished to substantiate a hypothesis that lighting intensity would affect workers' productivity. He borrowed five factory workers from Western Electric and brought them to an observation laboratory. They would work as normal putting together telephone relays as Mayo's two research colleagues varied the lighting. Unfortunately, as the switches were changed there were no effects. It was then determined to examine the effects of varying rest breaks, lunches, and daily or weekly working times. The observers were instructed to observe, but not to interfere with the work, and simply make the workers feel comfortable so they could get on with the job. Presumably, Mayo wanted to try and avoid 'contaminating' the test environment. So the observers asked the workers when breaks would suit them, and things like what meals they would prefer. Otherwise they stayed out of the way. Again, productivity went up when breaks were introduced, when meals were given, and also when an hour was taken off the day. But even more curious, productivity continued to improve when these benefits were *removed*. Mayo generated a large amount of data and findings, which he later wrote up,[76] but he did not exactly get what he wanted.

The proper interpretation of the Hawthorne experiments became an important point of debate, and it has remained one of the most important experiments in psychology and the workplace. What came to be known as the 'Hawthorne effect' is still widely discussed today. This term appears to have first been coined by Herbert Simon, to mean at a great level of generality that 'the very act of observing people in organizations and making them the subject of study and experimentation may well change their attitudes and behavior'.[77] Quite what changes might

[73] CD Wrege and AG Perroni, 'Taylor's Pig-Tale: A Historical Analysis of Frederick W Taylor's Pig-Iron Experiments' (1974) 17 *Academy of Management Journal* 6.

[74] FW Taylor, *The Principles of Scientific Management* (London, Harper & Row, 1911) ch 2.

[75] Ibid.

[76] E Mayo, *The Human Problems of an Industrial Civilization* (New York, Macmillan Company, 1933).

[77] HA Simon, 'Recent Advances in Organization Theory' in SK Bailey, *Research Frontiers in Politics and Government* (The Brookings Institution, 1955) 28.

result was left open, but the more important view was to follow. 'We now have', said Simon,

> a considerable body of evidence to support the participation hypothesis—the hypothesis that significant changes in human behavior can be brought about rapidly only if the persons who are expected to change participate in deciding what the change shall be and how it shall be made.[78]

On this theme, in 1968, sociologist Philip Blumberg looked back at the archives Mayo left, and highlighted the one absolutely solid finding.[79] Workers in the test lab consistently outperformed those who stayed in the factory in productivity. Even stranger, the workers seemed happier at work, and began to socialise with each other more after their shifts. Among the interviews were several statements about how they were glad to escape the authoritarian managers back at the factory.[80] But Mayo's main objective was to show how workers can be made productive, so the employer can appropriate the gains.[81] Blumberg concluded this is why Mayo missed the same conclusion that Simon was drawing: that what was making the Hawthorne workers more productive was their new ability to participate in workplace decisions. Even when benefits were taken away, the act of joining people in the process of decision (because it was genuine) meant that the staff had a reason to want to work more effectively. Productivity only dropped as the experiments continued toward 1932, and involvement in workplace decisions dropped away.[82] Participation in the workplace improved productivity.

Law and economics literature has since sought to ignore or side-line the view that meaningful workplace participation (and not simply information and consultation) could lead to productive gains. For instance, Oliver Williamson sought to address Blumberg's claims, albeit indirectly,[83] by pointing to alternative papers. These papers showed, said Williamson, that there was 'serious doubt that efforts to effect participation can be justified on profitability grounds'. Moreover 'evidence relating job satisfaction to productivity', said Williamson, 'discloses little or no association between the two'.[84] The difficulty is that the literature Williamson cited included Herbert Simon, who as we have just seen, did think there was evidence that participation improved productivity. If Williamson had attempted to address

[78] Ibid, 29.

[79] P Blumberg, *Industrial Democracy: The Sociology of Participation* (New York, Schocken Books, 1968) chs 2–3.

[80] Ibid, 25.

[81] See also, E Mayo, *Teamwork and Labor Turnover in the Aircraft Industry of Southern California* (Harvard, Harvard University Press, 1944).

[82] Blumberg, n 79, 37–39.

[83] OE Williamson, *The Economic Institutions of Capitalism* (New York, The Free Press, 1985) 269–70, cites S Bowles and H Gintis, *Schooling in Capitalist America: Educational Reform and the Contradictions of Economic Life* (New York, Basic Books, 1976) 79–80, for a quote from Blumberg.

[84] Williamson, ibid, 270. Job satisfaction obviously differs from participation itself. However, the evidence shows a clear positive correlation between job satisfaction and productivity. See D Ariely, E Kamenica and D Prelec, 'Man's Search for Meaning: The Case of Legos' (2008) 67 *Journal of Economic Behavior & Organization* 671.

the findings of Blumberg, he might have reached a different conclusion. If he had looked to chapter five of Blumberg's book, he would have seen a large catalogue of experiments up to 1968. If he had aimed to refute the findings, it would have been necessary to conduct a study demonstrating participation in the workplace has no positive effect on productivity. But he did not, probably because the evidence would have run counter to his argument.

C. Principles and Conclusions

This chapter has explored three of the most important fields of experiment for the workplace to come out of behavioural psychology. In the introduction, it was suggested that behavioural psychology was useful to develop a better positive theory of labour law, and that consequentialist reasoning could overcome the deadlock of conflicting conceptions of human rights. However, this argument came with a qualification: that deliberative debate takes place within a democracy. An assumption underlying all empirical study is that if consequences of different policies can be identified, it may be shown that common goals will be obtained. In a democracy, the common goal is to improve the lot of the many, not just the few.[85] Just as the existence of rights in law are, by themselves, of limited use to know what is the right thing to do, it is no good knowing all the consequences of every conceivable policy unless there is some idea of a goal.

The specific goal identified in this discussion was economic productivity, though admittedly this is more of a sub-goal. It forms part of a larger aim of human development or social justice, which must go hand-in-hand with democracy.[86] More economic productivity and growth means people can hold more property. But a right to property is primarily important because it serves as an expression of our personalities.[87] Justice means people getting what they are due. The ethical philosophy of human development is that our highest duty should be to strive to become better people and to help others do the same.[88] If it is accepted that we owe this duty as individuals, it follows that 'social' justice means a state where institutions are in place to bring forward everyone's 'capacity', for the 'utmost possible development of faculty in the individual human being', and to ensure 'the opportunity to develop individuality becomes fully actualized'.[89] To reach this goal, we should constantly revise our understanding of human rights in line with empirical evidence. In the abstract, the supposed conflict between deontology and

85 Thucydides, *History of the Peloponnesian War* (ca 411 BC) Book 2, para 37.

86 L Brandeis, 'The Living Law' (1916) 10 *Illinois Law Review* 461.

87 GWF Hegel, *Elements of the Philosophy of Right* (1820) §41.

88 B Spinoza, *On the Improvement of the Understanding* (1677) §§13–14.

89 T Paine, *The Rights of Man* (1792) Pt II, ch 3, S Webb and B Webb, *Industrial Democracy* (London, Longmans, Green and Co, 1920) Pt IV, ch 4, 847–49, AA Berle, 'Property, Production and Revolution' (1965) 65 *Columbia Law Review* 1, 17.

empiricism, between rights and utility, is overcome where a reflexive equilibrium is reached between principle and experience. In the real world, an ongoing process of social communication continually refines the public policies that achieve social justice.

But while a reflexive equilibrium between principle and experience in pursuit of social justice ought to be the goal of every democracy, it is plain that not everyone shares the same aim. Sometimes, the language of economic efficiency, or indeed social justice, is used as a veil for sectarian aims that favour the interests of the rich.[90] Sometimes people cannot be persuaded by evidence of the consequences, because they simply do not share the ethic of a democratic polity. So sometimes, just sometimes, discussion of the consequences—and a search for empirical evidence with it—must cease. Then, established rights and principles are to be followed, to 'let justice be done, whatever be the consequence'.[91]

But with this said, while deliberative, democratic discussion remains worth pursuing, the empirical evidence of the consequences of labour policy remains crucial. The ideology of social justice must differ from those which blithely proclaim the priority of rights for a particular group. Coupled to democracy, it must ground its legitimacy in the ability to persuade most people, most of the time, through reason and evidence. This chapter has contended that labour rights which counteract inequality of bargaining power promote economic productivity, because people who are fairly treated are motivated to work. It showed that security in terms and conditions of employment, particularly pay and potentially including job security, guard against productivity-decreasing distractions. It also recounted the evidence that workplace participation promotes productivity because a genuinely involved workforce will want to contribute more. Can behavioural psychology inform labour law? Yes, by confirming long-standing principles once more.

90 See, eg D Eggen, 'Bush Warns of Aggressive Economic Regulation. On Wall St, he Defends Bailout' *Washington Post*, 14 November 2008, 'If you seek economic growth, if you seek opportunity, if you seek social justice and human dignity, the free market system is the way to go'.

91 *Somerset v Stewart* (1772) 98 ER 499, per Lord Mansfield, holding slavery unlawful at common law.

7

Using Ethnographic Methods to Explore Labour Law Questions

AMY LUDLOW*

> You never really know a man until you understand things from his point of view, until you climb into his skin and walk around in it'.[1]

There is no single, uncontested definition of ethnography but it generally is said to entail a commitment to micro studies in 'natural' settings, to long term immersion in the field and to a focus upon internal culture and symbolic meaning. The use of ethnographic methods is most strongly associated with anthropology. However, in the world of work, ethnographic methods have been used particularly by sociologists and industrial relations scholars as a means by which to study organisational behaviour and discrete, often especially disempowered, or 'fringe' occupational communities. Sociologist Vicki Smith lists some of the themes in the workplace that have been explored ethnographically as autonomy, citizenship, informal relations, meaning, environments, ethics and change.[2] Examples of work ethnographies include Mayo's factory studies in the 1930s of the operation of payment incentives and their effects on productivity, studies of the coal industry, particularly Dennis, Henriques and Slaughter's 1956 study *Coal is Our Life*, Castles and Kosack's *Immigrant Workers and Class Structure* and Oakley's *The Sociology of Housework*.[3]

As is explored in a number of the chapters in this collection, there is a rich tradition of broadly socio-legal approaches to the study of work and relationships at work. However, but ethnographic methods are seldom used by lawyers in their research. This is perhaps because of their particular challenges upon which I

* Fellow in Law, Gonville and Caius College and Affiliated Lecturer, Faculty of Law, University of Cambridge. I am grateful for feedback on an early draft of this paper that was presented at the New Frontiers in Empirical Labour Law Research conference in Cambridge in April 2014 and feedback from Catherine Barnard on a first draft of this chapter. All errors are of course my own.

[1] H Lee, *To Kill a Mockingbird* (Philadelphia, Lippincott & Co, 1960) 196.

[2] V Smith, 'Ethnographies of Work and the Work of Ethnographers' in P Atkinson *et al* (eds), *Handbook of Ethnography* (London, Sage, 2007) 220, 220.

[3] See further, ibid, 220–33.

reflect in concluding this chapter.[4] In such a context, the aim of this chapter is to explore the potential, ideology and (to a lesser extent) challenges of using ethnographic methods to examine labour law questions, partly by reference to fieldwork I completed in 2011–12 at a prison that was being privatised. In the course of this work I became an 'accidental' ethnographer.[5]

My overarching argument is that the enquiry paradigm upon which the ethnographic method is based (the values and orientations from which ethnographic methods proceed) makes ethnography particularly well suited to explore vulnerability and 'precariousness' in work relationships,[6] which I take to be a central disciplinary concern for labour law. This reflects the traditional conception of labour law, based upon the inherent subordination of labour to capital and the employer, but it also encompasses wider developments in a now highly mobile and global field, such as the position of migrant workers and increased use of 'zero hour' contracts.[7] I also argue that ethnographic methods imply a collective and relational social ontology that challenges the neo-liberal ontological narrative and resonates with the values and presuppositions with which some, perhaps most, labour lawyers come to their discipline. To that extent this chapter highlights the power of ethnographic narrative for a critical and change-oriented 'transformative engagement'[8] with ideology and evidence.

A. Ethnography and the Ethnographic Enquiry Paradigm

Hammersley and Atkinson describe ethnographic work as usually having most of the following features:

1. The study is conducted in everyday contexts;
2. data is gathered from a range of sources but participant observation and informal conversation are primary methods of data collection;
3. data collection is relatively unstructured and open;

[4] As ever there are exceptions including Gabriella Alberti's recent work on migrant workers' experiences of working in London hotels and Morag McDermont's work on Citizens Advice Bureaux as increasingly important sites of 'legal consciousness' in (employment) disputes.

[5] A Ludlow, *Privatising Public Prisons: Labour Law and the Public Procurement Process* (Oxford, Hart, 2015).

[6] On precariousness, see G Standing, *The Precariat: The New Dangerous Class* (London, Bloomsbury, 2011).

[7] On the disciplinary nature of labour law, see especially G Davidov and B Langille (eds), *The Idea of Labour Law* (Oxford, Oxford University Press, 2011), C Barnard, S Deakin and S Morris (eds), *The Future of Labour Law* (Oxford, Hart, 2004), and H Collins, 'Labour Law as a Vocation' (1989) 105 *Law Quarterly Review* 468.

[8] This term is drawn from J Flood, 'Socio-Legal Ethnography' in R Banakar and M Travers (eds), *Theory and Method in Socio-Legal Research* (Oxford, Hart, 2005) 33, 36.

4. the focus is on a few cases that are studied in-depth; and
5. data analysis involves interpretation of the meanings, functions and consequences of human actions and institutional practices.[9]

As John Flood puts it 'Ethnography makes us simultaneously stand inside and outside the *mise en scene* as we research'.[10] The orientation of ethnographic work is exploratory and inductive. It produces texts that are not literal representations of the social situations under study but rather are 'artful products'; 'interpretation[s] of the society-as-reconstructed'[11] by both the researcher, who has in mind 'foreshadowed problems' from the literature,[12] and the reader, who 'read[s] into the text, based on [their] own background knowledge and assumptions'.[13] Ethnographic work strongly intertwines the personal and the intellectual.

With this working definition in mind, what is the philosophy and politics, or 'enquiry paradigm', upon which ethnography is based? The starting point in many texts on ethnography is for authors to draw a distinction between positivism and naturalism. Positivism is a philosophical movement that 'promot[es] the status of experimental and survey research and the quantitative forms of analysis associated with them'.[14] Positivism argues in favour of a scientific method modelled on the natural sciences: theory and hypothesis testing through theory neutral experimentation in which variables are controlled and the effect of the observer is minimised through the standardisation of data collection procedures. Through mostly deductive reasoning, the aim is to produce highly generalisable findings that form the basis for describing universal laws.

For positivists, ethnography produces 'subjective' data, 'mere idiosyncratic impressions of one or two cases that cannot provide a solid foundation for rigorous scientific analysis'.[15] In response to this critique, some ethnographers have advanced an alternative naturalist philosophy about the proper nature of social research. They have argued that the social world should be studied in its natural rather than experimental scientific state and, in place of a positivist attachment to a particular set of methodological principles, naturalists emphasise the importance of an attitude of respect and appreciation for the social world under study. Naturalism is allied with interpretivism; a view that the world is not subject to universal laws or straightforward causal relationships because human actions are based on, and suffused by, social and cultural meanings: intentions, motives, beliefs, rules, discourses and values. According to a naturalist perspective, it is only possible to understand the subject under study properly by exploring the subjective meanings

[9] M Hammersley and P Atkinson, *Ethnography: Principles in Practice*, 3rd edn (Abingdon, Routledge, 2007) 3.

[10] J Flood, n 8, 33.

[11] P Atkinson, *The Ethnographic Imagination: Textual Constructions of Reality* (London, Routledge, 1990) 2.

[12] B Malinowski, *Argonauts of the Western Pacific* (London, Routledge, 1922) 9.

[13] Atkinson, n 11.

[14] Hammersley and Atkinson, n 9, 5.

[15] Ibid, 7.

of social action. Consequently, positivism's quest for standardisation and its causal mechanical analysis and manipulation of variables are seen as misplaced and unable to yield a 'full picture'.[16]

B. The Potential of Ethnography for Exploring Labour Law Questions: Reflections from a Study at HMP Birmingham

Having briefly outlined the meaning of ethnography and explained something of its enquiry paradigm, I wish to reflect in most of the rest of this chapter upon the potential for using ethnography to explore labour law questions. These reflections are based upon an ethnographic study I conducted between 2010–11 of the public procurement rules[17] and the Transfer of Undertakings (Protection of Employment) Regulations 2006 (TUPE). In basic terms, the public procurement rules prescribe how EU governments or public bodies must source works, goods or services with a value exceeding at least £66,000.[18] The TUPE Regulations protect employees of businesses that are being transferred (by sale or outsourcing for example) by automatically novating (transferring) contracts of employment, providing some additional dismissal protection and imposing information and consultation obligations on the employer.[19]

The context for this research was the competitive tendering exercise for management of HMP Birmingham, a large local prison housing 1,500 men in the West Midlands of England. The competition launched in 2009 and concluded in 2011 with the award of a 15-year contract worth £316.5m to G4S. Birmingham is the first example of an operational public prison to be privatised in England and Wales (though others have since followed).

Fieldwork began at HMP Birmingham in November 2010. I expected that I would conduct interviews and focus groups over a two or three month period. Within the first month it became clear that this would be neither possible nor appropriate. First, it was apparent that my research participants, chiefly the staff at HMP Birmingham, were finding the competition process difficult. They felt vulnerable, anxious and uninformed and, consequently, they were reluctant to talk to me. It proved challenging to schedule formal appointments with people who

[16] Ibid, 7–10. For a 'defence' of ethnography, see, eg S Hillyard, 'What's (Still) Wrong with Ethnography?' in S Hillyard (ed), *New Frontiers in Ethnography*, Studies in Qualitative Methodology, Vol 11 (Bingley, Emerald Group Publishing Ltd, 2010) 1.

[17] Directive 2004/18/EC (OJ L 134, 30.4.2004, 114–240); implemented domestically in the UK as the Public Contracts Regulations 2006 (SI 2006/5).

[18] See www.ojec.com/Threshholds.aspx for detailed thresholds.

[19] The Regulations originate in the Acquired Rights Directive 77/187 ([1977] OJ L61/26). The Directive was implemented into national law in 1981 (SI 1981/1794) and in 2006 in its revised form (SI 2006/246).

did not understand my purpose in the prison and (understandably) distrusted strangers. I needed to cultivate trust and understanding.

Secondly, the course of the competition took unexpectedly interesting turns from a research perspective. I initially had intended to compare the use and experiences of the public procurement rules and TUPE at a privately managed prison that was party to the same competition as Birmingham. Although I had national research access permission, it was proving slow and problematic to obtain local permission. Later HMP Wellingborough, the only other publicly managed prison in the competition at risk of being privatised alongside HMP Birmingham, was withdrawn from the competition. Birmingham therefore became the most interesting prison in the competition from a labour lawyer's perspective because of its potential for management transfer from the public sector to G4S, with all of the workforce implications that flow from such a decision. Having spent only a few weeks in Birmingham it was clear that the process was being experienced at all staffing levels as much more complex and difficult than I had expected. The competitive 'landscape' was also less stable. I had assumed (erroneously) that the basic structure of the competition process would be clear at a national level and that it would have been explained to Birmingham's staff. Flowing from that assumption, I had presumed that law, particularly TUPE, would be important to staff and uppermost in the minds of the commissioning authority, the National Offender Management Service (NOMS: an Executive Agency of the Ministry of Justice). This proved not to be the case. I therefore needed to ensure my research methods captured the 'richness' and 'depth' of Birmingham's story and its evolution over time, beyond law and my (misjudged) assumptions.

I set about achieving my two methodological objectives, of cultivating trust and understanding and building a rich, deep research narrative, through conducting extensive, wide-ranging dialogue with staff. At first I perceived this to be merely 'informal', casual dialogue and a necessary, but somewhat distracting, precursor to the 'real' research that was to follow. However, as my time in the field increased, and I accepted the Governor's offer of keys, which gave me unrestricted, independent access to all parts of the prison, dialogue, observation and participation in all staffed areas of the prison became core research methods. Over time, and assisted by methodologically ambitious criminologist colleagues, I reformulated my research questions and methods ethnographically: the project evolved from a multicentred qualitative analysis of the operation of the public procurement rules and TUPE to a single case study exploring the staff experience and employment impacts of public service competition over 11 months of fieldwork. I became an 'accidental' novice ethnographer.

In looking for methodological guidance and, later, in reflecting upon the methodological journey I had taken at HMP Birmingham I was struck by the paucity of ethnographic legal research. This undoubtedly reflects the broader lack of empirical legal research in the UK as has been described in other chapters in this collection.[20]

[20] See particularly, H Genn, M Partington and S Wheeler, 'Law in the Real World: Improving Our Understanding of How Law Works' the Nuffield Inquiry on Empirical Legal Research, November 2006: www.ucl.ac.uk/laws/socio-legal/empirical/docs/inquiry_report.pdf.

However, even within the small group of legal scholars engaging in empirical work, ethnographies are rare. I would like to highlight three strengths of the ethnographic method that might be of particular advantage to labour law scholars. The first is theoretical, the second concerns the ethnographer's data collection standpoint and the method's potential strengths for building relationships with vulnerable research participants, and the third concerns output and impact. My argument is not that ethnography ought to be seen as the best method in all circumstances, but rather that ethnography ought to be seen as a valuable, long standing tool in a methodological tool box that labour lawyers might benefit from exploiting, particularly to explore vulnerability and 'precariousness' in work relationships. As Everett Hughes, one of the founding proponents of ethnography said, 'I am suspicious of any method said to be the one and only. But among the methods I should recommend is the intensive, penetrating look with an imagination as lively and as sociological as it can be made'.[21]

1. The Theoretical Attraction of Ethnographic Approaches to Labour Law Questions

As Ferrell has argued 'methodological choices inevitably intertwine with theoretical stances [and] political choices'.[22] Though these relationships are 'complex and subtle'[23] methodology can thus be seen as having both practical and theoretical or political dimensions: a researcher's choice of method shapes how the research is carried out (the types of data of interest, how data are collected and analysed, etc) but it also implies a certain understanding, a theory or politics, about the subject of study (here, labour law) and its normative underpinnings, and about being and the construction and functioning of the social world.

A common starting point for many empirical (perhaps particularly qualitative) studies of law is a belief in the possibility of, and relevance of interest in, a gap between law as it is conceived 'in books' and law 'in action'.[24] As Barmes has explored in her contribution to this collection, this is a jurisprudential challenge since it eschews the traditional, formalistic understanding of law as the sum of legislation and court developed jurisprudence. The 'centre of gravity' in empirical studies of law moves away from making sense of formal texts by reference to an internal 'science' of norms and principles toward gathering 'external' perspectives to understand how individuals and communities think about, accommodate, translate and are affected by law as a social institution in practice. Law is thereby repoliticised and implicitly contested at a very 'deep' level: the effectiveness, impact

[21] E Hughes, *The Sociological Eye: Selected Papers* (New Brunswick, Transaction Books, 1984).

[22] J Ferrell, 'Criminological Verstehen: Inside the Immediacy of Crime' in J Ferrell and M Hamm (eds), *Ethnography at the Edge: Crime, Deviance and Field Research* (Boston, Northeastern University Press, 1998) 25.

[23] A Liebling, 'Description at the Edge? I–It and I–Thou Relations and Action in Research' (presentation at the European Society of Criminology 14th Annual Conference, 12 September 2014), and forthcoming in a special issue of the *International Journal for Crime, Justice and Social Democracy*.

[24] This expression is most closely associated with R Pound, 'Law in Books and Law in Action' (1910) 44 *American Law Review* 15.

and importance of law are not assumed. Law is valued not for its internal consistency or own sake but because it produces the 'right' effects in practice. Of course this is not to say that many doctrinal legal scholars are not concerned with the law's effectiveness: my point is that the emphasis in doctrinal analysis is more inward-looking than empirical analysis' outward-looking, external perspective. Difficult questions are raised about how the formal legal system should take account of law in action.[25] A reflexive law approach provides one potential response to this: even if a legal system must remain 'operationally closed' to maintain its systematic integrity (by, eg maintaining judicial independence and the foreseeability of legal rights and obligations), the law can (and should) remain 'cognitively open' to insights arising from any divergence between formal rules and their practical application.[26]

In asserting that there is a possible and interesting 'gap' between law as it is conceived 'in books' and law 'in action', empirical methods also imply a particular understanding of being and the nature of reality—they imply a certain social ontology. Since my focus is upon ethnography my analysis is best limited here to qualitative (rather than quantitative) empirical methods in respect of which I would argue that an interpretivist ontology prevails. By this I mean a belief that reality is relative and multiple: individuals do not understand or respond to the same stimulus (law) in the same way; they disobey, prioritise or comply and do so for varying instrumental and normative reasons which will themselves condition individual future responses. There is thus no universal, straightforward or objective 'truth'. Reality is rather understood as highly complex, contextual and mobile.

Such an understanding of the nature of being can be seen as challenging the ontological assumptions embedded within the neo-liberal socio-political and neo-classical economic status quo that has come to dominate modern life. Tony Lawson has been among those at the forefront of describing and critiquing the ontology of heterodox economics. He has argued that the ontological presuppositions of mathematical modelling, upon which heterodox economics are based, are of a closed system comprised of isolated atoms in which event regularities occur ('whenever this, then that'). These presuppositions, he has argued, mischaracterise the nature of social reality. Consequently, heterodox economists are choosing the wrong 'tool' (social science method) for the social material with which they are dealing. Lawson puts forward an alternative social ontology of open systems of collective practices, social rules structured by matched rights and obligations, process, meaning, value, the emergence of new totalities from what existed before, and ontological and causal irreducibility.[27]

25 For analysis of how judges should take account of socio-legal scholarship, see B Hale, 'Should Judges be Socio-Legal Scholars?' (Socio-Legal Studies Association 2013 conference presentation, 26 March 2013).

26 S Deakin and R Rogowski, *Reflexive Labour Law, Capabilities and the Future of Social Europe* (Legal Studies Research Paper No 2011-04, Warwick Law School, 2011). The concept of reflexive regulation is most strongly associated with the sociological theory of autopoiesis posited particularly by Teubner and Luhmann. See R Rogowski and T Wilthagen (eds), *Reflexive Labour Law* (Deventer, Kluwer, 1994).

27 See especially, T Lawson, *Economics and Reality* (Oxford, Routledge, 1997) and *Reorienting Economics* (Oxford, Routledge, 2003).

Lawson's alternative social ontology resonates strongly with the interpretivisit ontology outlined above that seems implicit in qualitative empirical methods: rules are seen as distinct from, but important constitutors of, practices; entities are constituted and evolve in relation to one another rather than in silos. Furthermore, amongst the broad range of potential qualitative methods, it seems that ethnography can be seen as one of the methods that most strongly resonate with Lawson's alternative ontology and most strongly challenge the neo-liberal ontological narrative. This flows from the centrality of understanding culture within the discipline, which in many senses can be seen as a task that starts from an inherently collectivising and relational perspective. This is because understanding culture requires engagement with group norms and identities, both of which are understood and observed relationally, by reference to an individual's interactions with others. Thus, although an ethnographer might describe divisions, distinctions or dysfunctions within collectives and their relationships, it seems that most ethnographers start from a non-atomistic, relational position. Viewed in this way there seems to be quite a lot of common ground between this and the starting points of many labour lawyers, namely that the contract of employment is distinct from other contracts, not least in its strongly relational quality, and that workers are collectivised through their common position of subordination to capital.

There is a palpable dissonance between this ethnographic ontological position and the social ontology of 'hyper-individualism' that is presupposed by neo-liberalism. As Mary Wrenn has described

> neoliberalism teaches … that each individual should be accountable to herself, and in so doing, each individual's responsibility to others and to the collective is eroded. Society is then comprised entirely and solely of self-interested, atomistic individuals seeking to forward their own agendas'.

This encourages an 'increasingly fragmented notion of the self, one that is disconnected from any community, consisting of less of a coherent whole and more of an amalgamation of superficial commodified identities'.[28] My argument then is that in choosing qualitative methods, and particularly in choosing ethnographic methods, to explore labour law questions we are choosing a method that is rooted in a collective and relational ontology that seems to be well matched to some of the discipline's foundational presuppositions and orientations.

2. Working Ethnographically in the Field: Seeing Beyond Law and Adopting a Humanistic, Egalitarian and Non-Judgmental Research Philosophy

The second strength of ethnography that I would like to highlight pertains to how ethnographers work in the field. I have already suggested, by reference to my own

[28] M Wrenn, 'The Social Ontology of Fear and Neoliberalism' (2014) 72 *Review of Social Economy* 337, 347.

experience at HMP Birmingham, that lawyers may share a tendency to assume the importance or significance of law and, notwithstanding intentions to the contrary, may struggle to 'push beyond' thinking in narrowly legal terms. This is likely to manifest itself through how fieldwork is undertaken and how research questions are approached, structured and asked. As Ludema, Cooperrider and Barrett have argued, the questions we ask are 'fateful': our language of enquiry has important outcomes embedded in it and, through the choices we make in approaching, structuring and asking our research questions, we can 'significantly influence the destiny of … our social theory'.[29]

Since ethnography is an explicitly more fluid, relational and immersive research method, it offers a (longer) timeframe and (broader) perspective that affords researchers the opportunity to 'push beyond', or 'be liberated from',[30] conventional disciplinary ways of enquiring and thinking, to enable unexpected connections, relationships and impacts to be captured. In my Birmingham study I entered the field focused upon the understanding and operation of the TUPE Regulations, having assumed that the procurement itself would be managed relatively straightforwardly. In fact, TUPE was almost invisible until after the decision had been taken to award the contract to G4S. The significance of NOMS' management of the procurement process (more than the procurement rules per se), and its impacts upon the staff and prison, only arose empirically from time spent in the field looking (somewhat) beyond law and seeing the world through staff eyes. Likewise, when I observed prison staff voicing concern during the prison's transition to G4S about whether their right to carry batons was a term and condition of their employment, a non-ethnographic, narrower legal methodological focus might have led me to concentrate upon a contractual analysis and to miss the symbolic relationship between batons and public sector employment status and the 'classification struggle' around deprofessionalisation that lay behind the dispute. The highly inductive, long term and research participant driven nature of ethnographic methods helped to bring to the fore the field and its range of (non-legal) institutions, relationships, concerns and interactions.

Alongside helping to see 'beyond' law, and thereby fully mobilise a socio-legal perspective, ethnographic methods, and the modes of operating in the field that they require, seem to me to imply a particularly egalitarian (rather than hierarchical) and humanistic (rather than scientific) research philosophy. Working ethnographically focuses researchers upon 'building with others a common world of speech and meaning'. Ethnographic methods can help to build what Alison Liebling has described as 'I–thou' rather than 'I–it' relationships with research

[29] J Ludema, D Cooperrider and F Barrett, 'Appreciative Inquiry: the Power of the Unconditional Positive Question', P Reason and H Bradbury (eds), *Handbook of Action Research* (Thousand Oaks, Sage, 2001) 189. See also, J Ludema, 'From Deficit Discourse to Vocabularies of Hope: The Power of Appreciation' in D Cooperrider et al (eds), *Appreciative Inquiry: Rethinking Human Organization Toward a Positive Theory or Change* (Champaign, IL, Stipes Publishing, 2000) eds.

[30] This expression is drawn from J Flood, 'Socio-Legal Ethnography' in R Banakar and M Travers (eds), *Theory and Method in Socio-Legal Research* (Oxford, Hart, 2005) 33, 35.

participants: direct, equal, non-judgmental and giving relationships with the whole person rather than with only one aspect of them or with an identity that has been ascribed to them. 'I–thou' relationships are yielding rather than controlling and they grow sympathetic understanding ('*verstehen*').[31]

Such a research philosophy seems to be particularly important and helpful for accessing and learning from some of the most vulnerable, inaccessible, reticent or maligned research participants, which for labour lawyers particularly seems to include workers in precarious, atypical 'closed' or 'hidden' employment situations, such as migrant or illegal workers. At HMP Birmingham, staff were both somewhat 'hidden', in that they worked in a closed institution to which few people have access, and 'maligned', in that they had a longstanding collective reputation for cynicism, brutality in their treatment of prisoners and a hostility to change.

The prolonged informal immersion and relationship building inherent in ethnographic methods helps to build trust between researchers and such groups. Trust helps to diminish barriers and gaps between 'insiders' and 'outsiders'. As one senior officer at HMP Birmingham said: 'You can tell Amy how it is. You can trust her, she's sound, she's part of the furniture'. During my time at HMP Birmingham my outsider status became increasingly invisible. Male prison officers apologised less frequently for their bad language when I was in the room. Interactions became less structured, less predictable and less 'safe'. Conversations became more emotional, the 'party line' faded and the use protective mechanisms to 'cover' up anxiety and upset, such as of 'black' humour, diminished. Building trust and credibility in this way fosters openness and thereby improves understanding and research quality, though it also risks a researcher losing independence and 'going native' (on which see further section C, below). The ethnographic experience is thus both rich and deep; it enables us to get as close as we can to 'climbing into someone's skin and walking around in it'.

3. Output and Impact: The Power of Narrative for 'Transformative Engagement' with Ideology and Evidence

Ethnography produces narrative, 'authentic description'[32] of the social world under study as experienced and then reproduced in text by the researcher. Narrative has some immediate attractions, particularly in an academic world in which (a too narrow conception of)[33] 'impact'—producing research that is accessible to non-academic communities and 'makes a difference'—is prized: it is usually easy to relate to, and engage with, a text that is rich in vivid 'everyday' stories, examples,

[31] Liebling, n 23.

[32] A Liebling 'Being a Criminologist: Investigation as a Lifestyle and Living' in M Bosworth and C Hoyle (eds), *What is Criminology?* (Oxford, Oxford University Press, 2010) 518.

[33] Although others have also argued this, Liebling also makes this argument in n 32 in which she argues that 'Instead of compiling narrowly defined examples of "impact" for our research guardians, we should be asking, how might our research "enrich democracy"?'

experiences and quotes.[34] There is a directness about narrative that transcends the complexities of 'scientific' texts and captures our imaginations. As John Allen Paulos argued: 'In listening to stories we tend to suspend disbelief in order to be entertained, whereas in evaluating statistics we generally have the opposite inclination to suspend belief in order not to be beguiled'.[35]

But this is not to understate the intellectual worth, power and transformative potential of ethnographic research. As Van Maanen has argued, 'Narrative is not an ornamental or decorative feature designed to make ethnography more palatable or audience-friendly, but a cognitive instrument in its own right'.[36] Authentic, engaged and purposeful description can give voice to the disempowered, the estranged and the misunderstood; it renders the invisible visible, and the implicit explicit. To draw upon Alison Liebling's work, description can be 'dangerous'. Through description we articulate the moral implications of our work and thereby place a moral obligation upon practitioners and policymakers to act. We are able to make poor policy choices, or 'facile gestures' less defensible.[37]

Viewed in this way ethnographic methods, and the texts and analyses they produce, can help to reclaim the public democratic function of labour law, by repositioning employment relationships and disputes, too easily side-lined as merely private, isolated and individual, as matters of general public concern. Through ethnographic work we are able to elevate, intensify and (re)politicise 'ordinary' lived working experiences. Furthermore, what 'acts in the world' is not merely formally published research; it is rather dialogues, interactions and the messages and meanings taken from what we do and how we do it. Consequently, if the ethnographic method implies a collective, relational and complex social understanding of being and a humanistic, egalitarian and non-judgmental research philosophy, the decision to work ethnographically and the process of so working of themselves convey these values and politics. Our choice and deployment of method therefore can be seen as a distinct research output and impact, and a potentially deeply political act; all of which underlines the importance of making, articulating and defending our methodological choices carefully, consciously and courageously.

C. Conclusions

In this chapter I have presented some reflections about the strengths and potential of using ethnographic methods to explore labour law questions. I have argued

[34] Hillyard reflects upon the resonance between ethnographic methods and 'contemporary obligations to produce innovative research that "makes a difference"' in S Hillyard, 'What's (Still) Wrong with Ethnography?' in S Hillyard (ed), *New Frontiers in Ethnography*, Studies in Qualitative Methodology, Vol 11 (Bingley, Emerald Group Publishing Ltd, 2010) 1.

[35] Blog post in *New York Times*, 24 October 2010: opinionator.blogs.nytimes.com/2010/10/24/stories-vs-statistics/?_php=true&_type=blogs&_r=2.

[36] J Van Maanen, 'Afterword: Natives "R" Us: Some Notes on the Ethnography of Organisations' in D Gellner and E Hirsch (eds), *Inside Organisations: Anthropologists at Work* (Oxford, Berg, 2001) 256.

[37] Liebling, n 32.

that ethnographic methods have at least three key strengths. First, I have argued that ethnographic methods imply a collective and relational social ontology that challenges the neo-liberal ontological narrative and resonates with the values and presuppositions with which some, perhaps most, labour lawyers come to their discipline. Secondly, I have argued that there are analytical and access benefits of working ethnographically, namely in helping lawyers to see 'beyond' law to capture unexpected connections, relationships and impacts and to access and learn from vulnerable, reticent or marginalised communities whilst also taking proper ethical care of such research participants through an 'I–thou' (rather than 'I–it') research philosophy. Finally, I have argued that ethnographic work produces powerful and engaging narratives that elevate and systematically repoliticise 'ordinary' lived experiences, and, through careful description, place a moral obligation upon practitioners and policymakers to act.

However, all of this is not to suggest that ethnographic work is unproblematic, easy or alone sufficient to understand fully the complexities of social relationships and problems. Ethnographic work is very time consuming and (therefore) costly. Research time is a luxury that many who work in academic institutions struggle to find among other teaching and administrative responsibilities. Doctrinal research is in some senses an easier and quicker research 'win' in that it can be done mostly from an office or library within an academic institution and therefore can work more easily alongside other commitments. Research time is also increasingly constrained by some funders and commissioners of research who ask for rapid emerging findings and reports and prefer highly structured approaches to fieldwork which can eschew the 'messiness' of the social world and sit in tension with informal, immersive ethnographic methods. Emerging in mainstream research culture is some resistance to, or underestimation of the importance of, what Isabelle Stengers has called 'slow science' in favour of 'fast, competitive, benchmarked research'.[38]

Once ethnographic research has been resourced, plenty of further challenges await in the field and beyond. As John Flood has argued, ethnography is a 'messy process'. 'There are problems of entry, developing trust and empathy, recording interaction, and making sense of ethnography data'.[39] The researcher must find ways of growing open, trusting, but professional and ethical relationships, sometimes across sub-communities whose members are in conflict or tension. Such conflicts and tensions may require the researcher to develop his or her own multiple identities (or at least be sufficiently cautious to avoid appearing allied to one group over another, sometimes by pretending she knows less than she does) to garner acceptance and openness from all parties. In so doing an ethnographer treads a 'tightrope' between authenticity and inauthenticity and integrity and

[38] I Stengers, 'Another Science is Possible! A Plea for Slow Science' (Inaugural lecture of Chair Willy Calewaert 2011–12 VUB, Brussels, 13 December 2011).

[39] J Flood, 'Socio-Legal Ethnography' in R Banakar and M Travers (eds), *Theory and Method in Socio-Legal Research* (Oxford, Hart, 2005) 33, 40.

deception.[40] As relationships grow over time an ethnographer will be drawn deeper into the social world under study. He or she must find strategies to embrace and reap the rewards of that 'depth' but also manage the emotional and intellectual risks of 'going native': losing an analytical and independent thinking orientation, and becoming so emotionally intertwined with research participants and the research experience that the field is reshaped and it becomes impossible to analytically 'disentangle' yourself from the community under study.[41]

Having returned from the field a long iterative process of 'making sense' of the data begins; piecing together rich and usually voluminous data with instinct, authenticity and care. It can be difficult to disentangle what people did and said from what the researcher perceived them to do and say, which is itself shaped by the duration and intensity of fieldwork at any given point in time. Although ethnography recognises that there is no single, 'objective' truth, there are benefits here to having worked with a team in the field because readings of the data can be challenged and probed, and any individual presuppositions rendered explicit, by reference to the experiences of others. Other non-ethnographic forms of data can also help to explain and strengthen the emerging ethnographic narrative. Once again however, team research and the use of multiple methods can prove costly and can protract the analytical process, causing potential difficulties in a 'fast science' research climate.

In sum then, ethnography is a challenging but also in my view highly enriching research method. By reflecting upon the ontological orientation, values and perspectives of ethnographic methods, and the types of output ethnographies can produce, I have tried to make a case in this chapter for the increased use of ethnographic methods in labour law research. Beyond this narrow context though, I hope to have continued building the case, that runs throughout all of the contributions in this collection, for more empirical work that is methodologically diverse, creative and theoretically and politically reflective.

[40] For thoughtful reflections on these challenges, see B Fincham, 'Back to the "Old School": Bicycle Messengers, Employment and Ethnography' (2006) 6 *Qualitative Research* 187, 193–95.

[41] Though this is not to say that emotion is not a valuable source of ethnographic information in its own right. See further, C Sanders, 'Ethnography as Dangerous, Sad, and Dirty Work' in S Hillyard (ed), *New Frontiers in Ethnography*, Studies in Qualitative Methodology, Vol 11 (Bingley, Emerald Group Publishing Ltd, 2010) 101–24, and Y Jewkes, 'Autoethnography and Emotion as Intellectual Resources: Doing Prison Research Differently' (2012) 18 *Qualitative Inquiry* 63.

8

Collective Labour Law Explored

SONIA MCKAY AND SIAN MOORE*

The chapter demonstrates the value of empirical research in understanding the impact of collective labour law on key actors and in turn how they shape the statutory process and its outcomes. Research on the statutory trade union recognition procedure arising from the Employment Relations Act 1999, shows how an empirical approach, particularly one focussed on the workplace, can lead to a more nuanced understanding of labour law because it goes beyond analysis of legislation, legal doctrine and case law.[1] Such an approach highlights the interplay of structure (the legal and political framework and material conditions underpinning employment relations) and agency (the responses and behaviour of the actors) in a statutory model of collective representation. Concretely, we demonstrate how empirical research captures the fragility of worker support for unions consequent upon the fundamental imbalance of the employer—worker relationship.

A. Context

In June 2000 a new statutory trade union recognition procedure, under the Employment Relations Act 1999 (ERA99), came into force, giving UK trade unions that could demonstrate majority support for collective bargaining, a right to be recognised. While providing a process that could lead to statutory recognition, its primary aim was to encourage voluntary recognition though agreements reached between the parties. ERA99 was introduced following a lengthy period of decline in trade union density and an analysis of its subsequent operation over 14 years finds no evidence that it has either reversed such decline or increased

* Professor of European Socio-Legal Studies, Working Lives Research Institute, London Metropolitan University and Professor of Work and Employment Relations, Faculty of Business and Law, University of the West of England, respectively.

[1] S Moore and S McKay, *Statutory Regulation and Employment Relations: The Impact of Statutory Trade Union Recognition* (Basingstoke, Palgrave Macmillan, 2013).

collective bargaining coverage.[2] However, our aim in this paper is not to explore what the defects of the statutory scheme might be. Rather it is to show how empirical methods, analysis of the content of the decisions taken by the Central Arbitration Committee (the CAC or body charged with administering the statutory recognition procedure) alongside case studies of recognition claims at the level of the workplace, provide a context in which the impact of legislation can be better understood. The limitations of the statutory recognition process might have been predicted from analysis of the legislation itself; the complexity of the procedure that it establishes; the thresholds that it lays down for union membership and worker support; and the challenges of defining bargaining units deemed compatible with effective management. However, to understand why the impact of the legislation has been limited we argue that it is necessary to go beyond its content and to explore how key actors, unions, workers and employers, responded to the legislation and its requirements; but crucially to demonstrate how the dynamics of workplace relations represent constraints on the achievement of statutory recognition through the procedure.

B. For a Shift from Outcomes to Processes

The study of labour law has generally focused on the outcomes of case law decisions. Legislation has been explored, not through the lens of its impact on the day-to-day lives of those affected by it, but through the legal rulings engendered. Thus the analysis of case law is primarily doctrinal. Consequently only the small body of cases establishing precedent are the subject of legal study. While there is clearly a need to understand key interpretations, an exclusive focus on doctrinal study, to the exclusion of the overall body of cases, may fail to uncover the actual impact of legislation. There is a need to go beyond a focus on outcomes to look at 'processes'; the circumstances in which the recognition claim emerged, the key actors and their motivations and interests in lodging, pursuing or responding to the claim, as well as its journey through the CAC procedure and factors shaping the outcome.

By 2014 there had been over 800 claims to the CAC yet, a scan of legal text books dealing with the ERA will demonstrate that relatively few cases are referenced because most have not been significant in terms of their doctrinal impact. In a chapter in a 2012 book Lizzie Barmes showed how the content of case law decisions can be explored, not just for the legal doctrine that they contain, but also for the way that they illuminate the realities of workplace experience.[3] This is also our aim and

[2] N Brownlie, *Trade Union Membership 2011* (London, Department for Business, Innovation and Skills, 2012).

[3] L Barmes, 'Learning from Case Law Accounts of Marginalized Working' in J Fudge, S McCrystal and K Sankaran (eds), *Regulating Legal Work: Challenging Legal Boundaries* (Hart Onati Series, 2012). See also ch 3 of this collection.

we would argue that it is only by incorporating such understandings that it is possible to assess the actual impact of not only judicial rulings, but also those arising from the legal process (CAC decisions); this includes capturing their 'demonstration effect'—the way that such rulings shape the subsequent use of the legal process.

To understand the historical context of the legislation we utilise academic and grey literature as well as comparative data. Laws do not arise in a vacuum; their shape and sphere of operation take account of earlier and existing national and international models and their perceived efficacy. Moving beyond an interpretative paradigm permits an examination of the legislative context, including that appertaining to comparable legal systems. A study of legislation and legislative effect should, in addition to providing an interpretation, take account of history, context, actors and their positioning, comparisons and outcomes. It favours an approach that is multi-disciplinary and inter-disciplinary.

C. A Comparative Approach

The ERA99, and subsequent amendments in 2004, drew heavily on North American models of recognition and in particular on the US legislation in contrast to the more union-friendly Canadian legislation. This was despite the recommendations of a study commissioned by the UK Government in 2004 which had found that in the US 'the overwhelming consensus is that it [the law] fails to adequately protect the ability of workers to freely organise unions and engage in collective bargaining'.[4] However, this conclusion was insufficient to prompt the UK Government to consider alternative models. Additionally the UK legislation drew only on some aspects of the North American legislation, omitting those elements seen as more beneficial to trade union attempts to organise. In the US, for example, the legislation imposes a 'duty to bargain', an aspect excluded from the ERA99. Unions that fail to win a vote for recognition in the US are barred from making another application for one year; in the UK the bar on future applications lasts for three years. This suggests UK trade unions need to be even more cautious than their US counterparts in submitting a recognition claim.

D. History and Context

We took as the starting point for our research the need to locate the ERA99 statutory procedure within a history of union recognition, both in the UK and in other comparable legislative systems. The history of previous systems of recognition,

[4] J Goddard, *Trade Union Recognition: Statutory Unfair Labour Practice Regimes in the USA and Canada* (London, DTI Employment Relations Research Series No 29, March 2004).

both voluntary and statutory, is thus located within the concept of voluntarism which shaped the relationship between the social actors and the state prior to and up until the early years of the 1980s, when the Thatcher Government attempted to dismantle trade union organisation. The resulting decline in union density and collective bargaining coverage led the unions to demand a new legislative framework providing a route to recognition where there was employer opposition.

Without understanding why voluntarism held sway in the UK, when it was absent in comparable European models, it would be impossible to grasp why up until the early 1990s trade unions in the UK had not sought a statutory recognition process. The history of judicial intervention into the operation of trade unions was primarily seen as a negative one[5] and thus unions showed a reluctance to place their claims in the hands of the judiciary. Similarly without exploring why the previous two attempts at introducing a statutory framework for legislation failed, it is difficult to understand why the procedure was designed as it was. The history of failure, in particular of the Employment Protection Act 1975 (EPA75) to deliver recognition, informed the approach to ERA99. The legislation reflects caution; the principle of majority support was eroded by excessive legalism within a procedure that requires specific tests at each stage of the process. The legislation was also influenced by a changed political environment; it did not aim to promote collective bargaining, it specifically places restrictions on the scope of bargaining that can be imposed following recognition, whilst placing few constraints on employer advantage in the workplace. In part this also reflected a desire to maintain voluntarism, but in a period when trade unions were weaker, this meant that employer prerogative would trump.

Unions have been cautious in pursuing claims for recognition through the statutory route. Guided by the TUC[6] they were determined that informal criteria should be established to ensure that only those claims that were more likely to succeed than to fail—where there was demonstrable majority support for collective bargaining—would be submitted. Crucially, from the perspective of the CAC, there was similar reluctance to make decisions that were capable of being challenged in the courts, reflecting on the damage done to the authority of ACAS through legal challenges under the EPA75. Thus the fear of judicial review has been the mantra in CAC Annual Reports and the CAC has operated, cautiously and 'even-handedly' in its decisions.[7] From the perspectives of both the CAC and the trade unions, the legislation has been used strategically, but in a context of overall declining union membership and changes in the labour market and employer power (including the privatisation and contracting-out of public services), the result has been that the law has not been able to recover the ground unions had lost in terms of recognition in the previous two decades.

[5] Arguably from *Taff Vale Railway Company v ASRS* [1901] AC 426 onwards.

[6] For more information on this see the chapter by Sarah Veale in S Moore and S McKay, *Statutory Regulation and Employment Relations* (Basingstoke, Palgrave Macmillan, 2013).

[7] Moore and McKay, ibid.

E. CAC Reports—A Unique Source of Data

CAC reports on each decision made in regard to applications for recognition under the procedure and published on their website (www.cac.gov.uk) provide an incredibly rich source of data, shedding light not only on the operation of the legal process, but also on workplace industrial relations in the early twenty-first century. Our analysis is based upon at least 1,500 published decisions covering the various stages of the procedure, as well as data from CAC Annual Reports. These documents not only capture the CAC decision-making process, but also the behaviour of both parties within the procedure and offer a glimpse of the generation of recognition claims. In-depth interviews with CAC officers and panel members further illuminated the decision-making process.

Statistics from the CAC Annual Reports and analysis of CAC decisions focus upon the operation and outcomes of the CAC procedure over more than 10 years. They trace the level of applications, the proportion resulting in statutory or semi-voluntary agreements, level of support for recognition within the bargaining unit and how this is ascertained; rulings on the composition of the bargaining unit and on the ordering of 'automatic' recognition or ballots. They also provide information on CAC decisions over the method of bargaining and the fate of applications under the statutory de-recognition provisions. Analysis of these decisions identify pressure points for unions in the procedure, but also allows for consideration of how far these reflect upon the design of the procedure and/or the way that the CAC has interpreted Schedule A1 and the implications of its relative caution. Scrutiny of CAC decisions between 2000 and 2011/12 showed that consistently just half of the applications accepted resulted in recognition, that over one third of ballots were lost and that in just under a third of ballots the proportion of workers voting in favour of recognition in the ballot was below the membership level, as verified before the ballot.

The desire not to be challenged in the courts has encouraged a consensual approach by CAC panels and this can be seen in their determination of bargaining units, where the obligation that it is compatible with effective management means that it may impose the employer's alternative, generally to the detriment of the union. In such cases the union is obliged, if it wishes to continue with its application, to apply to represent a group of workers different from those for whom it initially gained a mandate. Further, the CAC's discretion to order ballots has undermined the 'automatic' route to recognition anticipated by unions during the design of the procedure; the CAC has ordered ballots where majority support for recognition has been established, placing the union in a position where it has to defend its claim in a potentially conflictual setting.

Analysis of CAC decisions also suggests that the procedure has become more legalistic, with a greater degree of reliance on case precedent; the employer and the union (as well as the CAC) are more reliant on case law citation. This dependency makes it more difficult to support the kind of informal process which might have been envisaged when the legislation was first established. We conclude from this that there is a disjuncture within the procedure between the implied absence of legalism—a relatively informal administration of recognition claims and emphasis on the avoidance of judicial intervention—and the reality of statutory recognition which has become shaped by legal precedent set by judicial review.

In addition to allowing us to explore the CAC's administration of the procedure, the depth of information in CAC reports allowed us to develop typologies of employer and trade union behaviours and strategies. Close examination of CAC decisions exposed the ability of employers to challenge the procedure at every stage. We define these strategies as pre-emption, contestation, and intervention, and have considered how the CAC has responded to such tactics and whether it has constrained employer intervention or whether employers have been able to undermine the operation of the procedure and the law.

CAC reports record how employers attempt to pre-empt recognition claims by establishing alternative channels of representation or employer defined representation, including non-independent unions or favoured independent unions. Once in the procedure they may genuinely test support for recognition, but they may also exploit legal technicalities or stall and delay the process to dissipate union support (the average length of time cases spend in the procedure has lengthened and this, of itself, negatively affects union support for recognition). Employers have attempted to influence CAC discretion by challenging likely support for recognition and there are examples where they have provided evidence which has led to the application being rejected, particularly in cases where the union cannot demonstrate majority membership and provides no other evidence of support. An analysis of trade union approaches exposed inadequacies and pinpointed the need to document high levels of support for recognition in the bargaining unit. CAC reports also show that employers have contested the union's bargaining unit arguing for larger bargaining units covering multiple workplaces, but also including wider occupational groups of workers. Where they have been successful unions have subsequently found it difficult to demonstrate support for recognition in the newly determined bargaining unit and where unions subsequently did not have a majority in membership in the revised bargaining units, ballots were called.

While in the recognition procedure the level of union membership may change due to fluctuations in employment levels, including labour turnover, non-replacement of leavers, redundancies and recruitment into the bargaining unit and any of these may be a result of an active employer strategy to block recognition. Case studies based upon CAC decisions illustrate how employers can appear to manipulate and dilute union support in the bargaining unit by purposively recruiting into the bargaining unit—something that could not have been identified from an examination of outcomes.[8]

[8] See especially, *GMB and JF Stone Investments Limited t/a The American Dry Cleaning Company* TUR1/492/2006.

CAC decisions demonstrate that in many cases where the union had majority membership, employers have not submitted any evidence to invoke any of the criteria which the CAC must take account of in determining whether there should be a ballot, allowing the CAC to grant automatic recognition. However, in others employers have actively sought to persuade the CAC to order a ballot on the basis of one or more of these criteria and, where they have produced evidence to raise doubts that a significant number of union members wanted the union to bargain on their behalf, unions have struggled to win subsequent ballots.[9] A number of CAC reports indicate the fragility of individual support for the union in the face of employer opposition, including where workers have signed both union petitions in support of collective bargaining and employer counter-petitions.[10]

F. Foregrounding Agency—Understanding the Actors and Agency

Whilst the provision and design of a legal framework has a role in restoring rights to representation for collective bargaining, the capacity of unions to mobilise support in the workplace is at least as important and this is defined by wider economic, social and ideological relationships. In particular the fragmentation of employment that has emerged from privatisation and outsourcing has implications for collective organisation. Our study of the impact of the ERA99 was underpinned by an analysis of union strategies, including eliciting the account of one of the key actors, the TUC,[11] whilst two surveys of unions gauged intent in their approach to the statutory procedure on its introduction and 10 years later. The longitudinal perspective allowed evaluation of unions' experience of the procedure, their changing strategies and any demonstration effect. The survey suggested that despite the decline in the use of the procedure and deceleration in the number of voluntary agreements signed in the shadow of the law,[12] securing recognition remained a priority for unions. It also found that the vast majority of respondents (85 per cent) considered that employer behaviour generally aimed to frustrate the legislation.

[9] See, eg *GMB and Varn International* TUR1/355/2004.

[10] See, eg *Unite and Eddie Stobart*, TUR1/750/2011.

[11] See especially, S Moore and S McKay, *Statutory Regulation and Employment Relations* (Basingstoke, Palgrave Macmillan, 2013) ch 3.

[12] The Labour Government's intention was that the statutory procedure should act as a last resort and it thus might be argued that the law had a larger 'shadow effect' particularly in the early years when those employers who were not adamantly opposed to recognition, reached voluntary agreements rather than wait for the formal application through the CAC. The TUC no longer systematically collects data on voluntary recognition agreements, but the union surveys shed some light on the early proliferation of voluntary agreements and drawing on ACAS data we were able to show that ACAS conciliation cases on recognition peaked at 385 in 2002–03, before beginning to fall again.

While unions may have expressed ambivalence towards the procedure, there is limited evidence of absolute reluctance to utilise it, albeit that its use has been confined to a relatively small group of unions. Strategically then, unions may be focussing upon organising for recognition, but they are not generating sufficient claims to sustain the level of statutory, and hence voluntary, recognition. The rationale that the law would encourage voluntary recognition, and that this was its primary purpose, does not stand up so well 10 years after its introduction.

We also conducted seven in-depth case studies of recognition and one of de-recognition at the level of the workplace.[13] Whilst CAC decisions document employer responses to claims once in the procedure, the case studies offered a fuller picture of employer behaviour in the workplace, illuminating the dynamics of recognition and derecognition claims from the perspective of workplace representatives and trade union officers involved in them. The case studies looked at the factors that give rise to unionisation, but also that then predicted success or failure in ballots through the procedure, and the interaction of employer and union strategies prior to and during the ballot period. Recognition ballots provide a crucible in which the behaviour of unions, union activists and employers can be studied, particularly since consistently throughout the period of its operation unions have lost a third of ballots held under the statutory procedure.

The following summaries of two of the case studies convey the importance of empirical research in illustrating the impact of the law at the level of the workplace, but also in highlighting the importance of agency and the role of key activists where employers both contested recognition in the procedure, but also intervened in the workplace to undermine support. Both have been anonymised to provide protection to the activists who provided data.

1. Case Study 1: Groomco

At Groomco the application for recognition for around 140 production workers covered one factory in a US multinational producing toiletries—it had never recognised unions in any of its plants worldwide. Unionisation was a result of changes to shift patterns and working hours and it was the impact upon work–life balance that caused anger.

The company had established a consultative committee with employee representation, but the imposition of changes in shift patterns exposed to employee representatives that this body gave them no real representation and they withdrew from it. The core group of employee representatives then became central to the

[13] See especially, S Moore and S McKay, *Statutory Regulation and Employment Relations* (Basingstoke, Palgrave Macmillan, 2013). The seven case studies represented union campaigns for recognition in which ballots were held under the statutory procedure.

campaign for union recognition. Since a small number of workers in the factory were in a union, the key activist, Ken, contacted the regional officer and undertook to increase membership to above the 50 per cent level needed to secure recognition. He and another activist met with the full-time union officer off-site to plan the campaign and talked to people face-to-face on both the day and night shifts. Ken played a key role in keeping the workforce updated on the campaign via email and a blog. Although the company had brought in US personnel to advise on opposing recognition, he perceived that this had backfired:

> That did the company no good, I think somebody coming across from such a high level trying to persuade people not to join the union, they were thinking hang on, there's something not right here, we'd better join the union.

In the context of such hostility Ken understood the importance of being identified with the union and in taking risks in challenging the employer:

> Somebody had to do it, I was there, I decided to do it and if you're going to achieve recognition you have to have somebody that's going to stand with their head above the parapet ... There was one meeting which again was reported back to me, in the early days before we got recognition, that the manager had said that the company knows who the troublemakers are and if we can get rid of them then there won't be any problems and my name was mentioned inevitably. I think it's a difficult situation because there's not many people that want to be seen to be associated with the union in that sort of situation ... I took the view that I was going to do it. If they chose to sack me as a result of doing that then I considered I would have enough ammunition and enough arguments to claim unfair dismissal and I was prepared to do that. So you don't do it ignoring that really. I'm fairly sort of motivated and quite prepared to stand up and make arguments against or for a particular cause that I believe in.

He reported that both prior to the application, and once in the procedure, the employer engaged the union in discussions that were unproductive and which activists felt were designed to delay the process. Although the CAC confirmed that the union had just over 50 per cent of the bargaining unit in membership it concluded that letters by six members of the bargaining unit stating that they did not want the union to be recognised constituted a qualifying condition for the holding of a ballot 'in the interest of good industrial relations'. The union argued that the letters had been written as a result of a sustained campaign by the employer at its instigation and without the opportunity for the union to put its case to the membership.

Ken had undertaken his own research on previous recognition campaigns and reported that the company utilised classic union avoidance tactics. Thus, even for Ken, knowledge of history, context and tactics was important in inoculating him against employer mobilisation. The union informed the CAC that the employer had instituted small group meetings at which briefings against union recognition took place, with at least one manager stating that recognition would lead to the factory closing—something subsequently denied by the company. Previous research suggests that the credibility of such threats in the eyes of the workforce is important;[14] when asked whether he thought that the workers believed that the plant would close if the union gained recognition Ken responded:

> Some, yes I mean—they really did, because they have this perception that American companies would do everything to avoid union recognition and will cut them off if they have union recognition because they see it as restrictive. So yes, they did believe that, quite a lot of them believed that.

Despite employer opposition 56 per cent of the bargaining unit voted in favour of recognition (from a membership level of 49 per cent). The case study demonstrates the adversarial nature of recognition, but how a strong union organising campaign with key activists led to a successful ballot.

2. Case Study 2: Foodco

Foodco provides a case study of where the union, despite demonstrating majority support for recognition on application, was defeated and where the issue of 'unfair practices' was raised. Unfair practices were introduced by the Employment Relations Act 2004 in response to union concerns about employer behaviour. However, they only apply from the beginning of the ballot period and any 'unfair practice' which occurs before this point in time is not challengeable—employers can legitimately campaign against recognition in a period when the union may have only limited or no access to the workforce and can carry out 'unfair practices' without a legal challenge. Foodco is a UK-owned food processing plant and the recognition claim, covering 290 hourly paid workers, was a result of an organising campaign around poor pay and conditions, bullying and victimisation. The workforce was employed through agencies, and three quarters were migrant workers.

The union had some individual success in grievance and disciplinary processes and this had a knock on effect for membership and it quickly built a core of eight or nine activists ensuring representation across the Polish, Kurdish and English speaking groups. It threw its entire local organising team into winning recognition and in the final months the whole of the regional organising team was involved, utilising a comprehensive organising model engaging with communities, national pressure groups and the media. All leaflets and mail-shots were in several languages and the union had Kurdish, Polish, Russian and Lithuanian organisers involved, holding events to bring the different migrant communities together.

The employer was implacably opposed to recognising the union and the day after the CAC accepted the application the company declared a 'no strike' recognition deal with another union, further frustrating the process until mediation by

[14] S Moore, 'Union Mobilization and Employer Counter-Mobilization in the Statutory Recognition Process' in J Kelly and P Willman (eds), *Union Organisation and Activity* (London, Routledge, 2004).

the TUC led to the other union withdrawing. At Foodco delay was seen as a key employer tactic, as the full-time officer explained:

> Stall it all the way through to give them more time to turn people against the union, because obviously we would have liked to have had a quick ballot, a quick response to it all, but it got dragged out and dragged out—anything they could challenge, they challenged.

Activists realised in the middle of the campaign that the company had engaged US anti-union consultants, the Burke Group (TBG), to advise on union avoidance. This was discovered when a member working on the factory gate alerted one of the local activists that two Americans had been signed into the site under the company name 'TBG', as the full-time officer reported:

> [The activist] phoned me straight away and said 'TBG' and of course, I knew about The Burke Group, I knew the company used them on Flybe. The alarm bells started ringing, so we kept our powder dry for a little while, a bit more investigating and yes The Burke Group were on site. It was two American guys ... but yes, they were on site and they were looking at employee surveys—that type of stuff. All through the campaign they weren't seen much on the shop floor at all, the pressure that these guys were putting on was more on the supervisors, management, 'this is what you go out and do' and indoctrinating the supervisors to go out and do their bidding really.

The strategy deployed by TBG at Foodco included 15 recognisable anti-union tactics and chimed with TBG's explanation of their 'behind the scene' methods.[15] The employer asserted that the union was making false promises on improvements to terms and conditions and predicted that union subscriptions would increase once workers had joined. It also claimed that the union was acting against the company because it had contacted an outside regulatory agency and this was used to label the union as an illegitimate 'third party'. An anti-union petition emerged, allegedly initiated by the workers themselves, but which the union was convinced had been produced by the consultants, with pressure put on workers to sign it. At the same time threats were made that the workplace was going to shut down and that migrant workers would be sent home. Foodco attempted to sack a key union activist, but this threat was withdrawn after the union placed external pressure upon the employer through the outside regulatory agency. Three key activists were disciplined on gross misconduct charges during the campaign, while one activist was prevented from returning from sick leave by the company claiming it needed to carry out a full 'risk assessment'—this left him at home on full pay until the end of the ballot period. Whilst ironically, consultants often claim that trade unions will invade the privacy of workers by obtaining information about their members, at Foodco management attempted to drive a wedge between a couple who both worked at the plant and were considered 'leaders' by stating to one: 'We're worried about your relationship with your wife, we'd ask you to not be involved in this

[15] See www.tbglabor.com.

campaign because it's going to put a strain on your relationship'. The full-time officer related how this was a pivotal moment for him:

> I think that's where it hit home to me that this wasn't just about work, people's private and personal lives were being dragged into it. And it became very personal then, I thought how dare these people put that type of pressure on a couple who have been married for 30 odd years. And all they wanted was the best for their fellow workers and this company were trying to drive a wedge between their relationship and it was just horrible.

Crucially the company recruited a group of Hungarian agency workers into the bargaining unit just before the ballot. The union claimed that they had been given contracts on the condition that they voted against the union in the ballot. This had added 60 new workers to the bargaining unit, none of whom had contact with union representatives and none of whom spoke English, but this was just days before the ballot and there was insufficient time for the union to respond:

> The 60 Hungarian workers they brought in before the ballot took place were told categorically 'if you vote for the union, then we're going to send you back to Hungary and you're going to lose your jobs'. The union response was to bring two Hungarian stewards from another campaign to the plant, but a crucial delay meant they did not have enough time to get through to the new staff. I think if we'd have used them for longer we may well have got into the Hungarian community more.

During the ballot period the access agreement allowed the union four mass meetings and individual surgeries. This was on the basis that the employer had equivalence, but the company made its meetings compulsory and the union reported that pressure was placed on workers not to attend union meetings. Only around six of nearly 300 workers attended the union's individual surgeries, the union reported that managers were 'loitering around' which discouraged workers from attending and even at the mass meetings they would stand at the staircase visibly observing who went in and out of the meeting—'there was clear intimidation'. The union reported that there were CCTV cameras inside the meeting rooms and although the union secured an agreement that any recording equipment would be turned off during their meetings, one of the security guards informed the union that cameras had been left on (although there was no sound it was capturing those in attendance). During the access period union officers were accompanied on and off the premises and in and out of meetings, with the employer ensuring that the meeting was closed after the half hour slot was up: 'We were escorted back to the room then, which didn't look very good for workers—saying the union had been escorted backwards and forwards, and virtually like we were prisoners'.

At the peak of the campaign, the Foodco canteen had an overhead projector on a loop that exhorted staff to 'Vote No!' in several different languages. The CAC access agreement stipulated that both unions and workers could send material to workers' addresses, but the union reported that the company generated another petition claiming to be from workers who did not wish to be contacted by the union. In this instance the CAC intervened and dismissed the attempt to derail the union's mail-shots to workers. The union made a further complaint to the CAC when a 'Vote No!' poster included the CAC logo, giving the impression it was official advice from the body assigned to oversee the ballot. The CAC objected to the company, but it was a week before it was taken down.

The union made a formal complaint that the employer had adopted unfair practices, alleging that the employer misled employees by suggesting that recognition would result in them having to go on strike, although the employer countered this by claiming that the accusations were imprecise and incorrect. The employer also pointed to behaviour by the union—not complying with notification procedures, over-running meetings and straying beyond designated areas. The union's complaint was dismissed by the CAC on the basis of lack of evidence and its inability to establish the effect of the employer's practices on the outcome of the ballot.

The union narrowly lost the ballot and the full-time officer commented that 'in the end they simply could not have known the extent to which the employer was prepared to go' and attributed defeat to the extent of resources the employer had invested in external consultants. He felt that the union could not have done much more in terms of its organisation and the campaign certainly deployed the vast majority of Bronfenbrenner and Juravich's comprehensive organising approach.[16] The union attempted to inoculate union representatives at training weekends and to prepare them to 'expect the unexpected'. Its strategy included an organising committee, house calls, one-to-one sessions, text messaging, whilst the campaign was also extended beyond the workplace mobilising external support and pressure.

The case study illustrates the contending factors that come into play during the statutory recognition process—the extent of resources employers are prepared to invest in defeating the union as well as union organisation and activity. The full-time officer was discouraged by the apparent lack of constraints on employer behaviour:

> I would be less likely to use the CAC now than I was before, because the practices the company were using, I thought would have constituted an unfair practice. And you know as I say, you've got to virtually shoot someone to trigger that, but I was disappointed really on that side.

This case study also allows reflection on what might constitute legitimate contestation over employee representation in the workplace. Of the seven formal complaints to the CAC of unfair practices between 2004 and 2011/12, none were upheld. Neither unions nor employers have made significant recourse to the unfair practices provision, despite evidence that employers continue to undermine the procedure.

[16] K Bronfenbrenner and T Juravich, 'It Takes More than House Calls: Organising to Win with a Comprehensive Union-Building Strategy' in K Bronfenbrenner, S Friedman, RW Hurd, R Oswald and R Seeber (eds), *Organising to Win: New Research on Union Strategies* (Ithaca, NY, ILR Press, 1998).

G. Conclusion

A multi-disciplinary approach drawing upon industrial relations, law and sociology provides a framework that moves beyond case law and individual legal decisions to locate the law in the employment relationship and the wider economic and political factors which define it. Such an approach shows that the efficacy of the statutory union procedure cannot be determined by an interpretive paradigm based only on a study of case law. One objective of the procedure was to encourage voluntary recognition in its shadow and this necessitates data on voluntary agreements. Surveys capturing the intent and perceptions of key actors, in this case unions, have shown that the statutory procedure itself shaped union strategies and promoted organising campaigns to secure recognition on the basis of majority membership. The *capacity* of unions to mobilise support in the workplace is at least as important as the provision and design of a statutory recognition procedure, but is influenced by wider economic, social and ideological relationships. This foregrounds the interplay of structure and agency in collective representation and organisation, a dynamic that is illuminated by workplace case studies, which provide a voice to the union activists who are central to recognition campaigns. They allow for reflection on the factors that constrain collective organisation; the potential for employers to frustrate the purpose of the legislation within and outside the procedure, the extent to which employers are prepared to invest resources into resisting union support in the workplace and the efficacy of union organising strategies, particularly the presence and confidence of activists. Such analysis clarifies the extent to which the limited impact of the procedure is a result of its design, or of wider union mobilisation and employer counter-mobilisation. The capacity for mobilisation, however, is a function of the structural forces that have reconfigured employment relationships since previous attempts to provide a statutory recognition process in the 1970s—the law does not operate in a vacuum.

9

No Longer a 'Secondary Force … in Labour Relations': A Mixed Methods Study of the Effect on Irish Trade Unions of the Industrial Relations (Amendment) Act 2001

TISH GIBBONS*

In the Republic of Ireland, unlike the UK, there is no statutory union recognition procedure for use in situations where employers refuse to negotiate with the trade union representing its workers. There is however, since 2001, a statutory means by which to resolve disputes between parties about issues such as rates of pay and general conditions of employment. The Industrial Relations (Amendment) Act of 2001 (the 2001 Act) provides that unions may refer the issues in dispute to the Labour Court,[1] which will issue a Recommendation that ultimately may be enforced by Circuit Court order. The literature focuses on the efficacy of the procedure; on whether the union or the employer 'won' the Labour Court Recommendation; its minutiae in terms of the exact award and the implications of various legal challenges. In this chapter I report on part of a recent research project which went beyond such examination of the paper outcome of the procedure and took an empirical approach.[2]

The chapter opens by exploring the background to the 2001 Act, the constitutional provision of the right to freedom of association and how it operates in practice. There follows a brief description of Irish industrial relations from its roots in UK traditions to a neo-liberal turn in the 1980s resulting in ever more contentious disputes about union recognition. The terms and usage of the 2001 Act are outlined and an explanation provided for its lack of use since 2007. My alternative

* Working Lives Research Institute, London Metropolitan University.

[1] Ireland's industrial tribunal

[2] T Gibbons, 'The Industrial Relations (Amendment) Act of 2001: Its Effects and the Implications for Workers and Trade Unions in Ireland' (unpublished D Prof thesis, Working Lives Research Institute, London Metropolitan University, 2014).

methodological approach adopted is outlined before presentation of the resultant data collected during 2012 and 2013. The data uncovers a dearth of collective bargaining; of trade union activity and of substantive benefits to the workers involved in claims under the 2001 Act. In concluding I argue that exploring events in workplaces in the years after the issuing of Labour Court Recommendations leads to less benign conclusions than those reached from a paper examination of the Recommendations alone.

A. Background

Ireland's 'unique constitutional environment'[3] underpins the development of the story of trade union recognition in Ireland albeit that the Constitution dates only from 1937 and there was de facto, though voluntary, trade union recognition in Ireland prior to independence. Article 40.6.iii of Bunreacht na hÉireann[4] provides, inter alia, that 'The State guarantees liberty for the exercise of … the right of the citizens to form associations and unions'. Nonetheless 'the Constitution does not confirm on trade unionists any right to have their union recognised'.[5] Notwithstanding the right to form an association, there is 'no corresponding obligation … to recognise that association for the purpose of negotiating the terms and conditions of employment of its members'.[6] The Constitution itself makes no mention of any right of disassociation, yet in the courts 'it has been readily implied'.[7] A further corollary advanced is that the right not to associate extends to employers who have the right not to associate with a trade union formed or joined by its employees.

While Article 40.6.iii also provides that 'laws may be enacted for the regulation and control' of such right to association, a 'hands-off' approach in terms of statutory regulation was nonetheless a fundamental feature of the 'voluntarist' nature of industrial relations in Ireland. Much like the UK, and until the latter decades of the twentieth century, the State's role was something akin to umpire: only intervening 'to address the pathological situation, i.e. when the employer–employee relationship goes drastically wrong'.[8] In Ireland, trade union fortunes declined towards the end of the twentieth century with density reducing from a high of over 60 per cent in the 1980s to little over 40 per cent by the millennium

[3] N Howlin and RC Fitzpatrick, 'The Feasibility of Mandatory Trade Union Recognition in Ireland' (2007) 29 *Dublin University Law Journal* 178.

[4] Bunreacht na hEireann—Constitution of Ireland (Dublin, Government Publications Office, 1937).

[5] *Nolan Transport (Oaklands) Ltd v Halligan* [1995] ELRI.

[6] *Dublin Colleges ASA v City of Dublin VEC* 31 July 1981 (HC).

[7] TJ Christian and KD Ewing, 'Labouring under the Canadian Constitution' (1988) 17 *Industrial Law Journal* 73, 75. See also, *Meskell v CIE* [1973] IR 121.

[8] C Fennell and I Lynch, *Labour Law in Ireland* (Dublin, Gill & Macmillan, 1993) 30.

and still reducing, coupled with an increasing dichotomy between union influence at the workplace and 'the rhetoric of partnership and involvement'[9] at national level. Employers were less inclined to deal with unions and there were some bitter strikes regarding trade union recognition. Traditional unionised industries closed while new or replacement industries, often US owned multi-nationals, became even more hostile to trade unions—a trend that spread to indigenous employers.

B. The Industrial Relations (Amendment) Act 2001

Years of lobbying by the trade unions contributed to the introduction of a Code of Practice on Voluntary Dispute Resolution introduced in May 2000 under Statutory Instrument No 145 of 2000. It provides that matters in dispute may be referred to the Labour Relations Commission (LRC)[10] who will appoint an officer to 'assess the issues in dispute' (section 2(1)) and to 'work with the parties in an attempt to resolve the issues'. If 'not capable of early resolution … an agreed cooling-off period should be put in place' (section 2(2)). In the event that issues remained unresolved 'the LRC shall make a written report to the Labour Court' who after consideration 'shall issue recommendations on outstanding matters' (section 2(5)). In order to investigate a dispute the Labour Court must first be satisfied that (per section 2(1)):

(a) [I]t is not the practice of the employer to engage in collective bargaining negotiations and the internal dispute resolution procedures (if any) normally used by the parties concerned have failed to resolve the dispute
(b) the employer has failed to observe a provision of the Code of Practice on Voluntary Dispute Resolution [SI 145/2000]
(c) the trade union … [has] not acted in a manner which … has frustrated the employer in observing a provision of such code of practice
(d) the trade union … [has] not had recourse to industrial action after the dispute in question was referred to the Commission.

Recommendations shall 'have regard to terms and conditions of employment, and to dispute resolution and disciplinary procedures in the employment concerned' (section 5(1)) and 'shall not provide for arrangements for collective bargaining' (section 5(2)). Where the dispute remains unresolved 'the Court may, at the request of a trade union … make a determination' (section 6(1)) and if not implemented 'on the application of a trade union … the Circuit Court shall, without hearing the employer or any evidence … make an order directing the employer to carry out the determination' (section 10). Unlike recognition legislation in the

[9] J Kelly, 'Foreword' in D D'Art and T Turner (eds), *Irish Employment Relations in the New Economy* (Dublin, Blackhall, 2002).

[10] Conciliation and advisory service.

UK, there is not a membership threshold or any compulsion to demonstrate who is involved in the claim.

1. Use and Disuse

Trade unions initially made little use of the procedures provided. Within a year trade unions concluded that the 'voluntary leg' had 'completely failed to achieve its aim of voluntarily resolving disputes about union recognition' and called for the procedures to be 'streamlined to ensure expeditious processing of referrals'[11] and to guard against 'pretence co-operation' by employers.[12] They successfully lobbied for an amendment and the Industrial Relations (Miscellaneous Provisions) Act 2004 shortens the timescale involved in resolving disputes, which resulted in 'a major growth in the referrals'.[13] Thus the number of Recommendations issued varies each year, from a slow start in 2002 with just two cases, increasing 10-fold by 2004 to 21 cases; 31 in the two subsequent years before reducing drastically, to no Recommendations in 2008 as reflected in Table 1 below.

Table 1: Labour Court Recommendations under the 2001 Act 2002–11

Year	2002	2003	2004	2005	2006	2007	2008	2009	2010	2011
No of LCRs	2	9	21	31	31	9	0	2	2	2

Source: www.labourcourt.ie

The dramatic reduction in the number of cases being processed from 2007 onwards is due to legal proceedings arising from a case taken against Ryanair. Public sector union IMPACT referred a case to the Labour Court under the provisions of the 2001 Act involving the pilots employed by Ryanair, the issues in dispute centring on training; contracts of employment and redundancies. Ryanair argued there was no trade dispute within the meaning of the Act because they *did* engage in collective bargaining and there *did* exist internal dispute resolution procedures that had not failed to resolve the dispute.[14] The Labour Court did not agree and found that it was not Ryanair's practice 'to engage in collective bargaining

[11] Irish Congress of Trade Unions, *Report of Working Group on Trade Union Recognition* (Dublin, Irish Congress of Trade Unions, 2002) 2.

[12] Ibid, 3.

[13] Labour Relations Commission, *Annual Report 2006* (Dublin, Labour Relations Commission, 2006) 8.

[14] Industrial Relations News, 'Ryanair—Union's Claim Gets Green Light from Court' (2005) 6 *Industrial Relations News*, 3 February 2005.

negotiations as the Court understands that expression';[15] that there was a trade dispute; that there were no dispute resolution procedures at the company, and therefore found in favour of the applicants, IMPACT. Ryanair sought and was granted permission by the High Court to challenge the Labour Court findings. The High Court rejected Ryanair's arguments[16] and upheld the Labour Court Recommendation. Ryanair appealed to the Supreme Court, which overturned the High Court decision and quashed the Labour Court Recommendation.[17]

Crucially however, for the 2001/2004 Acts, the Supreme Court was also 'sharply critical of the approach and procedures of the Labour Court'.[18] The Labour Court subsequently identified seven legal issues arising from the judgment that impinged on how future cases would proceed, including disclosing the identity of union members and relying on legal rules of evidence and witness testimony, a major change for a 'court of reasonableness and fair dealing ... enhanced with the spirit of cooperation not compulsion'.[19] The effects were far-reaching with a drastic reduction in the number of cases referred under the 'voluntary leg' and in the numbers being referred and recommended upon by the Labour Court. While many expressed concern at this 'forcing the Labour Court to assume many of the characteristics of a more formalised court setting'[20] unions have in any event voted with their feet and have entirely ceased to use the process they now say was 'annulled' by the Supreme Court decision; 'it is now redundant ... the lesson is clear—diplomacy does not work'.[21]

2. Is the 2001 Act a Help or a Hindrance?

Despite the relatively short time span between the promulgation of the Act in 2001 and the effective abandonment of its procedures in 2007, there exists a compact body of literature on the subject. D'Art and Turner use two case studies to examine the effectiveness of the 2001 Act 'in creating conditions for union recognition'.[22] While acknowledging the small sample size they conclude that the Act is 'inadequate' in 'facilitating members seeking union representation and recognition'.[23]

[15] Labour Court Recommendation No DECP051.

[16] *Ryanair v Labour Court* [2005] IEHC 330, 15 October 2005.

[17] *Ryanair Ltd v Labour Court* [2007] IESC 6, 1 February 2007.

[18] E Gilvarry and B Hunt, 'Trade Union Recognition and the Labour Court: Picking up the Pieces after Ryanair' in T Hastings (ed), *The State of the Unions: Challenges Facing Organised Labour in Ireland* (Dublin, Liffey Press, 2008) 174.

[19] A Kerr, 'National Report Ireland' in *The Evolving Structure of Collective Bargaining in Europe 1990–2004* (research project co-financed by the European Commission and the University of Florence, 2005): eprints.unifi.it/archive/00001163/01/Irlanda.pdf, 3.

[20] Gilvarry and Hunt, n 19, 168.

[21] J O'Connor, '2007 Policy Speech (Bantry) by SIPTU President, Jack O'Connor' *Industrial Relations News*, 13, 14 April 2007.

[22] D D'Art and T Turner, 'Union Organising, Union Recognition and Employer Opposition: Case Studies of the Irish Experience' (2006) 26 *Irish Journal of Management* 165, 165.

[23] Ibid, 178.

Their earlier work surveyed full time union officials from eight trade unions and also concluded that the Act was inadequate, again in terms of achieving recognition.[24] Roche concludes the procedures may at least have had a 'modest beneficial effect on union organisation'.[25] Otherwise, the focus of prior research is on documentary analysis of just some of the Labour Court Recommendations[26] and the effect of the Ryanair judgments.[27] Conclusions vary from D'Art and Turner's prediction that the procedures were 'likely to be a dismal failure'[28] to Cullinane and Dobbins' finding in 2014 that the procedures were 'moderately successful for a short period in generating pay rises, improved employment conditions and better access to procedures for union members in non-unionised firms'.[29] There is a need to broaden this knowledge of the effects of the 2001 Act; to see beyond the Recommendations; to look at the long-term effects for trade unions and to also look right into the workplace to those who must live with the consequences of the 2001 Act.

C. Questions and Methods

Attempting to go beyond the Labour Court Recommendations necessitates a different approach to methods. A paper examination alone leaves three central questions unanswered:

(a) To what extent do workers stay in membership of the trade union that took the case on their behalf?

[24] D D'Art and T Turner, 'Union Recognition and Partnership at Work: A New Legitimacy for Irish Trade Unions?' (2005) 36 *Industrial Relations Journal* 121.

[25] WK Roche, 'The Trend of Unionisation in Ireland Since the Mid-1990s' in T Hastings (ed), *The State of the Unions: Challenges Facing Organised Labour in Ireland* (Dublin, Liffey Press, 2008).

[26] M Doherty, 'Representation, Bargaining and the Law: Where to Next for the Unions?' (2009): doras.dcu.ie/17034/1/Doherty, _NILQ_Revised_Submission_Trade_Unions.pdf; M Doherty, 'When You Ain't Got Nothin', You Got Nothin' to Lose … Union Recognition Laws, Voluntarism and the Anglo Model' (2013) 42 *Industrial Law Journal* 369; C Higgins, 'The "Right to Bargain" Law—Is It Working?' *Industrial Relations News* 45, 29 November 2001; B Sheehan, 'Multinational Wins Employee Representation Case' (2004): www.eurofound.europa.eu/eiro/2004/12/inbrief/ie0412202n.htm; N Cullinane and A Dobbins, 'Considering the Impact of the "Right to Bargain" Legislation in Ireland: A Review' (2014) 43 *Industrial Law Journal* 52.

[27] M Doherty, 'Union Sundown? The Future of Collective Representation Rights in Irish Law' (2007) 4 *Irish Employment Law Journal* 96; T Dobbins, 'Firm Considers High Court Challenge Over "2001–04" Pay Ruling' *Industrial Relations News* IRN 7, 20 February 2007; B Sheehan, 'Labour Court's Guidelines for 2001–04 Cases in the Wake of "Ryanair" Judgment' *Industrial Relations News* 14, 17 April 2007; B Sheehan, 'No "Independent Enquiry" into "Ryanair" Case—Bruton' *Industrial Relations News* 35, 26 September 2012.

[28] D D'Art and T Turner, 'Union Recognition in Ireland: One Step Forward or Two Steps Back?' (2003) 34 *Industrial Relations Journal* 226.

[29] N Cullinane and A Dobbins, 'Considering the Impact of the "Right to Bargain" Legislation in Ireland: A Review' (2014) 43 *Industrial Law Journal* 52, 52.

(b) What can be said of the levels of activism and the nature of collective bargaining encountered amongst those who have remained in trade unions?
(c) Are there substantive benefits for the workers as a result of taking a claim under the 2001 Act?

An answer to question (a) could only be determined by examination of union membership records and/or the provision of the information by the trade unions themselves. Determining whether or not collective bargaining was conducted at such workplaces and/or the extent of worker activism, as posed in question (b), could not be determined by such counting. This was achieved by means of a survey of the union staff currently responsible for those workplaces that had come through the 2001 Act procedures asking them to account for the collective bargaining arrangements at each workplace and levels of activism of the members thereat. Trying to uncover whatever substantive benefits might have accrued to workers (question (c)) was a more difficult question to answer and therefore a representative sample of cases was chosen for closer study.

Cullinane and Dobbins report that 'union officials were found to be frequently un-contactable and/or unwilling to participate'[30] in their own research and very few union members or activists have been the focus of any such research on this question. The author's study was unique in addressing both of those problems. Response rates from union officials were exceptionally high and union members and activists were interviewed in nine of the 10 cases selected for closer study. My previous employment in the Irish trade union movement is likely to have contributed to this unique level of access.

1. Answering Question (a): Where are they now?

Prior research pays scant attention to the long-term implications for workers and their trade unions subsequent to the issuing of Labour Court Recommendations. The Recommendation is seen as the end of the process. Taking the view that a Recommendation is but a milestone in a union organising campaign, forces a different approach to methods. It becomes necessary to take account of subsequent events and to explore the extent to which those involved have remained in membership of, and active in, the trade union which referred the case. All nine trade unions who participated in Labour Court hearings under the 2001 Act were contacted early in 2012; given a list of workplaces where they had taken cases and asked if these workplaces remained in membership of their union and if so to provide the name and contact details of the official with current or potential responsibility in each case.

Six trade unions responded and provided information on 89 (92 per cent) of the 97 workplaces where cases were taken. The three unions that did not respond were responsible for a total of eight cases, six of which involved 'poaching', a

[30] Ibid, 61.

union attempting to represent workers where another union already has negotiating rights. Given the nature of such 'poaching', there are unlikely to be members remaining in those unions. Those cases fail at the preliminary stages of the 2001 Act procedures as employers can demonstrate that they bargain collectively albeit with a different union. Of those 89 workplaces reported upon by participating unions, just less than a quarter (n=23) were no longer registered with those unions, meaning all of those members registered at that employment had resigned their membership or otherwise ceased to pay union dues.[31] There thus remained registered with unions a total of 66 (74 per cent) of the original 89 companies where cases were taken under the 2001 Act by participating unions. The union organiser with potential responsibility for each was identified, contacted and invited to complete an online questionnaire aimed at uncovering the nature of collective bargaining and levels of worker activism at each location. Ten cases were deemed unsuitable for inclusion in the survey due to merger and acquisition activity or redundancies involving the grade concerned with the original claim. There thus remained 56 workplaces for inclusion in the survey of which 48 responses were received representing a survey response rate of 86 per cent. These 48 responses represent 54 per cent of the cases taken by participating unions and 50 per cent of all cases taken under the 2001 Act.

It was expected that unions would be reluctant to provide exact membership figures for each workplace so questions regarding numbers or even density were not therefore included in the questionnaire. During the process of tracking each workplace back to the referring union and contacting the current servicing official however, indications were given in confidence of the level of membership in each workplace. In order to preserve that confidentiality, numbers of members are expressed in Table 2 below according to whether membership is in single or double figures for those workplaces reported upon in the survey.

Three-quarters of workplaces had membership in single figures, a good half of those recording just one or two members; none had membership in treble or

Table 2: Membership Levels

Membership Levels	No of Workplaces (n=48)
Membership levels of 10 or more	11
Membership levels of less than 10	32
Zero membership	3
Unknown	2

[31] Unions maintain membership records, organised by place of employment. If all members in a workplace resign or if they all remain in arrears for a particular length of time (which varies from union to union), that workplace is removed from the records.

higher figures. The lack of comparators is a problem but membership levels such as this are unlikely to be representative of the Irish trade union movement as a whole.

Member joining patterns could be discerned in 45 of the workplaces involved in the 2001 Act by reference to some unions' membership records and lists of members or copies of application forms on file. Those patterns were as follows:

— Seven workplaces record no new members after the issuing of the Labour Court Recommendation;
— Twelve workplaces show some joining activity immediately after the issuing of the Recommendation but which then ceases;
— Twenty-two workplaces have gaps of between one and five years between the issuing of the Recommendation and the next newly recruited member at that workplace;
— Four workplaces show a similar and ongoing pattern of new members each year before and after the issuing of the Recommendation.

It was not possible to determine the extent to which membership patterns such as these can be explained by high levels of union density in each workplace and/or because there were no new employees for unions to recruit. However, three of the four workplaces that demonstrate a consistent and ongoing pattern of new members and increases in membership are also those which report better outcomes in terms of bargaining and activism, explored in question (b) below.

2. Answering Question (b): Bargaining and Activism

Respondents were asked three main questions about the union membership at each workplace: their collective bargaining status; their representative structure and the most recent industrial relations issue raised and resolved at each workplace. For bargaining status, respondents were asked to describe the members at each workplace according to one of the following options: (a) these members were not known to them[32] and/or were no longer paying union dues; (b) there were some confidential members but who had little contact with the union; (c) the union represents members on an individual basis only; (d) there is an active core of members but without bargaining rights; or (e) there are full collective bargaining rights. Table 3 below outlines the responses regarding bargaining status.

Half of all workplaces reported on (n=24), while still on the union's national records were unknown to the local union officials for their area and/or the members had ceased paying union dues, perhaps indicating in some cases more recent closures and/or resignations from the union, see group (a) in Table 3 below. In group (b) there were a total of six workplaces (13 per cent) where there were some

[32] Paying union dues to a central body or by bank electronic transfer and have no contact with their local union branch office.

Table 3: Collective bargaining status

Status	**Total**	**%**
(a) Unknown to respondent or non-paying	24	50%
(b) Confidential membership with little contact with union official	6	13%
(c) Individual representation only	9	19%
(e) Active core of members but without recognition	7	15%
(f) Full bargaining rights	2	4%
Totals	48	

confidential members who seldom contacted the union, confidential in the sense that their membership was unknown to the employer and they never sought the union's representation. Nine workplaces (19 per cent) involved a membership that the union represented on an individual basis only (group (c)). There was an active core of members but without full bargaining rights in seven cases (15 per cent) (group (d)) and in two cases (4 per cent) (group (e)), the respondents chose full bargaining rights as the option which best described the current status of the members at that workplace. These then are the categories to which union officials assigned each workplace and which are used for comparison purposes for the rest of the research project.

Where respondents chose the first status option indicating that the members at the relevant workplace were unknown to them and/or were actually no longer in membership (group (a)), the survey skipped to the end of the questionnaire as the subsequent questions regarding representative structure and issues raised and resolved would not be relevant. As this option was chosen in 24 cases, there remained 24 continuing cases for the remaining questions.

Representative structure was determined by asking respondents to answer 'Yes', 'No' or 'Don't know' to a range of questions regarding the existence of shop stewards, elected committees or elected safety representatives at each location and to also answer in the same manner regarding the activities of these representatives outside the workplace. Table 4 below outlines the total positive responses, which demonstrate a reliance on just one representative at workplaces; 15 or 63 per cent of workplaces had one elected shop steward though only a third of these, five or 21 per cent of total responses, reported the additional existence of an elected representative committee. There is an elected safety representative in a quarter of the workplaces (n=6); in five workplaces the union had succeeded in getting paid release for meetings or training. Activity outside the workplace was minimal; in only two cases was there any reported involvement within unions at internal administrative levels such as branch, region or division or external to unions at, for example, Trades Council. In nine workplaces respondents report the lack of any representative structure, that is: no shop steward, no committee, no safety representative, no involvement in their particular union internally or on outside bodies.

Table 4: Representative structure

Representative Structure	Total	%
No of cases being reported on	24	
There is an elected shop steward	15	63%
There is an elected representative committee	5	21%
There is an elected safety representative	6	25%
One or more representatives are active at other levels in the Union	2	8%
One or more representatives are active at Trades Council or other TU body	2	8%
One or more representatives have been released with pay to attend training or union meetings	5	21%

Not surprisingly the likelihood of there being a representative structure increased the further a workplace was along a rough continuum between group (b) who rarely contacted the union to group (e) with full bargaining rights. Both workplaces in group (e) with 'full bargaining rights' reported the existence of shop stewards, of elected representative committees and the acquisition of paid release. One of these also reported the existence of an elected safety representative. All seven workplaces in group (d), with an active core of members, reported the existence of an elected shop steward; two of these also included an elected representative committee and one had secured paid release. This is reflected in Table 5 below.

Table 5: Bargaining status and representative structure

Bargaining Status and Representative Structure	Total	Shop Steward	Elected Committee	Elected Safety Rep	Other internal activity	External activity	Paid release
Group (b)—Rare or no contact	6	1	—	—	—	—	—
Group (c)—Individual Representation	9	5	1	2	1	2	1
Group (d)—Active core	7	7	2	2	1	—	1
Group (e)—Full bargaining rights	2	2	2	1	—	—	2

Respondents were asked to report on the nature of the most recent industrial relations issue raised and resolved at those workplaces under examination. Twelve of 21 workplaces reported a collective issue half of which concerned rates of pay; the others were hours of work (2) and one each of redundancy, pension, transfer of undertakings and one collective disciplinary issue. The two workplaces with full bargaining rights in group (e) both reported collective issues (pay and hours respectively). Of the seven workplaces reporting an active core of members but without full bargaining rights (group (d)), pay (n=3) and hours (n=1) featured again and along with one transfer of undertakings case represented five collective issues raised at those workplaces. The other two issues raised in group (d) workplaces concerned individual disciplinary matters. Not surprisingly, individual issues dominated in groups (c) and (b). There is then a connection between bargaining status and representative structure; the further a workplace is along a continuum between 'rare contact' with the union official and 'full bargaining' the greater the likelihood that there is a shop steward, an elected committee and a safety representative. There is also a greater likelihood that collective issues are dealt with as opposed to individual disciplinary issues which are more likely at the other end of the continuum.

Combining the answers to questions (a) and (b) paints a somewhat bleak picture of the aftermath of Labour Court Recommendations. Figure 1 summarises the membership, bargaining and representative status of the workplaces involved.

Although two-thirds of workplaces remain nominally on union registers, actual numbers are sparse; activism is low and collective bargaining almost non-existent. Of 97 workplaces where unions sought the assistance of the Labour Court under the 2001 Act between 2002 and 2007, 66 are still recorded on union membership records at national level. Fifty-six of those were suitable for inclusion in a survey of full time union officials with current responsibility for those workplaces. Of 48 responses, only 24 are in contact with their local union official; less than one-third

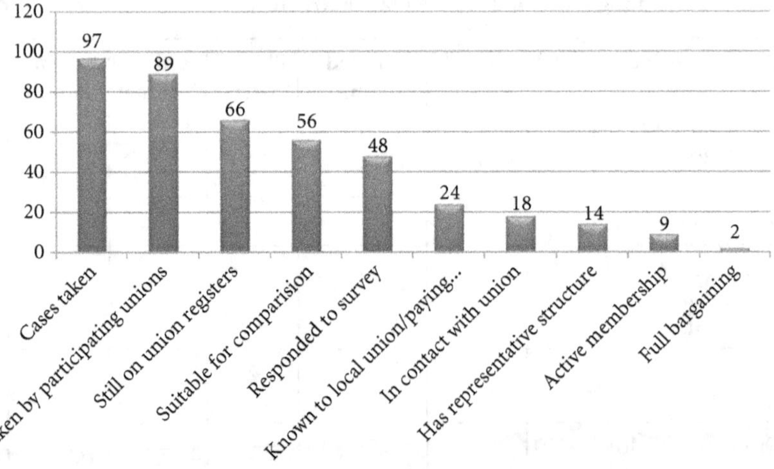

Figure 1: Membership, bargaining and representative status

of workplaces (n=14) have any elected trade union representatives and collective bargaining is conducted in just 4 per cent of workplaces (n=2).

3. Answering Question (c): Substantive Benefits

Some in the trade union movement defend the 2001 Act on the basis of its usefulness in improving the terms and conditions of employment of union members, that is those who would never be able to negotiate such improvements for themselves.[33] To assess this point, 10 cases were selected for closer examination, two each from groups (a)–(e) as outlined above and chosen to be reasonably representative of all cases taken in terms of economic sector and geographic location. Table 6 provides anonymised details about the 10 selected cases.

Table 6: Ten selected cases by bargaining status, economic sector and location

Workplace Name	Bargaining Status	Economic Sector	Location
Deltrans	Group (e)—Full bargaining	Transportation and storage	Urban Mid-West
Pegasus	Group (e)—Full bargaining	Transportation and storage	Urban East
Ard-na-Gaoithe	Group (d)—Active core	Services	Rural West
Garry's	Group (d)—Active core	Manufacturing	Urban South-East
Rosses	Group (c)—Individual representation	Manufacturing	Urban South-East
Canalcon	Group (c)—Individual representation	Manufacturing	Rural North
Blackwater	Group (b)—Confidential/ rare contact	Health	Urban West
Oakchurch	Group (b)—Confidential/ rare contact	Services	Rural Midlands
Led-Pack	Group (a)—No contact	Transportation and storage	Urban Mid-West
Knockrada	Group (a)—No contact	Health	Rural Midlands

[33] J Shanahan, 'Has the Supreme Court Decision Killed the 2001–04 Acts?' *Industrial Relations News* IRN 26, 11 July 2007; T Dobbins, 'Unresolved Union Recognition Question Back on Social Partnership Agenda' *Industrial Relations News* IRN 16, 1 May 2007.

A total of 36 interviews were conducted across these 10 cases. The union official who referred the original case, and where different, the officials with current or potential responsibility were interviewed in all cases. Interviews were also held with a mixture of current and former members, activists and shop stewards in all cases except Oakchurch where there were no existing members and no contact details available for former members.

Regarding the substantive benefits achieved from the Labour Court Recommendations, in four of the 10 cases, Deltrans, Pegasus, Ard-na-Gaoithe and Garry's, the terms of their respective Recommendations were implemented and represented a substantial improvement in the pay and conditions of workers at those locations. Only the workers *directly* involved in the claim at Oakchurch were successful. They were seasonal workers not hired for the subsequent season and the improved rates of pay were not applied to subsequent employees. At Rosses the Labour Court Recommendation did not provide any gains as such but confirmed agreement reached during the 'voluntary leg' at the LRC. Workers at Canalcon, Blackwater, Knockrada and Led-Pack never benefitted from the substantive terms of their respective Labour Court Recommendations. The Recommendations were not implemented and for a variety of different reasons, no Determinations were ever issued which would have forced the implementation.

There is then a strong connection between the bargaining status of a workplace (groups (a)–(e)) and whether or not there were improvements in pay and conditions of employment as a result of the implementation of the Labour Court Recommendations. The best results were achieved in groups (e) and (d)—Delpack, Pegasus, Ard-na-Gaoithe and Garry's.

D. Discussion

Ireland is at a crossroads where trade union recognition is concerned. The procedures introduced in legislation in 2001, and amended in 2004 with the aim of resolving disputes on recognition, have failed to satisfy either side and have fallen into disuse as a consequence of Ryanair's legal challenge. Trade unions are lobbying for, and Government Ministers are promising and will soon deliver, amended legislation. Determining the specifics of any such new legislation needs to be informed by discovering and acknowledging any limitations in the existing legislation, including limitations specifically separate from those caused by the Ryanair judgments which might in any event be resolved. It is essential to know what other effects participation in the legislative procedure might have, on membership levels for example, and on whether the procedure would let 'union recognition in by the back door'.[34]

[34] S Creaton, 'Ruling Delivers Severe Blow to Defiant Airline' *The Irish Times*, 15 October 2005.

Taking membership levels first and seeking to determine whether or not workers remain in unions and remain active, on the evidence of this study, they do not. Excluding the 10 cases not suitable for inclusion in the survey and the eight cases where officials did not respond, this leaves 71 workplaces whose membership status is known and for 47 or 66 per cent of those it is confirmed that they are no longer in membership of the union which referred the original case to the Labour Court; union registers contained no reference to 23 workplaces and while a further 24 were on national registers they were unknown to local union officials and/or had ceased to pay union contributions. There may be economic reasons for this level of attrition and in the absence of comparators it is not possible to attribute all of the loss of membership to the taking of cases under the 2001 Act. However levels of activism are also low. Only 14 out of 24 workplaces in contact with their union official have some kind of a union representative structure, nine of which report an active membership. In two (4 per cent) of 48 cases reported on in the survey, the local union official reports the existence and exercise of full bargaining rights. Unlike membership levels, economic decline can hardly be responsible for low levels of activism; intuitively it should increase activity at least with negotiations on redundancies, lay-offs or pay cuts. Union density levels particularly in small workplaces could be a factor, but as with membership levels, the union movement could not have continued in existence if those levels of membership and activism were representative of the movement as a whole.

Does the 2001 Act provide trade union recognition 'by the back door' or otherwise? If assessing this question by reference to the cases in this study, that is those cases that proceeded through the 'voluntary leg' to the 'fall-back' procedure at the Labour Court, then the answer has to be a resounding 'no'. Of the 48 workplaces examined in the survey, in only two cases was there found what union officials recorded as 'full bargaining rights'.

Trade unions have campaigned for legislative measures to deal with the question of trade union recognition though there seems little debate, much less research, to support the view that such measures are the best way of dealing with recognition disputes. In the absence of comparisons with other means of resolving the situation it is not possible to rank the various means according to which is best or worst. In terms of the pertaining issue of trade union recognition, what can be said is that the 2001 Act does not address the question at all. It side-steps it and deals with the substantive issues in dispute and makes no provision for collective bargaining or any 'continuous association of wage earners'[35] at the workplace. It also side-steps the issue in a macro political sense; the discussion on union recognition in Ireland now centres on fixing what Ryanair broke. The results of this study would indicate that that is the wrong debate for trade unions. Fixing what Ryanair broke will not address the other problems identified in this study such as low retention of members and low levels of activism even amongst retained members. In addition, any appreciable improvement in pay and conditions seems only

[35] S Webb and B Webb, *History of Trade Unionism*, 2nd edn (London, Longman, 1920) 1.

to be found in those situations where collective bargaining emerged (despite the Act's stated prohibition on providing for it) and should be attributed to this fact rather than to Labour Court Recommendations alone.

E. Conclusion

The provisions of the Industrial Relations (Amendment) Act 2001 have been found to be ineffective in providing for union recognition;[36] modest in terms of usefulness in union organising[37] and 'moderately successful'[38] in delivering pay increases and better terms and conditions of employment to workers involved in the claims.[39] Such are the findings when research is limited to an examination of the Labour Court Recommendations alone and/or a focus on a small sample. This project sought to go beyond the Labour Court Recommendation in each case to understand the real effects on those who must live with its consequences, the workers. Figure 1 graphically demonstrates the aftermath of the Labour Court Recommendations. A total of 97 workplaces were the subject of cases taken to the Labour Court under the Industrial Relations (Amendment) Act 2001. The current membership status of 71 workplaces is known and barely one-third, or 24 workplaces in total, record any actual union membership during 2012 and 2013. Membership levels are low, most record single figures. Activism as measured by the existence of a representative structure and the nature of issues raised and resolved is even lower. Substantive benefits to workers in terms of improved conditions at work arising from implementation of the Labour Court Recommendations were not much in evidence. Collective bargaining, surely the purpose of trade unions, is found in only two cases. Altogether this represents a far less benign conclusion than any reached from examination of the Labour Court Recommendations alone.

[36] D D'Art and T Turner, 'Union Recognition in Ireland: One Step Forward or Two Steps Back?' (2003) 34 *Industrial Relations Journal* 226; D D'Art and T Turner, 'Union Recognition and Partnership at Work: A New Legitimacy for Irish Trade Unions?' (2005) 36 *Industrial Relations Journal* 121; D D'Art and T Turner, 'Union Organising, Union Recognition and Employer Opposition: Case Studies of the Irish Experience' (2006) 26 *Irish Journal of Management* 165.

[37] WK Roche, 'The Trend of Unionisation in Ireland Since the Mid-1990s' in T Hastings (ed), *The State of the Unions: Challenges Facing Organised Labour in Ireland* (Dublin, Liffey Press, 2008).

[38] N Cullinane and A Dobbins, 'Considering the Impact of the "Right to Bargain" Legislation in Ireland: A Review' (2014) 43 *Industrial Law Journal* 52.

[39] J Shanahan, 'Has the Supreme Court Decision Killed the 2001–04 Acts?' *Industrial Relations News* IRN 26, 11 July 2007; T Dobbins, 'Unresolved Union Recognition Question Back on Social Partnership Agenda' *Industrial Relations News* IRN 16, 1 May 2007.

Part C

What Do We 'Do' With Empirical Work? Making Empirical Work 'Count'

10

Using the Delphi Method to Advance Legal Reform: A New Method for Empirical Labour Law Research?

ALYSIA BLACKHAM*

In navigating and mediating the interests of capital and labour, labour law remains a contentious subject of partisan attention, never far from the political agenda.[1] This constant change and political reform jeopardises the predictability and consistency of labour law, making it difficult for employers and workers to know where they stand. Further, there is limited political and legal consideration of how to address long-term issues facing the labour market, and few lasting or strategic reforms are put in place.

The use of doctrinal legal research methods in legal scholarship perpetuates this situation. Doctrinal methods are primarily geared to critiquing, interpreting and developing coherent accounts of existing legal provisions, rather than developing broad-ranging proposals for change.[2] In this context, alternative analytic processes offer considerable potential to take a deeper and more critical look at long-term labour issues.

This paper explores the use of the Delphi method as a structured group communication process for dealing with complex labour law problems. Drawing on a case study of responses to the ageing workforce, this paper appraises the challenges and potential benefits of the Delphi method in empirical labour law research. It argues that the Delphi method has significant potential to be used in labour law. However, the method poses major practical challenges for researchers and participants, and requires care and perseverance in its implementation. This paper

* Turpin-Lipstein Fellow and College Lecturer in Law, Clare College, University of Cambridge and Affiliated Lecturer, Faculty of Law, University of Cambridge.

[1] H Collins, KD Ewing, and A McColgan, *Labour Law*, Law in Context (Cambridge, Cambridge University Press, 2012) 5.

[2] See P Chynoweth, 'Legal Research' in A Knight and L Ruddock (eds), *Advanced Research Methods in the Built Environment* (Wiley-Blackwell, 2008) 29; M van Hoecke, 'Legal Doctrine: Which Method(s) for What Kind of Discipline?' in M van Hoecke (ed), *Methodologies of Legal Research: What Kind of Method for What Kind of Discipline?*, European Academy of Legal Theory (Oxford, Hart, 2011) 17; T Hutchinson and N Duncan, 'Defining and Describing What We Do: Doctrinal Legal Research' (2012) 17 *Deakin Law Review* 83, 110.

therefore highlights the strengths and limitations of using the Delphi process as an adjunct to traditional legal doctrinal methods.

A. The Delphi Method

The Delphi method is a structured group communication process that allows individuals to deal with complex problems as a group.[3] Where knowledge is uncertain or imperfect, the Delphi method can achieve reliable group consensus[4] and identify divergence of opinion on hypothetical future scenarios.[5] The Delphi method is very effective for exploring solutions in policy areas with high levels of uncertainty[6] and can eliminate distractions and distortions in group discussions by allowing responses to be anonymised.[7] The method is therefore more effective at generating new ideas and exploring future scenarios in areas of uncertainty than traditional face-to-face communication.[8] At a practical level, the Delphi method allows participants to think through responses, promoting careful and thoughtful contributions, while the anonymity of responses ensures open and honest discussion.

While a range of Delphi structures can be used, a policy Delphi is designed to identify all possible policy options and examine and estimate the impact, consequences and acceptability of particularly policy options.[9] It also allows respondents to react to and assess different viewpoints on policy issues.[10] Therefore, it is particularly well suited to coordinating and structuring respondents' thinking around how complex labour law issues might develop and evolve in the future[11] and provides a constructive forum for discussion, the building of consensus[12] and the clarification of different ideas and viewpoints on labour law issues.[13]

[3] HA Linstone and M Turoff, 'Introduction' in HA Linstone and M Turoff (eds), *The Delphi Method: Techniques and Applications* (Reading, Addison-Wesley, 1977) 3.

[4] G Aichholzer, 'The Delphi Method: Eliciting Experts' Knowledge in Technology Foresight' in A Bogner et al (eds), *Interviewing Experts*, Research Methods (Basingstoke, Palgrave Macmillan, 2009) 252–53.

[5] M Rayens and EJ Hahn, 'Building Consensus Using the Policy Delphi Method' (2000) 1 *Policy, Politics, & Nursing Practice* 308, 308.

[6] See A Rotondi and D Gustafson, 'Theoretical, Methodological and Practical Issues Arising out of the Delphi Method' in M Adler and E Ziglio (eds), *Gazing into the Oracle: The Delphi Method and Its Application to Social Policy and Public Health* (London, Jessica Kingsley, 1996) 42.

[7] Aichholzer, n 4.

[8] E Ziglio, 'The Delphi Method and Its Contribution to Decision-Making' in M Adler and E Ziglio (eds), *Gazing into the Oracle: The Delphi Method and Its Application to Social Policy and Public Health* (London, Jessica Kingsley, 1996) 22.

[9] M Turoff, 'The Policy Delphi' in HA Linstone and M Turoff (eds), *The Delphi Method: Techniques and Applications* (Reading, Addison-Wesley, 1977) 83.

[10] Ibid.

[11] Aichholzer, n 4, 259.

[12] Rayens and Hahn, n 5, 309.

[13] W Rauch, 'The Decision Delphi' (1979) 15 *Technological Forecasting and Social Change* 159, 163.

The RAND Corporation first used the Delphi method during the Cold War to estimate Soviet nuclear capabilities for the US Air Force.[14] The method has since been used a handful of times in legal and socio-legal research, including for examining the impact of legal rules and how laws operate in practice,[15] offering solutions to law-related problems,[16] developing taxonomies and definitions of legal phenomena[17] and criteria to evaluate policy initiatives,[18] and exploring the future of interactions between law and society.[19] While the Delphi method has been used to answer a range of legal and semi-legal questions, it has rarely been used to inform the process of law reform. This is an area where the Delphi method could add significant value, particularly in developing legal responses to long-term labour law issues.

B. Ageing as a Challenge for Labour Law

A key long-term issue facing UK labour law is demographic change. The UK population is 'ageing rapidly'[20] and it is projected that England will experience a 51 per cent increase in those aged over 65 and a 101 per cent increase in those aged over 85 from 2010 to 2030.[21] As the 'baby boom' generation of the 1960s approaches the state pension age, the median age of the UK population continues to advance upwards, being projected to rise from 39.7 years in 2010 to 42.2 years in 2035.[22]

[14] N Dalkey and O Helmer, 'An Experimental Application of the Delphi Method to the Use of Experts' (1963) 9 *Management Science* 458.

[15] JP van Gigch and R Hommes, 'A Study of How Correctional Counsellors and Psychologists Agree upon Pre-Sentence Recommendations' (1973) 15 *Canadian Journal of Criminology and Corrections* 93; B Dziurzynski, 'FDA Regulatory Review and Approval Processes: A Delphi Inquiry' (1996) 51 *Food and Drug Law Journal* 143.

[16] HG McDonald and CP Kirsch, 'Use of the Delphi Method as a Means of Assessing Judicial Manpower Needs' (1978) 3 *Justice System Journal* 314; SJ Young, AT Pittman, and JO Spengler, 'Best Case Scenario: The Development of a Teaching Tool For Sport Law' (2004) 14 *Journal of Legal Aspects of Sport* 1.

[17] MF Hudson, 'Elder Mistreatment: A Taxonomy with Definitions by Delphi' (1991) 3 *Journal of Elder Abuse & Neglect* 1.

[18] E Guglyuvatyy, 'Identifying Criteria for Climate Change Policy Evaluation in Australia' (2010) 7 *Macquarie Journal of Business Law* 98.

[19] KN Wright, 'A Delphi Assessment of the Effects of a Declining Economy on Crime and the Criminal Justice System' (1982) 46 *Federal Probation* 36; LF Travis, V O'Leary, and V Castelluccio, 'The Future of Sentencing and Parole: A Delphi Reassessment of Sentencing and Parole Reforms' (1985) 10 *Criminal Justice Review* 45; SJ Young and LM Jamieson, 'Perceived Liability and Risk Management Trends Impacting Recreational Sports into the 21st Century' (1999) 9 *Journal of Legal Aspects of Sport* 151.

[20] Select Committee on Public Service and Demographic Change, *Ready for Ageing?* (HL 2012–13, 140, 14 March 2013) 7.

[21] Ibid.

[22] Office for National Statistics, 'UK Population Projected to Reach 70 Million by Mid-2027' (October 2011): www.ons.gov.uk/ons/rel/npp/national-population-projections/2010-based-projections/sum-2010-based-national-population-projections.html; see also European Commission, *Active Ageing and Solidarity between Generations: A Statistical Portrait of the European Union 2012* (Luxembourg, Publications Office of the European Union, 2011) 27.

Population ageing will have consequences for many industries and government services, including housing, pensions, health and social care, and employment. The proportion of older workers is likely to increase substantially in coming years. Advancements in medical care and improved living conditions mean that individuals are living longer and can reasonably expect substantially more productive, healthy working years in their old age.[23] Further, inadequate pensions may compel older workers to continue in employment: according to 2012 figures, 10.7 million individuals in Great Britain are likely to have insufficient income in retirement.[24] This will be compounded by reforms to state pensions, which are gradually increasing the state pension age to 67 years of age by 2028.[25] Financial considerations will increasingly compel older workers to stay in employment. As a result, older workers are likely to become a significant feature of the UK labour market in coming years: it is projected that workers over 50 will constitute 31 per cent of the UK workforce in 2020, and that the number of workers aged over 65 will increase from 582,000 in 2005 to 775,000 in 2020, an increase of 33 per cent.[26]

Despite the significant consequences of population ageing for labour law, government and society are still 'woefully underprepared' for demographic change following a 'collective failure to address the implications' of ageing.[27] Few laws specifically address population ageing, meaning few employers are considering the implications of ageing for their workforce, and even fewer are proactively responding to the needs of older workers. Existing laws have limited potential to effectively address and accommodate demographic change. Therefore, the Delphi method is a useful tool for developing new legal options to respond to the ageing workforce.

C. Existing Legal Responses to the Ageing Workforce

1. Doctrinal Measures

While older workers will constitute a significant proportion of the UK workforce in years to come, there are few UK laws that promote the employment of older workers or encourage employers to actively support an ageing workforce. The key legislative provision that supports older workers is the prohibition of age discrimination in the Equality Act 2010 (UK) (c 15) ('the Act'),[28] which adopts Council

[23] European Commission, n 22, 18.

[24] Select Committee on Public Service and Demographic Change, *Ready for Ageing?* (HL 2012–13, 140, 14 March 2013) 7.

[25] HM Treasury and HM Parliament, *Autumn Statement 2011* (London, Stationery Office, 2011) 23.

[26] V Madouros, *Projections of the UK Labour Force, 2006–20*, Labour Market Trends (London, Office for National Statistics, January 2006) 20–21.

[27] Select Committee on Public Service and Demographic Change, n 24.

[28] Older workers may also benefit from other, general legislative provisions, like the right to request flexible working, occupational health and safety requirements and employment rights generally. However, age discrimination legislation is the only area of law specifically affecting older workers.

Directive 2000/78/EC of 27 November 2000 establishing a general framework for equal treatment in employment and occupation ('the Framework Directive')[29] into UK law. The Act prohibits direct and indirect discrimination, harassment and victimisation in the workplace on the grounds of age, during recruitment, in setting the terms of employment, deciding to award promotions and provide training and in dismissal (s 39). However, less favourable treatment on the grounds of age is not discrimination if the treatment is shown to be 'a proportionate means of achieving a legitimate aim' (s 13(2)). This does not apply to any other protected characteristic. Indirect discrimination may also be justified using the same test (s 19(2)).

The Act includes a number of specific exceptions to the prohibition of age discrimination in employment, including for:

- Occupational requirements which are a proportionate means of achieving a legitimate aim (Sch 9, s 1(1));
- Service in the armed forces (Sch 9, s 4(3));
- Benefits based on length of service that:
  - relate to a period of service of up to five years duration; or
  - relate to a period of service exceeding five years duration and which the employer reasonably believes fulfil a business need (Sch 9, s 10);
- The national minimum wage (Sch 9, ss 11–12);
- Enhanced redundancy payments (Sch 9, s 13); and
- Contributions to personal pension schemes (by order of a Minister) (Sch 9, s 16).

The Act allows (but does not require) employers to take positive action that is a proportionate means of:

- Enabling or encouraging persons who share a protected characteristic to overcome or minimise disadvantage connected to that characteristic;
- Meeting the needs of persons who share a protected characteristic which are different from the needs of persons who do not share the characteristic; or
- Enabling or encouraging persons who share a protected characteristic to participate in an activity in which their participation is disproportionately low (s 158(1)–(2)).

Similarly, positive action may be taken in recruitment and promotion to address a disadvantage or disproportionately low participation (s 159). However, a person with a protected characteristic may only be treated more favourably if: they are as qualified as the other person; the employer or company does not have a policy of treating people who share the protected characteristic more favourably in recruitment or promotion; and the action is a proportionate means of overcoming

[29] OJ L 303/16.

or minimising the disadvantage, or promoting participation in the activity (s 159(3)–(4)).

While positive action is allowed under the Act, employers are unlikely to take advantage of the provisions, as positive action is seen as too risky and resource intensive to be beneficial, and may lead to a 'potential minefield' of legal action if employers 'get it wrong'.[30] Rather than being helpful to employers, the sections are a 'trap for the well intentioned'.[31] The drafting of the sections makes them 'too dangerous [for employers] to use safely',[32] limiting the possibility of positive action in the UK.

The Act also establishes a public sector equality duty, requiring public authorities or people exercising public functions to, in exercise of their functions, have due regard to the need to:

- — Eliminate discrimination, harassment, victimisation and conduct prohibited by the Act;
- — Advance equality of opportunity between persons who share and do not share a protected characteristic, including by:
  - — removing or minimising disadvantages suffered by persons who share a protected characteristic that are connected to that characteristic;
  - — taking steps to meet the particular needs of persons who share a protected characteristic; and
  - — encouraging persons who share a protected characteristic to participate in public life or activities in which their participation is disproportionately low; and
- — Foster good relations between persons who share a relevant protected characteristic and persons who do not share it, including by tackling prejudice, and promoting understanding (s 149).

A review of the public sector equality duty was conducted in 2013 'to establish whether the Duty is operating as intended'.[33] The Steering Group concluded that it was too early to make a final judgement about the impact of the duty, as it was only introduced in April 2011, and the available evidence was inconclusive, particularly in relation to the associated costs and benefits of implementing the duty.[34] The Group recommended the government consider conducting a formal evaluation of the duty in 2016.

[30] Thomson Reuters, 'Positive Action: Tie Breaks in the Recruitment Process', *Prolegal*, 2 May 2012: www.prolegal.co.uk/legal-news/tie-breaks-in-the-recruitment-process.htm.

[31] A Hoggarth and L Taft, 'Legal Insight: Positive Discrimination—a Trap for the Well Intentioned?' *HRZone*, 10 May 2012: www.hrzone.com/topic/recruitment/legal-insight-positive-discrimination-trap-well-intentioned/120274.

[32] Kingsley Napley, '"Positive Action"—Will it Make Any Difference?' 12 May 2011.

[33] HM Government, 'Review of Public Sector Equality Duty' (*GOV.UK*, no date) www.gov.uk/government/policy-advisory-groups/review-of-public-sector-equality-duty-steering-group.

[34] Government Equalities Office, *Review of the Public Sector Equality Duty by the Independent Steering Group* (London, Government Equalities Office, 6 September 2013) 11.

In sum, the Act provides less protection for age discrimination in employment than other forms of discrimination,[35] particularly as both direct and indirect age discrimination may be justified as a 'proportionate means of achieving a legitimate aim'. This provides significant scope for employers to undermine the principle of equal treatment on the grounds of age. In the hierarchy of discriminatory grounds, age therefore 'occup[ies] the lowest rung'.[36] Further, positive action to enable older workers to participate in employment is likely to be rare, and the public sector equality duty is significantly circumscribed.[37] Therefore, existing laws have limited potential to effectively address and accommodate demographic change.

2. Practical Implementation of UK Age Discrimination Law

Given the doctrinal limitations of the Act, it is unsurprising that it has had limited impact in practice.[38] Few employers are adopting proactive measures to support ageing workers, and very few are actively seeking to recruit older workers. The 2011 Workplace Employment Relations Study found only 3 per cent of employers surveyed had special procedures to encourage applications from older workers. This was down from 5 per cent in the 2004 survey. Further, while 78 per cent of employers had an equal opportunity policy in place that explicitly mentioned age, less than 10 per cent had processes in place to monitor promotions and pay rates for discrimination.[39] It appears that many employers are not well prepared for the growth in older workers, with most adopting a compliance-focussed approach to age discrimination laws.[40]

Further, the law appears to be having limited success at improving employer attitudes towards older workers. The 2011 Special Eurobarometer on Active Ageing found that, in the last two years, 4.38 per cent of UK respondents had

[35] H Meenan, 'Age Discrimination in the EU and the Framework' in M Sargeant (ed), *The Law on Age Discrimination in the EU* (Alphen aan den Rijn, Kluwer Law International, 2008) 18; M Sargeant, 'Age Discrimination' in M Sargeant (ed), *The Law on Age Discrimination in the EU* (Alphen aan den Rijn, Kluwer Law International, 2008) 3, 5; M Sargeant, 'The European Court of Justice and Age Discrimination' [2011] *Journal of Business Law* 144, 146.

[36] C McGlynn, 'EC Legislation Prohibiting Age Discrimination: "Towards a Europe for All Ages"?' in A Dashwood et al (eds), *Cambridge Yearbook of European Legal Studies*, vol 3 (Oxford, Hart, 2000) 294; see further *R (Age UK) v Secretary of State for Business, Innovation and Skills* [2009] IRLR 1017 [20].

[37] S Fredman and S Spencer, *Delivering Equality: Towards an Outcome-Focused Positive Duty—Submission to the Cabinet Office Equality Review and to the Discrimination Law Review* (June 2006) 9; L Dickens, 'The Road is Long: Thirty Years of Equality Legislation in Britain' (2007) 45 *British Journal of Industrial Relations* 463, 473.

[38] This may also reflect the broader limitations of law in achieving social change: indeed, the link between law and social change is far from clear. See R Cotterrell, *The Sociology of Law: An Introduction* (London, Butterworths, 1984) 68.

[39] B van Wanrooy et al, *The 2011 Workplace Employment Relations Study: First Findings* (URN 13/1010, London, Department for Business, Innovation and Skills, January 2013) 34–35.

[40] This conclusion will be explored further in a subsequent publication.

been a victim of old age discrimination and 13.4 per cent had witnessed old age discrimination in the workplace or in seeking employment.[41] Further, the majority of respondents saw the exclusion of older workers from training (71.9 per cent) and employers not viewing older workers positively (68.2 per cent) as important factors in individual decisions to retire.[42] The practical efficacy of age discrimination laws therefore remains doubtful, particularly in effecting attitudinal change.

The Act's limited success at achieving practical change may reflect its dubious doctrinal and institutional foundations. The Act adopts a 'reflexive law' approach,[43] attempting to tailor regulation to particular contexts and integrate formal legal devices with self-regulation.[44] It provides significant scope for internal regulation by workplaces and few prescriptive 'command and control' regulations.[45] In implementing the Act, government departments have emphasised the creation of employer networks (such as the Age Action Alliance), the production of good practice guides and case studies, and holding forums to encourage discussion between organisations.[46] This reflects the strong focus on deliberation within and between organisations in reflexive regulation, including through the dissemination of best practice.[47]

While reflexive regulation may increase law's 'regulatory potential',[48] it will only be effective where it provides legal incentives for internal organisational action and scrutiny,[49] mechanisms for effective deliberation and participatory decision-making (such as collective bargaining),[50] and an external body to back-up and enforce regulations where voluntary methods fail.[51] While the Act adopts a reflexive law strategy, the UK equality framework lacks the institutional requirements for effective reflexive regulation in practice. In particular, there are few legal incentives for internal scrutiny and action in the private sector and limited information 'flows' regarding equality matters,[52] the public sector equality duty is significantly

[41] Eurobarometer, *Active Ageing* (Special Eurobarometer 378, Brussels, European Commission, January 2012) 33.

[42] Ibid, 49–50.

[43] See C McCrudden, 'Equality Legislation and Reflexive Regulation: A Response to the Discrimination Law Review's Consultative Paper' (2007) 36 *Industrial Law Journal* 255.

[44] S Deakin, C McLaughlin, and D Chai, 'Gender Inequality and Reflexive Law: The Potential for Different Regulatory Mechanisms' in L Dickens (ed), *Making Employment Rights Effective: Issues of Enforcement and Compliance* (Oxford, Hart, 2012) 118.

[45] See McCrudden, n 43.

[46] See, eg DWP, *Opportunity Age: Meeting the Challenges of Ageing in the 21st Century* (London, Department for Work and Pensions, 2005) 21.

[47] McCrudden, n 43, 259–60; Deakin, McLaughlin and Chai, n 44, 119.

[48] G Teubner, The European University Institute Press Series (Zenon Bankowski (ed), A Bankowska and R Adler (trs), *Law as an Autopoietic System* Oxford, Blackwell, 1993) 97.

[49] B Hepple, 'Agency Enforcement of Workplace Equality' in L Dickens (ed), *Making Employment Rights Effective: Issues of Enforcement and Compliance* (Oxford, Hart, 2012) 64–65.

[50] McCrudden, n 43, 260; Deakin, McLaughlin, and Chai, n 44, 120.

[51] Hepple, n 49, 55.

[52] See S Deakin and R Hobbs, 'False Dawn for CSR? Shifts in Regulatory Policy and the Response of the Corporate and Financial Sectors in Britain' (2007) 15 *Corporate Governance: An International Review* 68, 70.

circumscribed[53] and there is no duty to consult relevant interest groups in making equality decisions.[54] Barnard, Deakin and Hobbs have therefore argued that the UK lacks the basic institutional structures for effective reflexive law, particularly given the low levels of union representation in UK workplaces.[55]

To achieve effective reflexive regulation in the UK and, thereby, enhance the efficacy of the Act, Hepple, Coussey and Choudhury recommend the imposition of positive duties on private sector employers to achieve employment equality or fair participation, in addition to the public sector equality duty.[56] Imposing a positive duty on employers, including on the ground of age, would encourage a more proactive and less compliance-focussed organisational response to the equality framework.[57] Further, it would shift the responsibility to organisations to identify and address unlawful discrimination, irrespective of whether an individual complaint has been received.[58]

Imposing a duty on the private sector would probably generate significant consternation amongst employers and encounter substantial political resistance. The Act currently limits positive duties to public bodies, on the assumption it would be 'unfairly onerous' to apply them to the private sector.[59] However, the private sector has 'potential strategic importance' in addressing inequality given it employs the vast majority of the UK workforce.[60] Private and public sector equality duties 'harness the energies' of those in the best position to promote equality and achieve structural change.[61] It is also potentially unfair and practically problematic to create a division between the public and private sectors.[62] Therefore, the imposition of positive duties to achieve employment equality on private sector employers should be seriously considered.

It is also necessary to consider the practical content of any positive duty that might be placed on employers, and how it would be enforced. Hepple, Coussey and Choudhury propose the duty include obligations to:

— Conduct periodical reviews (once every three years) of employment practices to determine whether certain groups are enjoying fair participation in employment;

[53] Fredman and Spencer, n 37, 9; Dickens, n 37, 473.

[54] See further, B Hepple, M Coussey, and T Choudhury, *Equality: A New Framework—Report of the Independent Review of the Enforcement of UK Anti-Discrimination Legislation* (Oxford, Hart, 2000) 57–58; see also Hepple, n 49, 64–65.

[55] C Barnard, S Deakin, and R Hobbs, *Reflexive Law, Corporate Social Responsibility and the Evolution of Labour Standards: The Case of Working Time* (Working Paper 294, Cambridge, ESRC Centre for Business Research, December 2004) 23.

[56] Hepple, Coussey, and Choudhury, n 54, 59–65 and 69–72.

[57] L Dickens, 'Equality and Work-Life Balance: What's Happening at the Workplace' (2006) 35 *Industrial Law Journal* 445, 447; Fredman and Spencer, n 37, 6–7; Dickens, n 37, 474.

[58] Fredman and Spencer, n 87, 6–7.

[59] S Fredman, *Discrimination Law*, Calderon Law Series (Oxford, Oxford University Press, 2002) 178.

[60] Fredman and Spencer, n 37, 8; see also Dickens n 37.

[61] Fredman, n 59, 176.

[62] Ibid, 178.

- If certain groups are not enjoying fair participation in employment, draw up and implement an 'employment equity plan' in consultation with interest groups to address barriers to participation and make reasonable adjustments to secure fair participation; and
- Disclose the results of periodical reviews and equity plans in company reports, to employees and to employee representatives.[63]

A failure to comply with these requirements could be used as evidence in proceedings for unlawful discrimination. Further, the Equality and Human Rights Commission could secure written undertakings or deliver notices directing employers to comply with the requirements and, if not complied with, apply to an Employment Tribunal for enforcement.

D. Using the Delphi Method to Examine Proposals for Reform

Positive duties to achieve employment equality could be a key reform for promoting the employment of older workers. However, there has been limited academic consideration of whether this would be practicable in the UK context. Instead, it appears that positive duties have been abandoned in recent academic commentary, on the assumption they would be seen as unacceptable by government, lobby groups and employer bodies. Therefore, to illustrate how the Delphi method could be used to investigate labour law policy options, this study examines the introduction of positive duties as one example of a contentious future labour law scenario.

1. Research Procedures

a. Sample Selection

In a previous research study,[64] qualitative expert interviews were conducted with 17 active participants in community affairs who had special knowledge regarding older workers.[65] The experts were purposively sampled, using a literature review, lists of individuals and organisations consulted during government reviews, media articles and online databases,[66] with further respondents being identified

[63] Hepple, Coussey, and Choudhury, n 54, 71; see also F McAndrew, *Workplace Equality: Turning Policy into Practice* (London, Equality and Diversity Forum, November 2010) 19–20.

[64] The results of which will be published elsewhere.

[65] M Meuser and U Nagel, 'The Expert Interview and Changes in Knowledge Production' in A Bogner et al (eds), *Interviewing Experts*, Research Methods (Basingstoke, Palgrave Macmillan, 2009) 24.

[66] R Stake, 'Qualitative Case Studies' in Y Lincoln and N Denzin (eds), *Strategies of Qualitative Inquiry*, 3rd edn (London, SAGE, 2008) 130.

via theoretical[67] and snowball sampling.[68] The experts represented government, trade unions, employer groups, lobby groups, the judiciary and academia. At the conclusion of the in-person expert interviews, these same experts were invited to participate in a Delphi survey.

As noted by Turoff,[69] 'A policy question is one for which there are no experts, only advocates and referees'. In this survey, the experts were participating in their roles as advocates and lobbyists, with strong and partisan views on the issues at hand. Therefore, it was foreseeable that this Delphi survey might not generate consensus. However, it could still clarify and articulate the experts' views on particular scenarios and issues.[70] Given the partisan nature of the responses, care was taken to ensure the expert group was as representative of different perspectives as possible.[71]

b. The Delphi Process

The policy Delphi method adopted in this study was a multistage process with two asynchronous rounds of online surveys. The process involved:

- Initial measurement of opinions (Round 1);
- Data analysis;
- Design of a subsequent questionnaire based on initial responses; and
- Second measurement of opinions (Round 2).[72]

Between rounds, participants were provided with statistical group feedback about the beliefs of other participants to promote consensus.[73]

The first survey consisted of eight policy 'options items' to elicit opinions on the desirability and feasibility of policy scenarios.[74] Drawing on the qualitative expert interviews, meaningful hypothetical scenarios were created which might represent the future of law and policy structures affecting older workers.[75] These scenarios acted as 'straw models', presenting different perspectives on how the employment of older workers might evolve, to promote deep discussion amongst participants.[76] Scenarios were drafted to comprise no more than 20 words and

[67] KM Eisenhardt, 'Building Theories from Case Study Research' in AM Huberman and M Miles (eds), *The Qualitative Researcher's Companion* (Thousand Oaks, Sage Publications, 2002) 13; JM Corbin and AL Strauss, *Basics of Qualitative Research: Techniques and Procedures for Developing Grounded Theory*, 3rd edn (Thousand Oaks, Sage Publications, 2008) 117.

[68] T May, *Social Research: Issues, Methods and Process* (Buckingham, Open University Press, 1993) 100; L Webley, 'Qualitative Approaches to Empirical Legal Research' in P Cane and HM Kritzer (eds), *The Oxford Handbook of Empirical Legal Research* (Oxford, Oxford University Press, 2010) 934.

[69] M Turoff, 'The Design of a Policy Delphi' (1970) 2 *Technological Forecasting and Social Change* 149, 151.

[70] Ibid, 153; Rauch, n 13, 163.

[71] WN Dunn, *Public Policy Analysis: An Introduction*, 4th edn (Harlow, Prentice Hall, 2007) 181.

[72] Rayens and Hahn, n 5.

[73] Ibid.

[74] Ibid.

[75] Aichholzer, n 4, 262.

[76] Rotondi and Gustafson, n 6, 43; Ziglio, n 8, 20.

with sufficient specificity to enable their effective analysis.[77] Participants were also given the opportunity to suggest additional or different policy options during the first survey round.[78] As it is beyond the scope of this paper to report on all eight options items, this paper will present the results from one item:

> Employers have a positive duty to achieve employment equality, including for older workers.

In the survey, participant experts were asked to identify scenarios that were likely to be important, desirable and feasible.[79] Definitions of these terms were provided to ensure respondents had a similar understanding of what the terms meant (see the Appendix).[80] Questions were assessed on a four-stage assessment scale (1 = very low or negative, 4 = very high or positive).[81] No option was provided for participants to make a neutral response. This decision was made as neutral responses provide little information in survey analysis.[82] Further, not providing a neutral option may force respondents to think about the issue to the point where they are able to adopt a non-neutral stance.[83] Participants were also asked to rate their confidence in their assessment of each scenario (1 = no confidence, 4 = high confidence). Self-rating is a meaningful way to identify expertise and can improve the accuracy of responses.[84] Participants were invited to make comments regarding their selection and/or suggest other scenarios[85] and/or suggest changes to the wording of existing scenarios.[86]

The second survey included five elements:

1. 'Goal items' to evoke opinions about the desirability of particular policy goals and objectives.[87] These items were also intended to expose the assumptions underlying the experts' conflicting positions in the first round;[88]
2. Re-worded scenarios from the first survey to clarify or further develop scenarios in response to participant comments. Changing the wording of a policy option is often necessary in a policy Delphi, and can positively impact upon the level of consensus achieved;[89]

[77] HA Linstone and M Turoff, 'Evaluation—Introduction' in HA Linstone and M Turoff (eds), *The Delphi Method: Techniques and Applications* (Reading, Addison-Wesley, 1977) 232.
[78] Rayens and Hahn, n 5, 310.
[79] Ziglio, n 8, 19; Aichholzer, n 4, 263.
[80] Turoff, 'The Design of a Policy Delphi', n 69; Turoff, 'The Policy Delphi', n 9, 85.
[81] Aichholzer, n 4, 263.
[82] Turoff, 'The Policy Delphi', n 9, 90.
[83] Ibid; Rayens and Hahn, n 5.
[84] Linstone and Turoff, 'Evaluation—Introduction', n 77, 234.
[85] Aichholzer, n 4, 264.
[86] Turoff, 'The Policy Delphi', n 9, 93.
[87] Rayens and Hahn, n 5; Dunn, n 71, 183.
[88] Dunn, n 71, 182.
[89] Turoff, 'The Design of a Policy Delphi', n 69, 161.

3. Repetition of scenarios that led to disagreement in the first round, with the aim of allowing participants to revisit or reconsider their original opinions in light of the feedback provided;
4. New scenarios posed by respondents in the first survey round; and
5. New implementation scenarios, posing possible means of implementing scenarios that achieved a strong level of consensus in the first round.

Between the surveys, participants were provided with the median response for each question and a summary of comments made by other participants, to allow these responses to be taken into account in the second survey.[90] The surveys were pretested with five colleagues to identify confusing or ambiguous questions.[91]

In other reported Delphi studies, three survey rounds have been sufficient to attain stable responses from participants, with further rounds only antagonising participants with excessive repetition.[92] In this study, consensus appeared to have been achieved on many issues following the second survey round, making a third survey unnecessary. This is consistent with previous studies, which have found that changes tend to be limited to the early rounds of a Delphi.[93] Further, as found in other studies, the motivation and commitment of participants declined during the second round of the Delphi,[94] making a third round impracticable.

The Delphi was conducted online using a Google Forms survey tool. Google Forms was selected as it offered a free, accessible, streamlined and user-friendly mechanism for conducting an online roundtable. This created challenges for experts from government departments, as the hosting website was blocked by some government servers. Where this occurred, in Round 1 experts were asked to complete a hard-copy version of the survey, with the researcher manually entering the responses into the online database. For Round 2, the survey was hosted on a server that mirrored the Google Forms website, allowing it to be accessed by all respondents.

The response rate for each round of the Delphi is included in Table 1 below. To encourage a higher response rate, the researcher met with most respondents in person as part of the expert interview process, to develop stronger relationships and commitment; provided respondents with an extended period of time in which they could answer the survey; encouraged experts to respond by sending out follow-up emails (up to two follow-up emails were sent for each round, as required); and emphasised the importance of individual respondents contributing given the need for diversity of opinion.

[90] Aichholzer, n 4, 267.
[91] Turoff, 'The Policy Delphi', n 9, 93.
[92] Linstone and Turoff, 'Evaluation—Introduction', n 77, 229.
[93] Aichholzer, n 4, 267.
[94] Ibid.

Table 1: Response rate for Delphi roundtable by survey round

Round	Number of participants	Response rate	Period of survey
1	13	76%	May–July 2013
2	8	62%	October 2013–January 2014

Table 1 hints at the difficulties encountered in maintaining participant enthusiasm throughout the Delphi process, both in the declining response rates and the period over which the survey was conducted. These issues are explored further below.

E. Results

1. Means of Analysis

Rayens and Hahn recommend two criteria for measuring the degree of consensus in a Delphi survey.[95] First, it is necessary to consider the inter-quartile range (IQD) of an item. On a four point Likert-type scale,[96] an IQD of more than 1.00 indicates a degree of disagreement.[97] However, the IQD is not sufficiently sensitive to distinguish between degrees of agreement when IQD = 1.00.[98] Therefore, the percentage of respondents who are generally positive about a scenario may be used as a secondary criterion of consensus.[99] Following Rayens and Hahn, this study regarded both: (1) scenarios having an IQD of more than 1.00; and (2) scenarios having an IQD of 1.00 and receiving positive responses from between 40 and 60 per cent of respondents as having a degree of disagreement worthy of further exploration in Round 2.[100]

Prior to analysis, responses were adjusted to exclude respondents who self-identified as having 'no confidence' in their response to ensure a minimal level of knowledge about each area.[101] Following this adjustment, the answers of two respondents were excluded for two scenarios in Round 1 (four answers in total); and the answers of one respondent were excluded for five scenarios in Round 2 (five answers in total).

[95] Rayens and Hahn, n 5.
[96] That is, a four-stage assessment scale (such as: 1 = very low or negative, 4 = very high or positive).
[97] Rayens and Hahn, n 5, 312.
[98] See further ibid.
[99] Ibid.
[100] Ibid, 312–13.
[101] Aichholzer, n 4, 267.

2. Round 1 Results

The results from Round 1 are included in Table 2 below. The table provides: the number and per cent of experts who were generally positive about the scenario; the inter-quartile range of the responses; and a summary of respondent comments. Both original and confidence-adjusted results are provided

Table 2: Round 1 results—positive duty scenario

<table>
<tr><th>Scenario</th><th colspan="3">Desirable</th><th colspan="3">Feasible</th><th colspan="3">Important</th><th colspan="3">Confident</th></tr>
<tr><td></td><td>%</td><td>n</td><td>IQD</td><td>%</td><td>n</td><td>IQD</td><td>%</td><td>n</td><td>IQD</td><td>%</td><td>n</td><td>IQD</td></tr>
<tr><td>Employers have a positive duty to achieve employment equality, including for older workers (n = 12)</td><td>84</td><td>10</td><td>1</td><td>84</td><td>10</td><td>1</td><td>75</td><td>9</td><td>1.25</td><td>92</td><td>11</td><td>1</td></tr>
<tr><td>Confidence adjusted (n = 11)</td><td>82</td><td>9</td><td>1</td><td>82</td><td>9</td><td>1</td><td>73</td><td>8</td><td>1.5</td><td></td><td></td><td></td></tr>
<tr><td colspan="13">Summary of comments:
This duty could be modelled on the public sector equality duty.
Positive discrimination should be a last resort, but may be useful in some circumstances.
The question is unclear. It is necessary to define employment equality. Does this mean a statutory duty?
The duty will require enforcement to be effective. Unless it is directed to tackling a specific issue it is likely to be pointless.
The government is unlikely to adopt this given it will increase the burden on business.
It is easier to argue that measures should be age-neutral.
This is already in place under the current legislation.</td></tr>
</table>

While a significant majority regarded the scenario as desirable and feasible, the IQD for both original and confidence-adjusted results indicated a degree of disagreement over whether the scenario was important. The comments also demonstrated significant confusion regarding the scenario itself, what it might entail in practice, how it would be enforced, and whether it was already in place under the Act. Given this confusion and concern, it was surprising that the vast majority of respondents regarded the scenario as feasible.

3. Round 2 Results

The scenario was redrafted for Round 2 to address the confusion evident in Round 1. Respondents were again provided with a summary of the Round 1 comments in the survey itself, and were invited to reconsider the scenario with an additional clarification:

> Amended Scenario 7: A statutory duty is imposed on all employers (public and private) to achieve employment equality.
> The content of the duty might include:
>
> — Conducting periodical reviews (eg once every three years) of employment practices to determine whether certain groups are experiencing fair participation in employment;
> — If certain groups are not experiencing fair participation in employment, drawing up and implementing an 'employment equity plan' in consultation with interest groups to address barriers to participation and make reasonable adjustments to secure fair participation; and
> — Disclosing the results of periodical reviews and equity plans in company reports, to employees and to employee representatives.

The results from Round 2 are included in Table 3.

Table 3: Round 2 results—amended positive duty scenario

Scenario	Desirable			Feasible			Important			Confident		
	%	n	IQD	%	n	IQD	%	n	IQD	%	n	IQD
A statutory duty is imposed on all employers (public and private) to achieve employment equality.	87.5	7	1	37.5	3	1.25	75	6	1.25	100	8	.25
Summary of comments: Public authorities already need to give consideration to this because of the statutory public sector equality duty. Existing provisions affecting the private sector (including those that allow but do not require positive action) are unlikely to be strengthened, particularly under the current government.												

Having clarified the scenario, the results demonstrated increased disagreement between the respondents. The majority of respondents no longer regarded the scenario as feasible, though this generated significant divergence of opinion.

The respondents were also divided on whether the scenario was important. The comments indicate that respondents doubted the potential to achieve this reform under the current government, particularly in the context of a deregulatory governmental agenda.

F. Analysis

1. Evaluation of the Positive Duty

The results of the Delphi survey indicate that the introduction of a positive duty on employers to achieve employment equality still has theoretical merit in the UK context. A vast majority of Round 2 respondents (87.5 per cent) thought such a duty would be desirable. However, the respondents were divided on whether this change was important. This may indicate that a positive duty is not seen as a priority for governmental reform or, alternatively, that other reforms should take precedence.[102]

Respondents also disagreed about whether the introduction of a positive duty was feasible, particularly given government austerity measures and the 'red tape challenge'. The Coalition Government has 'set a clear aim' to reduce 'the overall burden of regulation'[103] and eliminate 'unnecessary burdens on business'.[104] The government's 'default presumption [is] that burdensome regulations' must go, and Ministers must proactively make a case for retaining 'burdensome' rules.[105] The government has a 'vision' of a labour market 'with minimal intervention by the Government'.[106] In this context, the respondents' concern about feasibility is wholly reasonable: it is unlikely that new regulations will be imposed on business in this climate.[107]

The positive duty generated significantly different responses in the two rounds. Following its rewording and clarification, the scenario received a markedly less

[102] Reforms that achieved consensus regarding their importance in the survey included workplaces adopting an age management approach; making easily accessible information and guidance available to employers; effective leadership; and the extension of the right to request flexible working arrangements. These reforms will be discussed in a later publication.

[103] Cabinet Office, 'About Red Tape Challenge' (Red Tape Challenge, no date) www.redtapechallenge.cabinetoffice.gov.uk/about/.

[104] Department for Business, Innovation and Skills, *Flexible, Effective, Fair: Promoting Economic Growth through a Strong and Efficient Labour Market* (URN 11/1308, London, Department for Business, Innovation and Skills, October 2011) 7.

[105] Cabinet Office, n 103.

[106] Department for Business, Innovation and Skills, n 104, 4.

[107] That said, the right to request flexible working was extended to all UK employees in 2014, extending regulation on business. However, the reforms also removed the statutory procedure for considering such requests. Therefore, while the reforms extended the burden on business, it was simultaneously 'cutting red tape'.

positive reception. The surprisingly positive response in Round 1 may therefore be attributable to a lack of clarity or inadequate explanation of the scenario, or to conflicting interpretations of the scenario. Confusion occurred despite the survey being extensively pre-tested and piloted. This reflects a fundamental challenge of the Delphi method: while the literature suggests limiting scenarios to 20 words, and framing scenarios broadly to allow for discussion, this may lead to misunderstanding or confusion, both between the researcher and the respondents and between different respondents. This will affect the veracity of respondents' assessments and reduce the validity of the exercise. However, generating prescriptive future scenarios, or providing detail about how a scenario might be implemented, defeats the purpose of the Delphi discussion. This remains a fundamental challenge of the Delphi method.

2. Utility of the Delphi Method at Achieving Consensus

Substantial disagreement remained at the end of Round 2 for this scenario. Ideally, a third survey would have been conducted to delve further into the lack of consensus. However, the motivation and commitment of participants appeared to decline during the second round of the Delphi,[108] making a third round impracticable. This is not an uncommon experience with Delphi surveys: respondents are busy and have other priorities. It is difficult to encourage respondents to participate in repeated rounds of a survey, particularly when they have already completed an in-person expert interview. While a number of strategies from the literature were adopted to encourage respondents to participate in this study (as discussed above), the Delphi method remains a very demanding experience for participants. Where a study involves senior officials or individuals in demanding roles, the Delphi method is likely to experience significant practical limitations, and will be frustrating and time-consuming to implement.

Despite these practical limitations, the Delphi method appears to be a very effective tool for achieving consensus. Given the positive duty scenario was re-worded and clarified between Rounds 1 and 2 of the survey, it is impossible to assess the utility of the Delphi method at achieving consensus on this particular question. However, the effectiveness of the method is evident from other scenarios in the survey. Across the whole survey, three of the eight scenarios achieved consensus in Round 1, a further three scenarios achieved consensus in Round 2, and two scenarios (including the positive duty) did not achieve consensus over the two rounds. On the face of it, the Delphi process was highly successful at achieving consensus.

It is possible that agreement was only reached because of a survival effect: two representatives of employer associations failed to participate in Round 2,

[108] This is visible in the limited written comments submitted in the survey and the declining participation rate.

potentially skewing the results. However, closer analysis of respondent behaviour over the two rounds shows that the survivor effect does not account for the consensus achieved. Table 4 below presents further analysis of the three scenarios where agreement was reached in Round 2 of the survey. A significant proportion of respondents changed their responses between Rounds 1 and 2, implying that the survey feedback may have moderated conflicting perspectives. The Delphi therefore appears to have resolved or reduced the respondents' disagreement across these three scenarios, supporting its efficacy as a consensus-building exercise.

Table 4: Change in responses between Round 1 and Round 2 where consensus was achieved

Question	Number of changed responses	Average change (absolute values)	% change
Work ability n = 8	5	1.2	62.5
Flexible working n = 8	3	1.3	37.5
Consultation n = 8	4	1	50

G. Using the Delphi Method in Labour Law Research

This study demonstrates the significant practical challenges in using the Delphi method to advance labour law research: the process can be time-consuming and demanding; maintaining response rates and participant enthusiasm is a constant challenge; scenarios may be misinterpreted or lead to confusion; and administering an online survey requires a level of technical expertise. That said, the method remains an excellent tool for exploring solutions in policy areas with high levels of uncertainty and divided opinion. Therefore, it is particularly well suited for developing long-term solutions and hypothetical scenarios for the advancement of labour law. As labour law continues to be a contentious area of government policy, the Delphi method provides new opportunities to constructively consider and generate consensus around policy options. While positive reform may be difficult in the context of a deregulatory governmental agenda, the Delphi method could also be a key means of assessing the impact of deregulation and austerity measures in employment.

While the Delphi method has significant potential to develop labour law, it is likely to raise additional challenges when used with labour *lawyers* as respondents. Lawyers are 'professional pessimists', expected to consider and plan for worst-case scenarios.[109] In creating something new, lawyers become 'mired in contemplating and planning for every possible mishap that might occur'.[110] While pessimism is helpful for the legal profession, it limits the potential for broad, unburdened thinking about future scenarios. Instead, lawyers consider the limitations and potential hazards of scenarios, and fail to distinguish the theoretical merit of an idea from its practical implementation. Policymakers or scientists may therefore be more comfortable participating in a Delphi study than lawyers.

The Delphi method may, therefore, need to be adapted to be used in labour law research. In the current study, respondents were reluctant to evaluate the *idea* of the positive duty without details of how it would be implemented, enforced and defined. This raises two options for researchers: first, this detail could be provided in the scenarios, creating a 'straw man' model for respondents to critique. However, this may lead to respondents becoming trapped in detail and neglecting to evaluate the broader merits of the scenario or idea. Second, respondents could be provided with additional background material regarding the nature and objectives of the Delphi process to contextualise their responses. While this material was already provided in this survey, it may be necessary to particularly emphasise that the scenarios are posited to generate argument and, rather than being fixed in stone, are merely a starting point for the development of solutions. It is doubtful whether this clarification would have affected the respondents' behaviour or responses in this survey.

H. Conclusion

This paper demonstrates the significant potential of the Delphi method for developing consultative and collaborative solutions to long-term labour law issues. As a result, the Delphi process is a worthy adjunct to traditional legal doctrinal methods. At the same time, the Delphi method poses a number of practical challenges in its implementation, particularly when drawing on lawyers as respondents. It may be that, over time, labour lawyers will become more accustomed to the demands of the Delphi method, just as they are with quantitative surveys. For this to occur, there will need to be a critical mass of labour law Delphi studies, which is likely to take some time. That said, given the significant potential of the Delphi method in contentious policy areas, this would be a very beneficial development.

[109] C O'Grady, 'Cognitive Optimism and Professional Pessimism in the Large-Firm Practice of Law: The Optimistic Associate' (2006) 30 *Law and Psychology Review* 23, 23; see also MEP Seligman, PR Verkuil, and TH Kang, 'Why Lawyers are Unhappy' (2005) 10 *Deakin Law Review* 49, 56.

[110] O'Grady, ibid, 24.

Appendix: Definition of Terms

For this survey, 'important', 'desirable', 'feasible', and 'confident' were defined as follows:[111]

Desirability

— Very desirable: will have a positive effect and little or no negative effect; extremely beneficial.
— Desirable: will have a positive effect and little or no negative effect; beneficial.
— Undesirable: will have a negative effect; harmful.
— Very undesirable: will have a major negative impact; extremely harmful.

Feasibility (Practicality)

— Definitely feasible: no hindrance to implementation; no research and development required; no political roadblocks; acceptable to the public and all other stakeholders.
— Possibly feasible: some indication this is implementable; some research and development still required; further consideration or preparation to be given to political or public reaction.
— Possibly unfeasible: some indication this is unworkable; significant unanswered questions.
— Definitely unfeasible: all indications are negative; unworkable; cannot be implemented.

Importance (Priority/Relevance)

— Very important: a most relevant point; first-order priority; has direct bearing on major issues; must be resolved, dealt with, or treated.
— Important: is relevant to the issue; second-order priority; significant impact but not until other items are treated; does not have to be fully resolved.
— Slightly important: insignificantly relevant; third-order priority; has little importance; not a determining factor to major issues.
— Unimportant: no priority; no relevance; no measurable effect; should be dropped as an item to consider.

[111] These definitions are adapted from Ziglio, n 8, 32–33, and Turoff, n 9, 91–92.

Confidence in Your Assessment of this Scenario

— High confidence: low risk of being wrong.
— Moderate confidence: some risk of being wrong.
— Low confidence: substantial risk of being wrong.
— No confidence: great risk of being wrong.

11

Labour Legislation and Evidence-Based Public Policy: A Case Study

ABI ADAMS AND JEREMIAS PRASSL*

The statistics provide the only way of finding out what is going on in our economy.[1]

Evidence-based policy-making has become a ubiquitous buzzword in UK governmental circles over the past 15 years, firmly embedded in the development and execution of policy across Whitehall's departments,[2] and unbroken by the formation of the country's first Coalition Government since World War II in May 2010.[3] In principle, this is to be welcomed: empirical evidence can improve the policy process in design, implementation, evaluation and feedback. At the same time, however, this central, multi-faceted role of empirical evidence suggests significant potential for negative impact if the underlying empirical methodology is itself flawed.

This is particularly true in the area of labour market policy reforms in the wake of the financial crisis, where difficult trade-offs between the competing interests of workers, employers and the state have to be held in careful balance, lest unintended adverse consequences be brought about.[4] The Coalition's plan to 'review employment and workplace laws, for employers and employees, to ensure they maximise flexibility for both parties while protecting fairness and providing the competitive

* Junior Research Fellow in Economics, Merton College, Oxford and Associate Professor in Law and Official Fellow, Magdalen College, Oxford. The materials in this contribution draw on a broader research project with Mark Freedland on the nature and regulation of zero hours contracts ('ZHCs'), and we are grateful to Alan Bogg, Hugh Collins, Anne Davies and the participants at the Cambridge Seminar on Empirical Labour Law in April 2014 for helpful criticism and comments. All responsibility for errors in the present piece remains with us alone.

[1] Alison McGovern MP, *Hansard* HC Deb 16 Oct 2013, col 754.

[2] See, eg BIS, *Guide to BIS 2012–13* (London, 2012) slide 6 (operational plan).

[3] See, eg the examples cited in J Rutter, *Evidence and Evaluation in Policy Making* (Institute for Government, London 2012) and the oft-cited illustration of the Prime Minister's behavioural economics team, known as the 'Nudge unit': see www.gov.uk/government/organisations/behavioural-insights-team (last accessed 24 July 2014).

[4] For an early assessment in the UK context, see M Freedland, N Countouris and J Prassl, 'Royaume-Uni' in M Escande-Varniol, S Laulom and E Mazuyer (eds), *Quel Droit Social Dans une Europe en Crise?* (Larcier 2012).

environment required for enterprise to thrive'[5] therefore raised important questions surrounding the government's reliance on empirical evidence in regulating changing labour markets.

The present chapter explores the role of empirical (and to a lesser extent, legal) evidence in recent governmental labour market policy and legislation.[6] In order to do so, we present a case study of the evidence used in the government's recent consultation document in preparation for the potential regulation of zero hours contracts (ZHCs). These work arrangements, which in essence provide no guarantee of work for employees, and do not oblige the latter to accept any assignments when offered, have become increasingly prevalent in public and political debates over the past three years,[7] with calls mounting from several directions for the government to take action against growing abuse.[8]

Following a series of House of Commons debates, research reports, and an 'informal information gathering exercise',[9] the Department for Business, Innovation and Skills (BIS) launched an official consultation on 'Zero hours employment contracts' in December 2013.[10] The Government's stated aim in this consultation was to seek 'to maximise the opportunities of zero hours contracts while minimising abuse and setting core standards that protect individuals'.[11] In encouraging individuals to engage in the consultation, Secretary of State Vince Cable MP suggested that the 'consultation document sets out the issues we have identified so far, seeks further evidence and invites views on a range of potential actions Government and employers can take'.[12]

With respect, however, this statement was deeply misleading: the issues in question were identified using inaccurate empirical evidence and the consultation's response form was designed to prevent a further exploration of alternative problems relating to the use of zero hours contracts. As the following discussion will demonstrate, the empirical evidence set out in the ZHC consultation is severely flawed in several aspects, painting an inaccurate picture on at least three levels: the legal position of workers on zero hours arrangements, the quantitative prevalence of such contracts, and the qualitative experience of those engaged as zero hours workers. On each level, empirical evidence was instrumental in producing

[5] HM Government, *The Coalition: Our Programme for Government* (Cabinet Office, London 2010) 10. See also, *Coalition Agreement for Stability and Reform: May 2010* (Cabinet Office, London 2010).

[6] This is, of course, not the only relevant factor: see notably the methodological discussion in P Davies and M Freedland, *Labour Legislation and Public Policy: A Contemporary History* (Clarendon Press, Oxford 1993).

[7] See, eg the stories collated at www.theguardian.com/uk-news/zero-hours-contracts (last accessed 25 July 2014).

[8] B Farhat, *Zero Tolerance Needed on Abuse of Zero Hour Contracts* (Press Release, TUC, London, 28 October 2013).

[9] See, for the latest version, D Pyper and F McGuinness, *Zero-Hours Contracts* (HC Library Standard Note, SN/BT/6553).

[10] BIS, *Consultation: Zero Hours Employment Contracts* (London, December 2013) (Consultation).

[11] Consultation, 4.

[12] Ibid.

an undeservedly benign impression concerning the operation of zero hours contracts in the UK labour market. In this sense, the consultation paper provides us with a model case study to explore some of the dangers and difficulties that can arise when using empirical evidence to inform public policy-making.

In order to develop this argument, the chapter is structured as follows: a first section outlines the consultation and the notion of zero hours contract work at its core. The remainder of the chapter than turns to a detailed criticism of the consultation's legal and empirical evidence. Section two briefly probes the legal claims made, to demonstrate that they are surprisingly narrow and simplistic. Section three then turns to the main focus of the consultation, viz empirical evidence which suggests that ZHCs are not a particularly widespread phenomenon in the UK economy, and that most workers in such arrangements are in fact content with their zero hours set-up. Upon closer scrutiny, however, neither of these claims can be sustained: given procedural flaws in the statistical sources, the numbers of ZHC workers are significantly understated, and the qualitative picture drawn of those recorded is furthermore far too rosy. Section four then links this failure of the empirical evidence to the consultation's flawed approach to the regulation of zero hours contracts, and concludes with potential lessons for future government consultations where empirical evidence is designed to play a crucial role in shaping policy recommendations.

Before turning to that discussion, three important caveats remain to be made. First, to note that the problems with empirical evidence identified in the zero hours consultation context are by no means isolated, and that our cautionary statements concerning the use and quality of empirical evidence translate across into a range of recent labour market policy consultations.[13] It should be recalled, second, that consultation documents represent but one step in a long pre-legislative process, and that individual aspects of the document discussed might subsequently change—indeed, the Office for National Statistics' approach to the measurement and qualification of zero hours work is in the process of undergoing a significant reorientation as a consequence of recent sustained critique of its traditional approach, which directly informed the consultation document under scrutiny.[14] It is nonetheless interesting to take a snap-shot of the consultation as such—not only to provide a clear case study of perhaps one of the most egregious (mis-) uses of empirical evidence in recent times, but also because legislative proposals laid before the House of Commons in the early summer of 2014 appear to confirm that key problems have been ignored.[15]

[13] See, eg BIS, 'Resolving Workplace Disputes: Government Response to Consultation' (November 2011); B Hepple, 'Back to the Future: Employment Law under the Coalition Government' (2013) 42 *Industrial Law Journal* 203.

[14] ONS, *Analysis of Employee Contracts that do no Guarantee a Minimum Number of Hours* (London, 30 April 2014).

[15] HM Government, *Queen's Speech 2014* (London, June 2014). See also Prime Minister's Office, *The Queen's Speech 2014—Lobby Briefing* (London, June 2014) 18.

The third caveat, finally, concerns the purpose of this chapter, and its place in the larger debate surrounding the regulation of zero hours work. Subsequent discussion will be focussed on the use of legal and empirical evidence in the government's official consultation launched in December 2013. As we have argued elsewhere with our colleague Mark Freedland, the overall project of 'regulating zero hours contracts' is a deeply questionable exercise in legitimating precarious work under the guise of addressing some of the worst problems associated with zero hours contracting.[16] Given limitations of space and scope, however, the present chapter does not engage with these broader questions as to regulatory strategy or detailed legal analysis.

A. The Zero Hours Employment Contracts Consultation 2013

Zero hours contracts are not a new phenomenon. Linguistically speaking, the widespread use of the term itself is a comparatively recent development: as an analysis of online search patterns reveals, the ZHC label has only been the subject of interest since late 2012.[17] Even the very notion of this neologism is however highly problematic—as subsequent sections will show, neither the 'zero hours' nor the contractual element of the label accurately reflect the reality of the underlying precarious work arrangement.

The fragmentation of work arrangements across multiple employers has been an ongoing concern for labour lawyers for several decades;[18] albeit under different terms, with such work historically characterised under the labels of 'casual' or 'atypical' work.[19] There have also been numerous attempts at legal regulation in this field: New Labour's White Paper on *Fairness at Work* in 1998, for example, included extensive discussion as to how to respond to employers' abusive practices of paying zero hours workers only for time actually worked on-site, thus shifting the risk of low turnover periods directly onto their staff.[20]

Thereafter, however, it took nearly 15 years for the problems surrounding zero hours work to resurge in public consciousness following wide-ranging austerity measures in the wake of the financial crisis. Extensive media coverage of the

[16] A Adams, M Freedland and J Prassl, 'The "Zero-Hours Contract": Regulating Casual Work, or Legitimating Precarity?' (SSRN Working Paper, at ssrn.com/abstract=2507693).

[17] See the Google Trends search at goo.gl/zXCxTk (last accessed 21 March 2014).

[18] J Prassl, 'The Notion of the Employer' (2013) *LQR* 380, 388ff.

[19] D McCann, *Regulating Flexible Work* (Oxford, Oxford University Press, 2008); L Dickens, 'Exploring the Atypical: Zero Hours Contracts' (1997) 26 *Industrial Law Journal* 262, 263.

[20] DTI, *Fairness at Work* (Cm 3968, London May 1998) 3.14ff.

problems facing zero hours contract workers[21] paved the way for an opposition debate day in Parliament.[22] This, in turn, led to the announcement of a consultation on 19 December 2013,[23] in preparation for legislation within the scope of the Government's labour market strategy.[24]

The main purpose of the consultation was to elicit responses to a series of questions ranging from the general use of ZHCs to more specific issues for employees and employers.[25] The consultation document was accompanied by an online form, to be completed by all respondents within three months; the relevant government department received over 30,000 responses over that period.[26] In terms of its procedural aspects, the consultation was therefore not as obviously flawed as other recent projects. The most (in-) famous example in that regard was the government's decision in 2012 to introduce a new employment status of 'employee shareholders'.[27] There, a BIS press release in October 2012 had already set out the contours of the new status when the government turned to implementing the new status at breakneck speed,[28] with the duration of public consultation reduced to a mere three weeks instead of the usual period of three months.[29]

Matters are, however, considerably more problematic as regards the consultation's substance. Section three of the consultation proceeds to set out the empirical evidence (to be evaluated in this chapter) that is used to identify and frame the issues for consultation. On the basis of this evidence, two particular areas of reform are identified: exclusivity clauses (which ban zero hours contract workers from entering into similar arrangements with another employer) and a broader category of 'transparency' issues.[30]

B. What is a Zero Hours Contract? The Legal Evidence

The consultation document opens with suggested answers to a series of questions surrounding the definition of zero hours contracts. Even though it notes

[21] See, eg several media outlets' sustained campaigns on point. A Stratton, 'Do Zero Hours Contracts Create Real Jobs?' (Newsnight, BBC News, 14 August 2012) available at www.bbc.co.uk/news/uk-19263787 (last accessed 24 July 2014).

[22] *Hansard* HC Deb 16 Oct 2013, col 744ff.

[23] See www.gov.uk/government/consultations/zero-hours-employment-contracts as updated (last accessed 25 July 2014).

[24] For a fuller overview of the legislative process, see www.parliament.uk/about/how/laws/new-laws/ (last accessed 24 July 2014).

[25] Consultation, section 5.

[26] BIS, Press Release, 'Zero Hours Contracts Consultation Closes With Over 30,000 Responses' (London 15 March 2014).

[27] See J Prassl, 'Employee-Shareholder "Status": Dismantling the Contract of Employment' (2013) 42 *Industrial Law Journal* 307, 311.

[28] BIS Press Release, http://news.bis.gov.uk/Press-Releases/No-capital-gains-tax-on-employee-share-ownership-for-new-employee-owners-68152.aspx (last accessed 1 August 2013).

[29] BIS, 'Consultation on Implementing Employee Owner Status' (London, October 2012).

[30] Consultation, section 4.

that 'There is no legal definition of a zero hours contract in domestic law', the consultation goes on to define the concept as 'an employment contract in which the employer does not guarantee the individual any work, and the individual is not obliged to accept any work offered'.[31]

This is further illustrated by means of a specific 'example of a clause in a zero hours contract which does not guarantee a fixed number of hours work per week': 'The Company is under no obligation to provide work to you at any time and you are under no obligation to accept any work offered by the Company at any time'.[32]

Discussion then turns to an analysis of the legal position of those working under zero hours arrangements, beginning with the assertion that 'Such contracts are legal under domestic law. If they are freely entered into, a zero hours contract is a legitimate form of contract between individual and employer'.[33] On the wording of the sample clause, however, this analysis is highly questionable.[34]

It is, first, difficult to see how on the basis of that clause alone, the arrangement could constitute a valid (global) contract at all, absent consideration and an intention to create permanent legal relations.[35] On the basis of individual arrangements, the circumstances on the ground, or indeed the contractual wording of a zero hours arrangement, specific facts might of course differ from those set out in the official guidance. The consultation document thus notes that 'An erroneous view is that individuals who work under zero hours contracts have no protection under domestic employment law, or that they cannot be an employee'.[36] Indeed, it then goes on to suggest that 'It is likely that the majority of individuals on zero hours contracts are either employees or workers'.[37]

Its is, however, highly unlikely that every arrangement along the lines set out by the government could be characterised as a contract of service, or even one of the newer subsidiary categories such as the worker concept. A detailed legal analysis of the position of zero hours contract workers is beyond the scope of the present discussion; suffice it to say, however, that the requirement of mutuality of obligation will frequently deny the existence of a contract of service,[38] or even a workers'

[31] Consultation, 11–12.

[32] Ibid.

[33] Consultation, 13.

[34] With the exception of the legality point: in a strict technical sense, the arrangements will of course be legal. In the vast majority of ZHC arrangements, doctrines such as public policy constraints and illegality will not be applicable in the absence of the commission of (another) legal wrong. See E Peel, *Treitel's Law of Contract*, 13th edn (London, Sweet & Maxwell, 2011) 11-011ff; 11-032ff.

[35] See G Treitel, 'The Agreement' and 'Consideration' in H Beale (ed), *Chitty on Contracts* 31st edn (London, Sweet & Maxwell, 2012) chs 2 and 3, respectively.

[36] Consultation, 14.

[37] Consultation, 15.

[38] See *Nethermere (St Neots) Ltd v Gardiner* [1984] ICR 612 (CA)632F–G, where mutuality of obligation was described as the 'sine qua non … of the existence of a contract of service … there must be mutual obligations on the employer to provide work for the employee and on the employee to perform work for the employer. If such mutuality is not present, then either there is no contract at all or whatever contract there is must be a contract for services or something else'.

contract.[39] In leading cases such as *O'Kelly v Trusthouse Forte*[40] and *Carmichael v National Power*,[41] individuals working as casual wine waiters and tour guides under arrangements akin to what is labelled as a zero hours contract today were held to fall outside the scope of collective representation protection and the right to particulars of employment, respectively. The law has developed somewhat since then, and it has proved possible on occasion to find that the parties had in fact undertaken mutual obligations on the facts of individual cases, as the decision in *Haggerty v St Ives* illustrates.[42] In the vast majority of ZHC scenarios, and particularly in those as stark as described in the government's model clause, mutuality of obligation will nonetheless continue to be the 'rock on which [the claimant's case] founders'.[43]

In the consultation document, finally, much is made of the 'misconceptions that an individual working under a zero hours contract can never be an employee'. This is said to be

> incorrect [as there is] case law from the Employment Appeal Tribunal (EAT) which considered the employment status of nurses who worked rostered hours under a 'zero hours contract agreement' providing critical care services [holding] that the nurses were employed under global contracts of employment.[44]

The referenced decision of *Pulse Healthcare*,[45] however, is no more than an ordinary application of the 'sham contracts' doctrine developed by the Supreme Court in *Autoclenz v Belcher*:[46] the written 'zero hours' clause in the nurses' contracts did not reflect the true agreement between the parties, who were highly-trained providers of specialist care services during fixed hours over long periods. The vast majority of truly precarious workers will therefore not be able to rely on that line of cases to bring their work arrangements within the scope of employment protective legislation.

As regards the legal evidence presented in the consultation document, several warning flags have therefore already been registered. Whilst it is of course true that some zero hours contract workers might be able to come within the scope of employment law,[47] this will not be the case for the majority of (truly) precarious zero hours contract workers, whose legal position will often be considerably less clear-cut than suggested by the government's evidence.

[39] As per *Byrne Bros (Formwork) Ltd v Bard and others* [2002] ICR 667. Though *cf* now *Clyde & Co LLP v Bates van Winkelhof* [2014] UKSC 32.

[40] *O'Kelly v Trusthouse Forte plc* [1984] QB 90 (CA).

[41] *Carmichael v National Power plc* [1999] UKHL 47, [1999] ICR 1226.

[42] *St Ives Plymouth Ltd v Haggerty* [2008] WL 2148113 (EAT).

[43] *Carmichael* (n 41) 1229.

[44] Consultation, 25 (Annex 2: Further Information on Employment Statuses).

[45] *Pulse Healthcare Ltd v Carewatch Care Services Ltd* [2012] UKEAT 0123_12_0608.

[46] *Autoclenz Ltd v Belcher* [2011] UKSC 41, [2011] 4 All ER 745; see A Bogg, 'Sham Self-Employment in the Supreme Court' (2012) 41 *Industrial Law Journal* 328.

[47] For a detailed analysis of potential avenues, see Adams, Freedland and Prassl, n 16.

C. The Prevalence of Zero Hours Contracts: Empirical Evidence

Empirical evidence on the use of zero hours contracts sits at the heart of the consultation document. Crucially for present purposes, the consultation asserts that 'From this [evidence] the Government has identified key advantages and concerns over the current use of zero hours contracts'.[48] Thus, the entire exercise has been heavily influenced by whatever validity this empirical evidence has.

When taken at face value, the empirical evidence presented does not suggest significant cause for concern. Statistics concerning the prevalence and characteristics of work under a zero hours contract are instead suggestive of a relatively benign labour market phenomenon; the prevalence of zero hours contracts appears relatively low,[49] with workers employed across a range of industries[50] and the majority content with the number of hours worked in an average week.[51] These statistics are primarily drawn from the Labour Force Survey (LFS), and supplemented with some additional evidence from the CIPD and the Workforce Employment Relations Survey.

Attention should first be drawn to estimates of the number of individuals on zero hours contracts in the UK. In the final quarter of 2012, responses to the Labour Force Survey suggested that a negligible percentage of the workforce, a mere 0.8 per cent, held a zero hours contract.[52] Indeed, the historical evidence presented in the document suggests that the percentage of workers on a zero hours contract has not exceeded 0.9 per cent of total employment since the early 2000s.[53] Although some qualification of this evidence is given, with the CIPD estimate of 1 million workers on a zero hours contract cited,[54] a difference in 'survey methodologies' is alluded to as the reason for discrepancies in the available evidence and little guidance is given as to how one should interpret the LFS evidence in the light of this large impact of survey design.[55]

1. LFS Survey Methodology

Despite some cautionary words concerning the LFS's survey methodology, empirical evidence drawn from this source forms the backbone of the empirical case that

[48] Consultation, 9.
[49] Ibid.
[50] Consultation, 10.
[51] Consultation, 12.
[52] ONS, 'Zero Hours Contract Levels and percent 2000–12' (*ad hoc* analysis, 31 July 2013).
[53] Consultation, 9.
[54] Ibid.
[55] Ibid.

is made in the consultation document.[56] The validity of the methodology used by the LFS thus underpins the quality of the majority of the statistics used to frame the zero hours contract debate. The LFS is the largest regular social survey of private households in the UK that is administered by the Office for National Statistics (ONS). Although the LFS is regarded as a high quality source of information on many labour market issues, the difficulties it faces in capturing certain forms of atypical work (such as zero hours contract work) have been noted.[57]

The LFS currently puts a question on zero hours contracts to respondents 'in employment' during the reference week in the second and fourth calendar quarters, that is during April to June and October to December.[58,59] Responses to the following question are used to identify employed respondents that work under a zero hours contract.[60] A respondent can provide up to three responses to FLEX10, with the first option used to define her 'main' working arrangement.[61]

Table 1: LFS survey question on zero hours contract work

Some people have special working hours arrangements that vary daily or weekly. In your (main) job is your agreed working arrangement any of the following ... *(up to 3 coded)*
a. flexitime
b. annualised hours contract
c. term-time working
d. job sharing
e. nine-day fortnight
f. 4.5 day week
g. zero hours contract
h. on call working
i. none of these
FLEX10 (Applies if in work during reference week)

[56] Eg every graph in section 3 of the consultation document uses BIS evidence from the Labour Force Survey.

[57] ONS, 'Estimating Zero Hours Contracts from the Labour Force Survey' (July 2013).

[58] ONS LFS, *User Guide*, vol 2—Questionnaire, Labour Force Survey (November 2013) 69.

[59] A respondent may be classed as being in employment even if they worked zero paid hours in the reference week if they consider themselves temporarily away from a job to which they will return, undertook unpaid work for their own business or a relative's business, or took part in a government training scheme considered as employment. See Questionnaire, n 58.

[60] This question was previously FLEX9D (ONS, n 57); Questionnaire, n 58, 69.

[61] The prevalence of, and trend in, zero hours contract work does not vary much depending on whether one considers 'main' or 'all' working arrangements (ONS, n 57, 2). This suggests that a zero hours contract is typically the main work arrangement for the majority of respondents currently identified as zero hours contract workers by the survey.

It is the responses to this question that yield the commonly discussed figures for ZHCs—in spite of several key limitations in identifying respondents who work under a zero hours contract. We discuss the three most salient methodological issues in the following paragraphs.

a. The 'In Employment' Criterion

First, only respondents who are considered to be in employment are asked about the nature of their work contract. Therefore, in practice, one's employment status comes to form a necessary element of the working definition of a zero hours contract in the LFS. This is not a problem for individuals who worked a positive number of paid hours during the reference week: they can be unambiguously classed as having been in employment. However, it appears that the employment criterion could be of issue for those who were not assigned any work during the survey reference week.

The latter group can still be classified as being in employment so long as they regard themselves as being temporarily away from a job to which they expect to return. In such cases, the Office for National Statistics argues that 'the continued existence of a contract of employment is the key determinant of their employment status'[62] and that this trumps the absence of paid work for their classification. Whether such an overarching contract of service can be found in all ZHC scenarios is however a difficult question, to be explored in the next section.

The ONS's practice is said to be in line with the internationally agreed definition of employment.[63] However, although the International Labour Organization's (ILO) definition of employment does allow for individuals to be employed yet 'not at work' under particular circumstances,[64] it is unclear whether the presence of a zero hours contract constitutes one of these circumstances. In fact, in the official resolution, individuals specifically excluded from employment are, among others, those 'on indefinite lay-off who do not have an assurance of a return to employment with the same economic unit'.

b. Definitional Ambiguity

The term 'zero hours contract' appears in the LFS survey without an accompanying formal definition (unless the survey respondent requests further clarification of the term). The problem of providing a precise definition of a zero hours contract is thus largely side-stepped by invoking the judgement of the individual; survey respondents must, in the first instance, identify with the label 'zero hours

62 ONS, n 57, 1.

63 Ibid.

64 19th International Conference of Labour Statisticians, Resolution I: Resolution concerning statistics of work, employment and underutilization, October 2013, 27(b), 6.

contract' without the term having been defined a priori. This practice is deeply problematic when individuals, or employers, apply alternative labels to zero hours working arrangements. In this instance, the concept is not necessarily defined in a consistent manner over time, nor between the LFS and the survey respondent.

In circumstances when clarification of the terms listed in FLEX10 is requested, respondents are provided with the following definition of a zero hours contract: '[A zero hours contract] is where a person is not contracted to work a set number of hours, and is only paid for the number of hours that they actually work'.[65]

Yet, in asking for definitional clarification, a respondent is likely to exclude themselves from being recorded as working under a zero hours contract, or, in fact, any of the listed categories in FLEX10, to be recorded as working under 'none of these' working arrangements. In the opinion of the LFS, in

> most cases a respondent who works any of these particular type of shift patterns will recognise the term and will require no further explanation. Where a respondent asks what is meant by the term it is unlikely they work such shift patterns and are generally coded as (8) [on call working] or (9) [none of these].[66]

The precise working definition of a zero hours contract embodied by the LFS is, therefore, deeply unclear. Definition is primarily a matter of respondent self-identification in the absence of official guidance. There is no framework embedded in the LFS to ensure that a consistent definition of a zero hours contract is applied by the survey over time, that a consistent definition holds between different survey respondents at any one time, and there are no mechanisms to ensure that the working definitions of the survey and respondent are congruent.

c. *Individual Responses*

Finally, the LFS is based upon the responses of individuals, who will frequently not have the necessary information about, or understanding of, their contractual situation to provide reliable evidence in this regard. For example, in an interview given to the Resolution Foundation, a further education lecturer in Bradford suggested that he 'had no idea [that he] had signed a zero-hours contract. When I applied for the job it was advertised as being for between three and twenty-one hours work a week'.[67]

In response to these difficulties, the ONS have begun to carry out a survey of businesses, who may be better placed to respond to questions about the contractual arrangements of their workers.[68] At the time of writing, however, results from this new approach were not yet available.

[65] *User Guide*, vol 3—Details of LFS Variables, Labour Force Survey, February 2014. www.ons.gov.uk/ons/guide-method/method-quality/specific/labour-market/labour-market-statistics/index.html.

[66] Ibid.

[67] Resolution Foundation, 'A Matter of Time—the Rise of Zero Hours Contracts' (London, Resolution Foundation, June 2013) 12.

[68] ONS Press Release, 'ONS Announces Additional Estimate of Zero-Hours Contracts' (22 August 2013).

2. The Quality of the Statistics

The identified limitations of the LFS methodology have had a significant impact on the statistical information on which recent discussions and policy proposals have been based: not only does the LFS substantially underestimate the prevalence of ZHCs; it also likely paints a biased picture of working conditions under such arrangements.

a. Underestimation

The LFS methodology has resulted in a gross underestimate of the prevalence of zero hours contracts. LFS estimates for the fourth quarter of 2012 suggested that 250,000 people were on zero hours contracts.[69] However, this figure seems incredible in the face of evidence from other sources. For example, Skills for Care estimates that 307,000 individuals were employed on zero hours contracts in the social care sector alone in May 2013.[70] Indeed, during the already-cited Parliamentary Debate in 2013,[71] the Secretary of State explicitly acknowledged the likely under-recording by the LFS.[72]

Under the instruction of Sir Andrew Dilnot, the Office for National Statistics revised its estimates of the prevalence of zero hours contracts in 2013 to reflect the evidence presented in independent estimates.[73] A check-box preventing people who do shift work from being asked about zero hours contracts has furthermore been removed in the most recent numbers; these revisions have led to a substantial increase in estimates of the prevalence of zero hour contracts. In the latest set of figures, the ONS estimates that 582,935 workers were on such contracts in 2013.[74] This is a significant rise from the official estimate of 250,000 zero hours contract workers in 2012 and represents a three-fold increase in the numbers of individuals on zero hours contracts since 2008 (as estimated by the LFS).[75]

[69] Note that these numbers were revised upwards from 200,000 to 250,000 in late 2013. See, eg ONS, 'Corporate Information: Zero Hour Contract Levels and percent 2000–12' (July 2013).

[70] A Dilnot, Zero-hours employment statistics, correspondence with Chuka Umunna MP, 7 August 2013.

[71] *Hansard* HC Deb 16 Oct 2013, col 754.

[72] Sampling bias and the presence of so-called 'check-and-block' questions are likely to have further contributed to the underestimate. FLEX10 is only asked in the second and fourth quarters of the years, making it likely that groups of seasonal workers employed under zero hours contracts are not covered by the survey (ONS, n 57). Furthermore, the ONS recommends that only responses from the fourth quarter of the year be used to estimate the prevalence of zero hour contracts because of a check in the LFS questionnaire in the second quarter that prevents an individual from simultaneously identifying themselves as working shift work and working under a zero hours contact because these two methods of working were previously considered incompatible by those designing the survey (ONS, n 57). This check has been removed in the most recent survey.

[73] ONS, Statement, 'ONS Urges Caution on Zero-Hours Estimates' (March 2014).

[74] Ibid.

[75] Authors' calculation from ONS data.

However, it is important to note that the recent rise in these estimates does not necessarily imply anything about underlying trends in the labour market. The jump in zero hours contracts observed in the latest LFS may simply be a product of changes in reporting behaviour, rather than changes in the prevalence of such contracts in reality. Indeed, the ONS in removing the shift work check cautioned that: 'there is potential for a step change in the data'.[76] Figure 1 below is suggestive of this, showing the change in the number of zero hours contracts as recorded by the LFS and the number of google searches for the term 'zero hours contracts' over time. Thus, comments in the media that rely on these new statistics as evidence of a *rise* in the numbers of people employed on zero hour contracts should be discounted. Mr Umunna's claim that 'these new figures from the ONS, following my request to Sir Andrew Dilnot last summer, confirm that there has been a huge rise in the numbers of people on zero-hours contracts since 2010'[77] is, therefore, not justified.

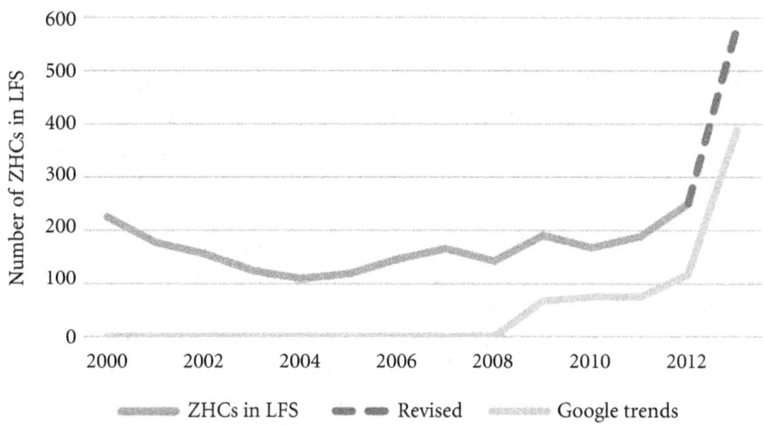

Figure 1: Estimates of zero hours contracts from the LFS and Google Trends estimate of searches for 'zero hours contracts'
Source: Authors' calculations from the LFS and Google Trends.
*See the Google Trends search at goo.gl/zXCxTk

At the time of writing, there remains great uncertainty about the actual prevalence of zero hours contracts even given the aforementioned upward revisions to the statistics. Available evidence suggests that the revised LFS estimates remain on the lower end of the likely spectrum and that zero hours contracts may not be as

[76] www.ons.gov.uk/ons/guide-method/method-quality/specific/labour-market/articles-and-reports/zero-hours-contracts.pdf (last accessed 10 March 2014).

[77] www.theguardian.com/uk-news/2014/mar/10/rise-zero-hours-contracts (last accessed 10 March 2014).

insignificant a feature of the labour market as current official statistics suggest.[78] The ONS continues to urge caution when using estimates drawn from LFS data and will publish statistics it considers to be more reliable upon the release of results from an employer survey that contains questions on the use of zero hours contracts.[79]

b. 'Not Missing at Random'

Media and Opposition attention has primarily focused on the fact that the LFS has understated the prevalence of zero hour contracts. However, statistics concerning the nature of work under zero hours contracts have also been used to define the issues for consultation. LFS statistics on the number, and variability, of hours that characterise work on a zero hours contract, and the distribution of such contracts across industries, appear in the consultation document and have helped to define the scope of the issues for consultation.[80]

The currently available data suggest that a diverse number of working arrangements are captured under the term zero hour contracts. Evidence from the LFS, Workplace Employment Relations Survey, and Chartered Institute for Personnel and Development (CIPD) surveys suggests that zero hours contracts are found in a range of industries, across all levels of the occupational ladder and are associated with varying degrees of permanency.[81] Certain themes emerging from the statistics run contrary to what one might expect. For example, Work Foundation analysis using LFS responses in the fourth quarter of 2012 found that the majority of respondents on zero hour contracts (~75 per cent) regarded the number of hours that they worked as sufficient and only 18 per cent of those on zero hour contracts were actively looking for another job, compared to 7 per cent of all employees. The CIPD found that almost half (47 per cent) of zero hour contract workers reported that they were satisfied with having no minimum contracted hours.[82] However, the CIPD presents a slightly more negative impression than the LFS with regards to worker satisfaction with their hours, finding that 38 per cent would like to work more hours. In addition, and again going against popular impressions, the LFS suggests that people in the top three occupational groups hold a significant proportion of zero hour contracts (43 per cent).[83]

For the statistics to give an accurate picture of working arrangements under a zero hours contract, the sample of individuals who self-identify as zero hours contract workers must be representative of the full population of individuals subject to such working arrangements. However, this condition is unlikely to be met.

[78] See, eg Chartered Institute for Personnel and Development, 'Zero-Hours Contracts: Myth and Reality' (November 2013).

[79] ONS Statement, 'ONS Urges Caution on Zero-Hours Estimates' (March 2014).

[80] Consultation, 10–12.

[81] Summarised in I Brinkley, 'Flexibility or Insecurity? Exploring the Rise in Zero Hours Contracts' (London, The Work Foundation, August 2013).

[82] Chartered Institute for Personnel and Development, n 79.

[83] Brinkley, n 82.

As was discussed in the previous section, it is acknowledged by the ONS that many individuals on zero hour contracts are likely either to be unaware of their contractual situation or do not identify with the term 'zero-hours'.[84] It is doubtful that the missing zero hours contract workers in the official statistics are 'missing at random'. Rather, it is plausible that those self-identifying as zero hour contract workers are predominantly those who have actively sought out such a working arrangement and/or are working for employers who have clearly set out the contractual terms that an individual is working under. If this is the case, individuals who are working under a zero hour contract arrangement as a matter of need and not want, and those working for less transparent employers, will be under-represented in the subset of respondents classified as zero hour contract workers.

It is likely that those respondents who have actively sought out a zero hours contract job are more likely to value the flexibility that such a working arrangement gives them. If so, it is plausible that these individuals are less likely actively to seek alternative employment and more likely to report high job satisfaction than those individuals who are forced to take a zero hours job out of need. However, this experience may not hold true for zero hours contract workers on average. Such themes arose in an interview with the Resolution Foundation given by a (self-identified) zero hours domestic care worker:

> I really value the flexibility of working on zero-hours because it allows me to fit other things into my life and if I don't get enough hours one week I can always make them up the next. I can see that for families with a mortgage the situation would be seriously nerve-wracking and of course I have to trust my line-manager to deliver those hours and that's far from ideal but it has worked for me so far.[85]

The current statistics, in relying on individual responses and the self-classification of respondents as zero hours workers, have therefore likely painted an unduly rosy picture of life under a zero hours contract, reflecting the 'danger … that the growth of part-time work is employer, rather than employee, led and is emerging to replace "good" full-time work with marginal part-time work'.[86]

D. The Uses and Misuses of Empirical Evidence in Labour Legislation and Public Policy-Making

Despite the many flaws thus identified in the consultation document's legal and empirical evidence, a press release issued shortly after the three-month

[84] ONS, n 80.

[85] Resolution Foundation, 'A Matter of Time—the Rise of Zero Hours Contracts' (London, Resolution Foundation, June 2013) 16.

[86] C McGlynn, 'Reclaiming a Feminist Vision: The Reconciliation of Paid Work and Family Life in European Union Law and Policy' (2001) 7 *Columbia Journal of European Law* 241, 259; citing S McRae, 'Part-Time Employment in a European Perspective' in E Drew et al (eds), *Women, Work and the Family in Europe* (Routledge, 1998) 111.

consultation period's close pronounced the exercise to have been successful, as in excess of 300,000 responses had been received.[87] Can that however truly be said to be a measure of the consultation's success?

In considering the impact of the problematic empirical evidence on the consultation's flawed approach to the regulation of zero hours contracts, it is important to keep in mind the oft-rehearsed methodological warning about uses and misuses of new techniques as tools of law reform.[88] By relying on information that overstated the legal protection of zero hours workers, underestimated the prevalence of such arrangements and mischaracterised the qualitative experience of individuals labouring under such arrangements, the consultation focused on issues far too narrow to address the core problems associated with the explosive growth of vulnerable employment in a highly fragmented labour market. In consequence, the resulting legislative proposal will do little to address the majority of problems associated with such work.

That said, at least one positive aspect can be said to flow, at least indirectly, from the consultation project. In recent policy documents, it is increasingly acknowledged that the ONS's lack of clarity is likely to have resulted in the misclassification of many atypical workers' employment arrangements. For example, the Chair of the UK Statistics Authority, Sir Andrew Dilnot, early on expressed his concern that individuals who did not recognise the term 'zero hours contract' were unlikely to correctly classify themselves in the relevant surveys.[89] In the late spring of 2014, that issue had finally begun to be addressed formally, through new statistical and survey methods and the introduction of a new label, *Contracts that do no Guarantee a Minimum Number of Hours*.[90]

In concluding, then, we suggest that three connected lessons might be learnt from our case study of the Government's 2013 consultation exercise surrounding zero hours contracts in the broader context of this volume exploring empirical labour law. First and foremost is the fact that empirical evidence matters—both positively and negatively. It can inform policy-making in design, helping to identify relevant areas and strategies for government action, implementation, exploring different approaches and ideas as to how the challenges identified might be tackled once a particular set of goals has been agreed, and evaluation and feedback once policies are in place, playing a crucial role in ensuring that any learning outcomes are fed back into future policy development and changes.

As a result, Second it is of paramount importance to ensure that the evidence supplied is accurate, both in terms of quantitative and qualitative information. It is only when options are explored on the basis of reliable empirical evidence that

[87] Press Release, n 24.

[88] As famously developed in the context of comparative evidence in O Kahn-Freund, 'On Uses and Misuses of Comparative Law' (1974) 37 *MLR* 120.

[89] A Dilnot, Zero-hours employment statistics, correspondence with Mr Umunna MP, 22 August 2013.

[90] ONS, n 14.

the full range of problems can be identified and solutions thereto proposed. One key problem with the use of empirical evidence in the ZHC consultation was the centrality of statistics drawn from the ONS' Labour Force Survey. Methodological problems with that data set therefore had a limiting impact on the entire consultation exercise. Such problems can, however, be overcome with relative ease, not least by relying on multiple sources such as, for example, expert reports.[91]

Finally, and perhaps most obviously, it is important that even in the context of evidence-based public policy-making, officials and ministers must ensure to keep an open mind, both as regards the validity of empirical information, and potential avenues to identify and address problems in the labour market. We hope that our discussion in this chapter will have contributed a small warning call in this regard: there is much to be said for empirical evidence to inform and shape labour law, as long as the relevant materials' limitations and their implications are understood and duly taken into account by all involved.

[91] A successful example of this multi-source strategy can be found in the current 'Review of the Balance of Competences'. See in particular, BIS, Department for Culture, Media and Sport, DWP, FCO et al, *Review of the Balance of Competences between the United Kingdom and the European Union: Social and Employment Policy* (London, 22 July 2014).

12

Creating a 'Virtuous Circle' Between Legal Empirical Research, Knowledge Exchange and Impact

SIMONETTA MANFREDI AND LUCY VICKERS*

A. Introduction

In this chapter, we reflect on our experience of what we have termed the 'virtuous circle' between empirical legal research, doctrinal research, leading on to knowledge exchange and impact.

By this we are referring to a process whereby we have developed our doctrinal research on an issue, from this we have identified research questions which we have tested using empirical research, and from the findings of this research we have developed knowledge exchange activities, which have helped ensure that our academic work has impact on non-academic users. This has in turn led, full circle, back to informing our doctrinal work.

We believe that by undertaking some of our research in this way, we are able to meet a number of different research agendas currently operating in UK higher education. First, we are responding to the call by the 2004 Nuffield Foundation *Law in the Real World*[1] Report which identified the need for conducting more legal empirical research in order to gain a better understanding of 'how the law works in the real world'. Secondly, by using our research to develop knowledge exchange activities we help meet the aims of many universities to diversify the range of research-related activity beyond academic research. Thirdly, the interactions that this process creates with non-academic end users help to meet the aims of ensuring that our work has impact. This not only meets the instrumental aims of universities keen to generate 'impact' as defined (and funded) through the REF

* Both authors are Professors at the Centre for Diversity Policy Research and Practice, Oxford Brookes University.

[1] H Genn, M Partington and S Wheeler, *Law in the Real World: Improving Our Understanding of How Law Works* (London, Nuffield Foundation, 2004).

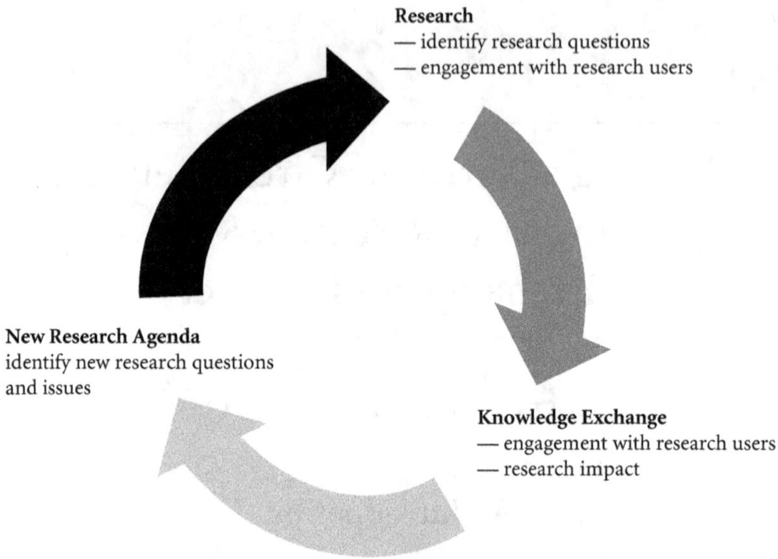

Figure 1: The 'virtuous circle' between research and knowledge exchange

process,[2] but it is of value in itself as we seek to use our research in practical as well as academic ways.

In the next sections we discuss our experience of using empirical research, borrowing methods employed by social science and business research to investigate organisational practice, in order to explore the implications of different aspects of equality legislation for the management of human resources in the workplace and to facilitate research impact. We also show how the findings from the 'impact' activities have fed back into both the doctrinal analysis and further empirical research. However, before turning to these aspects of our work we first provide some brief reflections on the epistemological and methodological considerations which have underpinned our work.

B. Epistemological and Methodological Considerations

In the context of our research, which is seeking to gain an understanding about the implications for the management of human resources of different aspects

[2] REF 2014 defines impact as 'an effect on change or benefit to the economy, society, culture, public policy or services, health, the environment or quality of life beyond academia'; the RCUK definition is 'impact is the demonstrable contribution that excellent research makes to society and the economy' cited in P Denicolo, *Achieving Impact in Research* (London, Sage, 2014).

of equality legislation, we have adopted an interpretativist perspective. This acknowledges that those involved in the implementation of equality law in the workplace, as well as those who are intended to be its beneficiaries, play a part in the construction of the reality around them which the law is seeking to regulate. It is by seeking to understand how these actors interpret and give meaning to their experiences of the law that we, as researchers, can reach a contextual understanding about the impact of equality law in the workplace. Of course, this understanding is itself mediated by the meaning making of the researcher, who is interpreting the interpretation of others. Thus reflexivity, and an appreciation of one's own socio-cultural position, is therefore important in this type of enquiry. Although it cannot be denied that the knowledge that we are generating is subjective, since it is based on the views and experiences of individuals, we would argue that it remains valid. It is only through the experience of those who are supposed to benefit from equality legislation in the workplace, and those who have to respond to the law at an organisational level, that we can access the reality of how the law interacts with organisational norms and management practices. This enables us to gain knowledge which will help to develop new understanding about equality law and advance doctrinal research.

In terms of methodology, in our work we have used qualitative research methods, such as semi-structured interviews and focus groups with participants working in a particular sector, and this method fits well with an interpretativist perspective. However, we have also used a 'mixed method' approach combining both quantitative and qualitative methods. It is arguable that these two distinctive methods should not be combined because they are associated with different epistemological approaches and more specifically that quantitative methods are predominantly linked to a positivist approach while qualitative to an interpretative approach.[3] However, equally, the use of mixed methods is gaining legitimacy within the research community since this approach, as highlighted by Bryman, is 'freeing the researcher to select whichever methods and data sources that might be reasonably used to explore a research problem in pursuit of rigorous and comprehensive findings'.[4] We have therefore chosen to undertake our research using mixed methods in order to secure a rich set of findings to inform our research questions.

As we discuss examples of our work in more detail in the following sections we will explain how we have applied these approaches to our research.

[3] A Bryman, 'Mixed Methods in Organisational Research' in DA Buchanan and A Bryman (eds), *Organisational Research Methods* (London, Sage, 2009) 517.

[4] Ibid, 518. Of course this does not mean that 'anything goes', because researchers must still be alert to the legitimacy of their knowledge claims; however a mixed method approach does release researchers from the straight-jacket of the paradigm wars of the late 20th century.

C. Investigating Age Equality and Retirement Policies through a Mixed Method Approach

Between 2008 and 2012 we undertook two consecutive projects funded by the Higher Education Funding Council for England (HEFCE) under its Leadership, Governance and Management[5] Scheme to research the implications for the management of human resources in the higher education sector of the 2006 Employment Equality (Age) Regulations[6] and of the subsequent abolition of mandatory retirement in 2011.

Both projects were undertaken in collaboration with key HE stakeholders: the Equality Challenge Unit (ECU), the Universities and Colleges Employers Association (UCEA), the Leadership Foundation for Higher Education, the University Association of Human Resources and the trade unions, UNISON and Universities and College Union (UCU). These project partners advised on the project, including advising on the design of the questionnaires used and the areas of questioning. Their involvement therefore helped us to design the project in a way which would be useful to end users, as well as to generate pertinent lines of enquiry for the research.

The research was conducted on a sample of 12 institutions, and involved a mixed method approach which encompassed both quantitative and qualitative research methods.

Prior to carrying out the research, our review of doctrinal research on age discrimination and retirement had identified a number of concerns. First, mandatory retirement is on the face of it discriminatory on grounds of age as it involves less favourable treatment and infringes individual dignity. However, some have sought to justify age discrimination and retirement on the basis that older workers have already enjoyed the benefits and advantages of youth—effectively they have had a 'fair innings' and so they should make way for younger workers. The issue of 'fair innings' is however contested[7] with questions asked as to whether it can really provide a robust justification for mandatory retirement.

A second area of academic debate surrounding retirement relates to the more pragmatic question of the 'business case' based on the benefits for employers of retaining older workers' skills and expertise. Again, the business case can be contested: it may be that the removal of retirement will cause difficulties in terms of

[5] S Manfredi, 'Developing Good Practice in Managing Age Diversity in the Higher Education Sector: An Evidence-Based Approach' (Oxford, Centre for Diversity Policy Research and Practice, 2008); E Halvorsen and S Manfredi, 'Managing Flexible Retirement and Extended Working Lives in Higher Education: An Evidence-Based Approach' (Oxford, Centre for Diversity Policy Research and Practice, 2011).

[6] SI 2006/2408.

[7] See S Fredman, 'The Age of Equality' S Fredman and S Spencer (eds), *Age as an Equality Issue: Legal and Policy Perspectives* (Oxford, Hart Publishing, 2003).

workforce planning, with suggestions that employers rely on retirement to generate turnover of staff; or removing retirement may enable valuable skills to be retained. Hence the 'business case' is not entirely clear when it comes to mandatory retirement. The business case may favour removal of retirement ages, or it may support their retention on the basis that this allows for better financial planning for businesses, as well as allowing staff to plan their careers.

A third area of debate relating to age discrimination involves the question of intersections between age discrimination and gender discrimination. The question here is whether retirement ages cause greater difficulties for women, who are more likely to have had interrupted careers. Thus, reliance on a business case or a 'fair innings' argument for retaining retirement could lead to an increase in gender inequality.

Matters such as these had been rehearsed in the academic literature and we designed our research to test out whether they reflected matters on the ground. Effectively we sought to determine whether the academic debates reflect 'law in the real world', to use the terminology of the Nuffield Foundation Report.[8] Moreover, we wanted to see whether the legal responses which had been made to these issues were 'fit for purpose' in the light of our findings about how things worked in practice. This then was the 'doctrinal research' starting point of our 'circle' and formed the background to our empirical study.

Thus, we started our empirical research with an on-line questionnaire to survey staff working in 12 higher education institutions across the country to explore their attitudes towards retirement and age discrimination. We chose this method because it would enable us to capture a wide range of views from staff in different occupational groups (eg academics, administrative staff, and manual staff) working in a sample of higher education institutions. In particular, in order to test the arguments highlighted above and identified through the doctrinal research, we designed a question to be included in the questionnaire, which was underpinned by these arguments, and we used a Likert scale to assess the strength of the respondents' views in relation to the arguments highlighted above. Table 1, below, shows how the question was designed (note however, that the version of the question which appeared in the questionnaire did not have the reference in brackets to the doctrinal arguments to which the questions were matched).

Other areas that we were able to investigate through the questionnaire included staff preferences and expectations about retirement and perceptions of age discrimination across different occupational groups working in the HE sector. One interesting dimension to studying these questions in the HE context is the range of employees within the sector. The researched group comprised a wide range of staff groups, including some lower skilled manual workers.

[8] Genn, Partington and Wheeler, n 1.

Table 1

Total responses: 6161	**Strongly agree**	**Agree**	**Neither agree nor disagree**	**Disagree**	**Strongly disagree**
It is important to have a fixed retirement age in order to enable younger employees to progress their career **('Fair innings' argument)**	4.2%	15.5%	33.9%	**36.2%**	10.2%
A fixed retirement age unfairly discriminates against older employees **(Age equality argument)**	13.6%	**45%**	26.4%	13.4%	1.6%
It is important to have a fixed retirement age in order to enable under-represented groups such as ethnic minorities and women to progress their career **(Competing claims with other equality strands argument, eg race and gender)**	1.2%	5.2%	32.8%	**43.4%**	17.4%
It is important not to have a fixed retirement age in order to enable HEIs to retain valuable expertise and specialist skills **'Business case' argument in support of no mandatory retirement age to tap into the resource of older workers**	15.5%	**46.1%**	26.3%	10.5%	1.5%
It is important to have a fixed retirement age in order to enable HEIs to manage their workforce effectively **'Business case' argument in support of a fixed retirement age for workforce planning**	1.7%	13.4%	**37.9%**	37%	9.9%

Over 6,000 respondents completed this questionnaire and such a large sample enabled us to disaggregate the data, undertake appropriate statistical testing, and obtain a more refined picture of staff perceptions of these issues by gender, different occupational groups working in the sector and different age groups. For example, other results from the survey suggested that many staff, especially male academics, wish to retire after the age of 65.

For the second stage of this project we adopted a qualitative method by undertaking focus groups with senior academics, who had responsibilities for managing other academic staff (eg head of departments/schools), managers of professional, support and manual staff. In particular we wanted to explore how these groups felt about the implications for the management of human resources of extending working lives past the normal retirement age of 65. We chose to use focus groups, because they offer the opportunity to bring together people with shared experiences of managing staff in different occupational categories, and to explore a variety of views in relation to the issues under investigation. Moreover, as highlighted by Bryman and Bell,[9] focus groups enable the researchers 'to study the way in which individuals make sense of a phenomenon and construct meanings around it' which to us was of particular interest given that we were exploring at the time a new phenomenon; namely the extension of working lives beyond the conventional retirement age of 65.

The findings from the focus groups with senior academics and managers of professional and support staff showed that institutions had a number of concerns about the implications of staff working past the age of 65 and the effect that this could have on access to jobs and career opportunities for younger people (ie they broadly seemed to support the 'fair innings' argument). These perceptions however, contrasted with the survey results for staff which indicated that overall respondents in all different age groups favoured the removal of mandatory retirement and showed very little support for the 'fair innings' argument.

In summary, one can see from the results of the research that there was a very mixed reaction to the 'fair innings' argument in practice, depending on whether the response was from the management perspective or that of a worker. The response to the 'business case' was similarly mixed.

1. Facilitating Research Impact

The research from this project was then used to develop a series of workshops and practical guidance (effectively knowledge exchange activities aimed at facilitating research impact) for senior human resource managers to help them shape their

[9] A Bryman and E Bell, *Business Research Methods* (Oxford, Oxford University Press, 2007).

institutional policies and practices in this area. Further workshops were commissioned by the Equality Forward and Equality Challenge Unit (ECU) for Scottish HEIs and FE colleges.

These workshops provided an opportunity to use the research findings to influence management responses within the sector to tackle age discrimination in the workplace as well as to manage the workforce without mandatory retirement. For example, we found that numbers of staff wanting to work beyond 65 were quite high, but that most only wanted to work for a couple of extra years. Few wanted to work into older age. This means that the scale of any anticipated problem of senior staff blocking progression of younger staff may be smaller than expected. Equally, we found that knowledge about pension entitlement was very low among all age groups, and this led some managers to decide to implement procedures to share information about pensions and retirement more widely within their institutions. Written feedback from those who attended these workshops showed how the research influenced their thinking and practice. For example, some reported that they 'used evidence from the research to tackle prejudice and stereotypes about older people, especially their performance in the workplace', or 'to think creatively about how work could be organised to extend working lives' and to consider more the 'links between equality strands'.

The findings from this research were used to develop a resource guide on managing flexible retirement and extended working lives specifically aimed at higher education institutions which were funded by the ECU. Our research findings were also utilised by lawyers in their briefings to clients in the HE sector and in the preparation of cases involving the enforcement of an employer justified retirement age in some higher education institutions. In this way, we feel that the research had direct impact on non-academic users, who welcomed the chance to discuss how they may tackle these issues, armed with the data we had discovered.

2. Completing the 'Virtuous Circle'

The completion of this 'virtuous circle' can be seen in the second phase of this project, in particular the development of a future agenda for research arising from insights from the knowledge exchange phases of the work. The workshops with HR managers in higher education had led us to conclude that many managers were intending to use stricter performance management policies to address any low level performance issues which had traditionally been ignored, with retirement being used as something of a benign performance management tool. The removal of retirement as an option had led many managers to suggest in focus groups that formal management processes would need to be introduced.

These findings were explored in the follow-up study, which indeed confirmed that managers were intending to take this step. The approach of courts to questions of 'dignity in retirement' is interesting to assess in the light of these findings, in practice suggesting increased use of performance management as a way to 'ensure' retirement. The CJEU has not allowed for 'collegiality' to justify age discrimination (*Petersen*),[10] effectively rejecting the argument that retirement can be justified as it enables managers to use it as a kinder proxy for performance management. However, the UK Supreme Court in *Seldon*[11] seemed to accept the idea that in some cases retirement may be used to avoid performance management and allow greater 'collegiality' in working life. We discuss this issue in some of our later academic work[12] and our case note on *Seldon*[13] in which we question whether the removal of retirement will in fact be beneficial to workers, as it may lead to increasingly heavy management processes being implemented in higher education and applied to all workers throughout their careers.

D. Equality in Research Careers: A Case Study Exploring the Impact of 'Reflexive Law'

Another example of work undertaken by using an empirical approach which has contributed to knowledge exchange and research impact is a project commissioned at the end of 2008 by the Equality Challenge Unit about the actual implementation of the equality guidance issued by the Funding Councils in respect of the Research Assessment Exercise (RAE) 2008 process. This research was intended to provide qualitative data to complement HEFCE's own quantitative review of the equality impact of the RAE 2008, and to assess the application of the equality duties to the process for selecting staff for inclusion in the RAE. The aim was to learn from the exercise and to produce recommendations for improving practice for the future Research Excellence Framework (REF) 2014. It was followed up by further research which we carried out between 2012 and 2013 with a sample of 32 academics at different stages of their career in four different institutions to explore to what extent they had benefitted from the equality guidance issues both for RAE 2008 and REF 2014.

Since we completed the first research project commissioned by the ECU focusing on RAE 2008,[14] we reflected back on this work with reference to the doctrinal research on 'reflexive law' which has provided us with a framework of analysis to revisit our past work and, more importantly, to inform our follow-up research in this area.

[10] Case C-341/08 *Domnica Petersen v Berufungsausschuss für Zahnärzte für den Bizirk Westfalen-Lippe* [2010] ECR I-47.

[11] *Seldon v Clarkson Wright and Jakes* [2012] UKSC 16.

[12] S Manfredi and L Vickers, 'Meeting the Challenges of Active Ageing in the Workplace: Is the Abolition of Retirement the Answer?' (2013) 4 *European Labour Law Journal* 250.

[13] L Vickers and S Manfredi, 'Age Equality and Retirement: Squaring the Circle' (2013) 42 *Industrial Law Journal* 61.

[14] S Manfredi and L Vickers, 'The Impact of the Process to Promote Equality and Diversity in the Research Assessment Exercise 2008' (London, Equality Challenge Unit, 2009).

We have considered the matter of equality within the REF 2014 process as a case study for the implementation of the Public Sector Equality Duty (PSED). This duty, found in section 149 of the Equality Act 2010, requires all public sector bodies to have due regard to the need to eliminate discrimination, advance equality of opportunity, and foster good relations between people with different protected characteristics. Our study of equality measures within the REF 2014 system can be viewed as a worked example of how the PSED works on the ground. In addition, doctrinal work by Hepple,[15] Fredman,[16] and McCrudden[17] on this issue has involved considering the concept of 'reflexive law' as a framework to analyse the PSED, and so we also considered this notion within our analysis. The PSED places responsibility for progressing equality on public bodies, employers and other actors who are in a position to bring about change.

The concept of 'reflexive law' has been presented as an alternative model of regulation to that of 'command and control', which aims to change behaviours by inducing forms of self-regulation. It is based on the idea that society is not structured in a hierarchical order with the law at the top but instead it is organised in a series of sub-systems, such as, for example, the workplace. Each of these sub-systems is autonomous, has its own language and operates according to its own logic and can respond to external stimuli by adjusting practices within its internal environment. To use the workplace as an example of an individual sub-system, when this 'receives a communication from the legal system, this filters through its own internal norms and culture'.[18] The advantage of adopting this regulatory model, at least in theory, is that it could be best placed to tackle structural and institutional inequalities by harnessing 'the energy of local actors' (and we would also add their 'know-how') 'who are best acquainted with the problems and potential solutions' as highlighted by Fredman.[19] Thus, if the former positive duties and more recently the Public Sector Equality Duty can be seen in theory as examples of 'reflexive regulation' the next question to be considered is whether this approach actually works in practice and the best way to investigate this is through empirical research.

The concept of 'reflexive law' as a framework for analysis can be applied to the research project commissioned by the ECU to investigate the impact of the process to promote equality and diversity in the RAE 2008. We argue that the HE sector is a sub-system with its own language which operates according to its own logic and that RAE/REF is a process of key importance within this sub-system. The broad aims of our research were to investigate methods adopted by HEIs to implement

[15] B Hepple, 'Enforcing Equality Law: Two Steps Forward and Two Steps Backward for Reflexive Regulation' (2009) 40 *Industrial Law Journal* 315.

[16] S Fredman, 'The Public Sector Equality Duty' (2011) 40 *Industrial Law Journal* 405.

[17] C McCrudden 'Equality Legislation and Reflexive Regulation: A Response to the Discrimination Law Review's Consultative Paper' (2007) 36 *Industrial Law Journal* 255.

[18] Hepple, n 15, 320.

[19] Fredman, n 16, 419.

the Funding Council equality guidance issues for RAE 2008; and whether this was sufficient to promote equality and more generally to comply with the requirements of the equality legislation which at that time provided for individual equality duties in the area of race, disability and gender.

The very fact that the Funding Councils had issued equality guidance for the RAE 2008 already indicated that the policymakers at sector level had responded to the external stimuli provided by the equality duties by modifying some of its practices relating to one of its key processes, namely the assessment of research outputs produced by individual academics. Prior to the introduction of the equality guidance the assessment of research outputs operated according to two major criteria which were: the high quality of research outputs and their quantity based on a norm of four outputs. In response to the equality duties HEFCE modified the 'quantity' criteria by allowing for a reduction of research outputs to take into account equality-related personal circumstances such as maternity leave; working part-time; disability and others, which might have impacted on the ability of an individual to produce four outputs. This showed that the policymakers within the sector, who were in a position to bring about change, had responded to the legislation and identified the rule about quantity of research outputs as potentially problematic and likely to indirectly discriminate against, for example, academic staff working part-time (likely to be women) or who had a period of absence due to maternity leave, etc and would find it difficult to comply with a requirement based on the norm of an academic working full-time who had not been affected by any of the equality-related circumstances mentioned above. However, the policymakers at this level also identified the need to engage other actors at the level of individual institutions and at the level of unit of assessments in order to bring about substantive change. Thus, they required individual HEIs to develop a Code of Practice to ensure the implementation of the Funding Councils equality guidance at a local level and to provide equality training to all those staff likely to be involved in the selection of academic staff for submission in the RAE. Equally they required all those involved in the assessment of the research outputs in the UoAs to apply the equality guidance and for this purpose they provided them with equality training.

Our research enabled us to investigate how far the initial response to the equality duty which resulted in the production of equality guidance for RAE 2008 by the Funding Councils had filtered through the different layers within the sub-system environment, namely individual institutions and UoAs, and had succeeded in harnessing the energy of local actors to find solutions in order to advance substantive equality within this process which is of key importance to academic careers.

1. Using Empirical Research to Assess the Effectiveness of 'Reflexive Law' as an Alternative Model of Regulation

Thus, looking at our past and current work through the lens of the 'reflexive law' model we have developed a framework of analysis, involving empirical research, which hopefully can provide a useful tool to assess to what extent equality legislation, and especially the PSED, has succeeded in achieving organisational change. It has also enabled us to initiate a 'virtuous circle' between research and knowledge exchange. We have articulated our framework of analysis into three levels which are summarised in Table 2 and explained below.

2. Level One: Formal Self-regulation/Compliance

At this level the main aim of the investigation was to assess what kind of formal self-regulation has taken place in response to the requirement of the positive duty to 'have due regard' to the need to 'eliminate discrimination', 'advance equality of opportunity' and 'foster good relations'. The focus of empirical research is likely to be on the analysis of documentation in the form of policies and other preparatory work evidencing how these have been developed and who has been involved in this process.

Applied to our study this involved undertaking desk-based research to review a sample of Codes of Practice, developed, as required by the Funding Councils, by a sample of 32 HEIs. This review started with a pilot based on RAE equality-related documentation of six institutions out of the total sample of 32 in order to identify a series of criteria, drawn from the Funding Councils guidance (more specifically RAE 03/2005 Annex G) against which to evaluate the institutional documentation and to ensure a consistent approach in the assessment process. This level of analysis showed that all the institutions in the sample had complied with the Funding Councils equality guidance and adopted a Code of Practice. However, some degree of variation emerged from different institutions especially in relation to involvement and engagement of the stakeholders. For example, in only a few cases was there clear evidence that institutions had consulted with the trade unions or other representatives of academic staff who were intended to be the beneficiaries of the Code of Practice.

Another significant difference emerged in the way the Code of Practice and its equality-related provisions were communicated to eligible academic staff to ensure that they all had an equal opportunity to disclose any equality-related personal circumstances which may have impacted on the number of research outputs that they were able to produce during the relevant period. Some institutions appeared to have been more pro-active than others in bringing the Code of Practice to the attention of their staff in establishing effective processes to facilitate disclosure of equality-related personal circumstances. Thus, this initial analysis suggested that although the duties had been formally met by self-regulation developed at sector level through the adoption of equality guidance and, at institutional level, through the adoption of a Code of Practice, in some institutions the policy response might have not gone beyond formal compliance.

Table 2: Framework of analysis

Level one formal self-regulation/compliance		
Sector level	Empirical methods of investigation and sample	Institutional level
Funding Councils' general equality guidance; research units of assessment specific equality guidance	Secondary research: documents analysis	Codes of Practice and other relevant documentation
Level two substantive self-regulation/compliance		
Interpretation and application of the equality guidance to individual submissions within units of assessment	Primary research: qualitative method underpinned by an interpretativist perspective; one-to-one to one semi-structured interviews with a sample of 'decisionmakers' both at institutional and at UoAs level	Steps taken to communicate Code of Practice and facilitate disclosure of equality-related personal circumstances; equality training provided to those involved in the selection process
Level three achieving cultural change and equality outcomes		
	Primary research: qualitative method underpinned by an interpretativist perspective: one-to-one to one semi-structured interviews with a sample of beneficiaries of the equality guidance (eg academics at different stages of their career)	Actual use of the equality provisions in the Code of Practice by individual academics; experienced impact of the equality guidance on departmental/ institutional culture beyond the RAE/REF

3. Level Two: Substantive Self-regulation/Compliance

This level enabled us to delve into greater depth on the response of the sector and of individual institutions to the equality duties and assess to what extent the self-regulation had gone beyond formal compliance; and to what extent the 'energy' and the know-how of 'local actors' (eg senior academics responsible for selection of staff for inclusion in the RAE 2008; panel and sub-panel chairs) had been harnessed to identify problems and solutions to bring about change that would eliminate discrimination and promote equality of opportunities within the RAE process.

The method of investigation that we selected to achieve the objectives of our research at this stage was a qualitative approach through one-to-one semi-structured interviews with a sample of people with an interest in this process whose position of responsibility either within the RAE (eg panel and sub-panel chairs) or at institutional level put them in a position to make change happen. We chose semi-structured interviews because they allowed us to design and use a list of predetermined questions informed by findings from the first level of analysis and from other relevant literature review. For example, the work of Rees[20] suggested that in RAE 2001, doubts about the interpretation of the equality guidance issued by the Funding Councils at the time might have led to exclude staff who could have been submitted pro rata, in order to 'play safe' by adhering to the norm of entering staff, typically on a full-time contract, with four research outputs. The semi-structured interview approach enabled us to ask questions designed to test this hypothesis and to explore whether the intervening changes to equality legislation since 2001 had provided a stronger stimulus to induce a more robust self-regulatory response, in the form of sector equality guidance capable of modifying the 'risk averse' behaviour of many institutions.

These two levels of investigation combined enabled us to identify some clear differences in the way HEIs had responded to the Funding Councils equality guidance. Some of the main issues that we identified included that: some institutions had not gone beyond formal compliance and failed to develop effective procedures to facilitate disclosure of equality-related personal circumstances compared to others which instead put reasonable steps in place to facilitate disclosure; some institutions had provided better equality training than others by using case studies which were designed to explore equality issues in the explicit context of selection of staff for inclusion in the RAE 2008; and there was some degree of inconsistency in the specific equality guidance issued by UoAs panel and sub-panels, especially in relation to the treatment of early career researchers, which may have resulted in the exclusion of some staff as no doubt institutions preferred 'to play safe'.

Overall the evidence collected showed that the 'reflexive approach' had induced a degree of self-regulation within the sector, modified the norm of the four research outputs by allowing for adjustments to take into account equality-related personal circumstances and harness, to different degrees, the energy and know-how of local actors to achieve change to promote equality. However, it also highlighted that the level of flexibility and openness which seems to be inherent to a 'reflexive approach' when interacting with the complexity of the sub-system in question, organised in different layers (eg sector level, institutional level) and relying on a range of local actors operating within these levels in different capacities, can produce inconsistent results in terms of promoting substantive equality. Furthermore even in those cases where it appeared that the 'reflexive approach'

[20] T Rees, *Measuring excellence in scientific research: the UK Research Assessment Exercise, in Gender and Excellence in the Making* (Brussels, European Commission, 2004).

had filtered through all the different layers of the sub-system and produced some positive results the analysis was still inconclusive unless it included the experience of the beneficiaries (ie research active academics). However, due to the project tight time frame (the findings from this research were needed by a certain date to inform HEFCE consultation for REF 2014 equality guidance) it was not possible to include a sample of beneficiaries within that project.

Relating this work back to our idea of a 'virtuous circle' between research, knowledge exchange and research impact, the findings and recommendations from this research were adopted by the Funding Councils to inform the equality guidance for REF 2014 thus having a direct research impact on sector policy in this area. Moreover we were commissioned by one university to design and deliver their equality training (knowledge exchange) for senior academics, including their Vice-Chancellor, in the run up to REF 2014. Finally, a new research agenda was identified about the need to investigate the experiences of potential beneficiaries of the equality duties in order to gain a full picture about the extent to which the 'reflexive approach' worked in practice. This has led us to add a third level to our framework of analysis, included in Table 2 above and described below by undertaking further research focusing on individual academics.

4. Level Three: Achieving Cultural Change and Equality Outcomes

The Government Equalities Office[21] indicated that one of the aims of the PSED was 'to bring about cultural change'. Furthermore as highlighted by Hepple[22] the change of wording from 'promoting equality' to 'advancing equality' signalled a change of emphasis and a focus 'on making progress on outcomes'. Therefore this level of analysis needs to focus on two broad questions which are: to what extent have the intended beneficiaries of the equality duties both as individuals and as a group actually benefitted from the policies and resulting practices put in place by the sector and HEIs in response to the equality duties?

In order to address these questions we carried out 32 one-to-one semi-structured interviews between 2012 and 2013 with a sample of academics at different stages of their career working in four institutions from different mission groups although all research focused. Once again the semi-structured interview method was chosen since, for the reasons already outlined above, we felt that it enabled us to achieve a balance between the areas that emerged from the previous research findings, which we wanted to explore with individuals, and the need for retaining sufficient flexibility during the interviews to enable the participants to make sense of their experiences.

[21] As cited in B Hepple, *Equality: The New Legal Framework* (Oxford, Hart Publishing, 2011).

[22] Ibid.

The findings suggest that the communication of the Code of Practice to staff in RAE 2008 was still inconsistent and some individuals had a vague or even no idea that it even existed. In comparison, the Code of Practice developed in the run up to REF 2014 had been better communicated across institutions and filtered through at departmental level. Thus, the strengthening of the equality guidance for REF 2014 appeared to have paid dividends. Several academics in our sample with equality-related personal circumstances were able to benefit directly from the application of the Code of Practice and were submitted with a reduced number of research outputs.

In terms of bringing about broader cultural change that would benefit groups of academics with protected characteristics, our findings suggested that there was a perception among some participants that this had begun to happen in their departments, especially for women who felt that their working environment was no longer seen as a 'care free zone',[23] where caring responsibilities are expected to remain invisible. Some female participants felt more empowered to challenge practices in their departments which, although intended to be gender neutral, appeared to have disproportionally affected female academics. However, on the one hand we identified some positive signs that change has begun to take place and it appeared to have been directed or stimulated by the RAE/REF equality guidance which in turn was developed in response to the equality duties; on the other hand the research findings also suggested that some entrenched academic practices—most notably an unspoken expectation that academics would undertake a lot of research work outside normal working hours and a normal working week—represented a major challenge for staff with caring responsibilities in the pursuit of their research careers.

There are a number of lessons that can be derived from the application of this framework of analysis in terms of collecting empirical evidence to assess to what extent the 'reflexive approach' of equality legislation may be working in practice at organisational level. The first one is that a focus on a particular activity (in the case of our research the RAE/REF), which is of key importance within a chosen sub-system, (in our case the HE sector), provides a useful starting point to collect meaningful evidence and remain focused on the research objectives while navigating through the complexity of the sub-system selected. The second one is that there are different organisational layers within the sub-system which are likely to be affected by the activity and that different actors are likely to be involved in translating the initial stimulus and ensuring that it filters down to the intended beneficiaries. The third one is the importance of researching the experience of the intended beneficiaries to assess whether the key aims of the legislation to change culture and advance equality have been achieved.

[23] K Lynch, 'Carelessness: A Hidden Doxa of Higher Education', CHEER/ESRC Seminar Series: Imagining the University of the Future, Seminar 2: What are the Disqualified Discourses in the Knowledge Society? (Centre for Higher Education and Equality Research (CHEER), University of Sussex, 2010).

So far it appears that there is insufficient empirical research on the application of the equality duties that have captured the experiences of the intended beneficiaries.[24] Therefore, this framework for empirical analysis about the application of the PSED could prove particularly useful in order to gather further evidence about the effectiveness of the duty until its next review.

Finally, to return to the premise of our chapter it can be seen how the application of this framework of analysis, implemented through the use of empirical research methods, has enabled us to meet a number of different research agendas as highlighted at the beginning of our chapter. We have established how the PSED is working on the ground, thus meeting the 'Law in the Real World' agenda; we have ensured that our findings and the recommendations from our research have had impact on non-academic users, as evidenced by the fact that they were adopted by the Funding Councils to inform the equality guidance for REF 2014; we have developed knowledge exchange activities underpinned by the research findings aimed at senior academics who are responsible for shaping and delivering their institutions' research agendas; and have provided empirical backing for theoretical assertions about the 'reflexive aspect' of the equality legislation. This has enabled us to generate new research arising from insights gained through this process.

E. Conclusions

In summary, what we hope to have shown in this chapter is how it is possible to form a virtuous circle from doctrinal research influencing the development of empirical projects, feeding to knowledge exchange, and also into the development of legal thinking in the area of age discrimination and retirement policies and on the response to the equality duties. These findings have resulted in academic articles[25] drawing directly on the projects, and have also influenced organisational practice in this area.

We conclude by saying that this 'virtuous circle' approach has helped us to gain a better understanding of the impact of equality legislation in the workplace and that it also provides a model which meets the research councils' objectives for academics to 'think creatively about knowledge exchange' and to maximise the impact of their research.

[24] K Clayton-Hathway, 'The Public Sector Equality Duty: Empirical Evidence Base' (Oxford, Centre for Diversity Policy Research and Practice, Oxford Brookes University, 2013).

[25] S Manfredi and L Vickers, 'Pensioning off the Mandatory Retirement Age: Implications for the Higher Education Sector' (2013) 33 *Legal Studies* 289; and 'Retirement and Age Discrimination: Managing Retirement in Higher Education' (2009) 38 *Industrial Law Journal* 343; 'Public Sector Equality Duty: Its Impact on Research Careers in HE' forthcoming.

INDEX

www.ingramcontent.com/pod-product-compliance
Lightning Source LLC
LaVergne TN
LVHW052322200926
848481LV00002B/640
9781509917068